The Glorious Life of

JESSICA KRAUT

An Adventure in Eastern and Indigenous
Religions and Philosophies

Carol V.A. Quinn

Rock's Mills Press
2018

Published by
ROCK'S MILLS PRESS
www.rocksmillspress.com

For information, please contact Rock's Mills Press at
customer.service@rocksmillspress.com.

In loving memory of my father, Michael Quinn
And for my Uncle Daddy

Thanks to the many people whose support made this project possible. A special thanks to my mother Judy Quinn, my husband Bogdan Chlebus, my stepdaughter Maria Chlebus, the Chlebus clan in Warsaw, my brother John Quinn, my sister-in-law Naomi Quinn, my nephew Jordan Quinn, and my niece Jillian Quinn for their unending encouragement and love. My unending gratitude and love to my father's caregiver, John-Mark Lambertson. A big hug and shout-out to Don Mather for his invaluable comments on an earlier draft. Thanks too to Frances Howard-Snyder, my workshop partner at the Philosophy and Fiction Writing Workshop in Oxford, June 2017, and Kim Hayashi whose wonderful stories inspired the character Chicken Eyes. I'd also like to thank my awesome students Noelle Helmer and Govinda Mishra for providing interesting and insightful ways to think about some of these Eastern philosophies, my awesome mentor Samuel Gorovitz, and my dear friends Sean McAleer and Randy Sunshine. Of course none of this would have been possible without my wonderful publisher and editor David Stover.

ANNOTATED TABLE OF CONTENTS
Eastern and Indigenous Religions and Philosophies

A JESSICA KRAUT BESTIARY
Images of Unusual Animals Featured in the Novel

Scarlet macaw (Adrian Pingstone)
Kinkajou (*Dictionnaire Universelle d'Histoire Naturelle*, 1849)
Motmot (Stephen Turner)
Tapir (LtShears)
pages 11–12

Gibnut (or paca) (Hans Hillewaert)
Pauraque (Andy Morffew)
Black howler monkey (Ryan E. Poplin)
Coati (Luna04)
pages 59–60

Spider monkey (Lea Maimone)
Slaty-breasted tinamou (Joseph Smit, 1869)
Ferruginous pygmy owl (Sky Jacobs)
Peccary (Cburnett)
pages 77–78

White-crowned manakin (Ana Agreda, Aves y Conservacion)
Agouti (Illustration from 1891 edition of *A Swiss Family Robinson*)
Red-eyed tree frog (Carey James Balboa)
Gray-headed kite (Hector Bottai)
pages 93–94

(Image credits in parentheses)

ONE

April 7, 2016

At two o'clock in the afternoon, a scarlet macaw escaped from the Los Angeles Zoo. Fifty-four minutes later, it flew through an open door at LAX, landing smack dab in the middle of Jessica Kraut's opened backpack. She took this as a sign. A sign from God that she should not go through with her plans. And so when she saw the fat black man with sad brown eyes holding a card that read "Jessica Kraus," she strode purposefully toward him with a smile.

"Miss Kraus?"

"Yes, I am Miss Kraus."

"My name is Aapo. I am taking you to Mr. Chan's. It's about a fifteen-mile drive…. That your bird?"

Jessica looked at the bird, now sitting atop her backpack preening its scarlet feathers. She wasn't sure how she was going to pull this off. But the alternative would be a miserable marriage to a miserable man who insisted she get a boob job and Botox right after their honeymoon.

"Yes, he's my bird. His name is … *Maya*." She smiled. It felt a little forced.

"Hello," Maya said in a squawky voice.

How is it that nobody has noticed him? If he's even a "him" (she wasn't)—but no one was paying any attention. Folks were grabbing their luggage, checking their cellphones, hugging their loved ones.

"You've only got a carry-on, right? You were instructed to only have a carry-on."

She nodded. "Yep, just a carry-on."

"OK, then follow me."

Jessica, Maya, and Aapo went out the door and to the parking garage, just as the *real* Jessica Kraus walked into baggage claim.

Jessica Kraut sat in one of the two leather wingback chairs in front of the marble fireplace. She reached for an apple in a wooden bowl atop the little round table. Reclaimed Russian oak, her host explained. Jessica took a bite and offered a piece to Maya.

"Lovely bird. Where'd you get it?" Mr. Chan asked.

Jessica was completely taken in by her host. He was positively striking, with brown skin, silver-black hair, moustache and goatee, and a smile that could charm even the most disagreeable of persons. He reminded her of her father (at least how she remembered him). She smiled.

Mr. Chan looked at Aapo who was standing by the marble pillar. "Grab another bottle of the Montrachet…. And a banana for the macaw." He smiled at Jessica. "Did you know that Aapo pulled off a heist with a peeled banana?" He chuckled.

Aapo shouted from the bar, "I left the peel *on*!"

"I, uh…" Jessica scrambled to come up with a story about the bird. Thankfully Mr. Chan forgot the question.

"You look just like your photograph. Your hair's a bit different. Darker than I expected. Very pretty."

"Thanks," Jessica said. She was glad that the real Jessica Kraus wasn't a different age, size, or color. She stroked the back of the macaw's head. It leaned down from

Jessica's shoulder and pulled at one of the buttons of her white blouse.

"Your uncle's done great work for us. I'm happy to bring his niece on board. Our flight for Belize leaves in about two hours…. Your uncle filled you in? I assure you that your macaw will be safe."

BELIZE? What have I gotten myself into?

Aapo arrived with the bottle of wine. He approached Jessica who extended her glass as he poured. He handed her the banana and then walked up to Mr. Chan to refill his glass. "Yu coulda lie suga outta bun …" he jested in his native Kriol, then repeated, "I left the peel *on*." He smiled. Even his smile looked sad.

Mr. Chan gave a hearty laugh and then said, "Well if dah no so, da naily so…." He addressed Jessica, "We'll be gone for about six weeks and pretty incommunicado. Why don't you go freshen up? Here, I'd like you to wear this *huipil*. You'll look beautiful in it with those green eyes." He handed her a brightly colored, elaborately embroidered shirt. Although Jessica did not know this yet, the pattern depicted the day keeper *Imox* (Crocodile) of the Maya calendar, symbolizing the dark hidden forces in the universe.

"The bathroom is just down the hall to the left," Mr. Chan continued. "Make any phone calls you'd like. Just remember to say that you're assisting in a Maya archeological dig. We'll be leaving for the airfield in about a half hour."

Jessica stood up and gave a nervous smile. She straightened her sage green skirt. "OK, I will."

Jessica washed up in one of the two marble basins, marveling at her host's love of this stone. She kept the golden faucet running to let the macaw have a drink. She put the stopper in. Maya stood under the faucet and let the water pour over her head and body. Then she jumped onto the (you guessed it) *marble* counter top, and shook and puffed her feathers. Jessica slipped on the *huipil*, pulled out her wallet from her purse, and grabbed Finn's business card. She looked at the Malibu address.

At the time it seemed like a smart idea, exciting even. She met Finn on a flight— Charlotte to LA. Finn spotted her as she boarded the plane. He paid the man next to him a hundred bucks to switch places with her, so that she could sit with him in first class. The man had only paid fifty dollars for the upgrade, and so he was more than happy to oblige. Finn all but convinced Jessica to move in with him during the five-hour flight. They spent a week together and she thought that life with him would be *good*. Certainly better than what awaited her back in Charlotte. She was certain that the scandal would break while she was gone, and *then* what would she do? And so when Finn asked her to marry him as he dropped her off at LAX for her return flight home, she said "yes." Of course "yes" came with a lot of strings. He would introduce her to the ladies at the Country Club. He'd give her a credit card, and they'd take her shopping, teach her how to dress and apply makeup. And she'd have to get her nails done. The dark hair would have to go. She'd have daily sessions with Carlos, the Brazilian model-turned-personal trainer, and she'd need to learn to play tennis with some of the girls at the Racquet Club.

"But can't I get a teaching gig, maybe at Santa Monica College or something?" Jessica had asked.

"Nope," he'd tell her. She'd live a different kind of life now. A *better* life. She quit her tenure-track job mid-semester, which utterly screwed her chances of ever getting a recommendation from her chair—or anyone else for that matter. The scandal would never break (her student kept his mouth shut), but Jessica would never know that, having shown her middle finger to that place.

She looked at Finn's business card again, then looked at herself in the mirror while twisting the obnoxiously ostentatious engagement ring that Finn had given her. She took it off, lifted the top off the toilet tank, and watched the ring sink to the bottom. She replaced the cover, picked up Maya and her purse and walked back to her host, accidentally dropping Finn's card on the floor as she did so.

After a five-hour flight, Jessica, Maya, Mr. Chan, and Aapo arrived at the Philip S.W. Goldson International Airport just outside Belize City. Though it was early April, 12:32 a.m., it was still a balmy 83 degrees. Jessica was disappointed that it was a new moon, disappointed that it was so dark, disappointed that she wouldn't be able to see anything on their two-plus hour drive to San Ignacio, where they'd get some rest before driving another fifty miles to the camp just outside the Chiquibul Forest Reserve.

"So what would I be seeing, if I could see anything? This used to be the capital of British Honduras, right?" Jessica asked.

Mr. Chan turned around from the front passenger seat of an old white Isuzu Trooper and answered, "It was—until 1970. It was almost completely ravaged by Hurricane Hattie in October '61. I was just a boy then. The new capital, Belmopan, was built inland…. We've been passing mostly mangroves and sand. We'll be getting into some low bush soon where you'd be able to see the wooden shacks of the villages, some with palm-thatched roofs, some brightly painted in yellows and greens. You'd be seeing the 'real' Belize, the Belize hidden from most tourists. You might think it a bit ramshackle by your standards, but I'd say it's got *personality*. Sorry we didn't plan the timing better, but you'll see plenty enough on your stay…. Hope you're not afraid of jaguars and snakes." He laughed.

"Jaguars and snakes…." Jessica repeated. She opened a bag of unsalted peanuts and a bottle of water, offering some to Maya. Aapo noticed through the rearview mirror and smiled.

"Actually, we call them 'tigers' here," Mr. Chan explained.

"I like that you named your bird 'Maya.' Did you know that the Maya people consider the scarlet macaw to be sacred? It represents the rising sun," Aapo said.

That's one of the few things that Jessica did know about her new (female) friend.

"Another sign from God," Jessica said so softly that only her bird could hear. *Who would have imagined that I'd name the macaw 'Maya' only to be coming up close to some Maya ruins?*

"As we move inland, the Maya Mountains would be more visible—if only we could see them," Mr. Chan offered. "We'll be reaching Belmopan in about an hour."

"I don't really know much about the history of this place," Jessica said. She was more than a bit freaked out about this strange land, about all of the growling and slithering things that were there, but that she could not see. She needed a distraction.

"We have quite a history," Mr. Chan began. "As you noted, we were formerly called 'British Honduras.' We didn't become an independent nation until 1981, though we've been called 'Belize' since '73. Of course Guatemala didn't recognize our independence until '91."

"Why's that?"

"A long history of territorial disputes going back to an 1859 treaty with Britain….

Anyway, the first British settlers, shipwrecked sailors known as the 'Baymen,' arrived here in 1638. Soon swashbucklers appeared from all over the place. They were mostly pirates targeting the treasure-loaded Spanish ships…."

"Pirates of the Caribbean," Jessica said and smiled. Maya was now comfortably perched on her lap. She turned her head, nuzzled into her back feathers, and closed her eyes to sleep.

"Many of the settlers became loggers, providing timber for export to Europe," Mr. Chan explained. "You know, Great Britain and Spain were great colonial rivals. Spain claimed dominion over the New World first, and they were constantly trying to oust the British settlers in order to reclaim sovereignty. There were frequent clashes, including all-out wars, over the cutting of logwood. Britain took control of the whole territory, declaring it a crown colony, in 1862. It wasn't exactly a friendly place to live, though: Indian raids, cholera outbreaks, attacks by neighboring Spanish settlements, hurricanes…."

"Did you know, Jessica, that hundreds of American Confederates fled to Honduras during and after the Civil War? My great, great grampa, Hermann, came to America from Germany in 1842, emigrating to Texas. Hermann had a big cotton plantation. When Texas seceded in 1861 and joined the Confederate States, he enlisted in the Confederate army a year before the draft. He moved to Honduras with his family in 1865, shortly after John Wilkes Booth shot Lincoln, when his son—*my great grampa*—was only five years old," Aapo said. "Not exactly proud of that family history, though it makes for an interesting story."

"Aapo has a very colorful family history." Mr. Chan chuckled. "His grandfather bootlegged during Prohibition. At sixty years old, he ran a fast boat from here to the US, smuggling and bootlegging whiskey. Made a fortune…."

"Then lost a fortune," Aapo interrupted.

"His grandfather married the daughter of a Baymen slave owner and his slave. Slaves were brought here to harvest the logwood. We emancipated them in the 1830s. Almost an entire generation before you did in America," Mr. Chan explained.

"My great, great gramma, Milly, was born a slave. Perhaps my grampa was rebelling against his own grampa's ugly slave past…."

"Or perhaps he just fell in love," Jessica interrupted. She smiled.

"Or perhaps he just fell in love," Aapo repeated and smiled back. "My grandparents raised me and my sister, Lottie, after our parents died. They were wonderful people."

"I lived with my grandparents for a time. They weren't so wonderful," Jessica said with a sour face. "And what about you, Mr. Chan?"

"Not much to tell, really. I'm mestizo—Q'eqchi and Spanish. In the late nineteenth century the Q'eqchi fled from forced labor in Guatemala and settled in several villages in the south. My great grandfather came here when he was twenty-four years old.

"Mr. Chan's grampa and great grampa were Maya priests," Aapo offered.

"Oh? Were you raised in a Q'eqchi village?" Jessica asked.

"No, my father escaped that life before I was born. Made something of himself."

Jessica could hear a tinge of shame in Mr. Chan's voice. Or perhaps it was disappointment. She couldn't tell. "What about the Maya people and their culture?"

"Your uncle didn't fill you in? He loves Maya art and philosophy," Mr. Chan said.

Jessica began twirling her hair. Maya thought it was a game and tugged at one of the strands. Aapo looked through the rearview mirror, clearly amused.

"Have you heard about the Popol Vuh? It's the Maya creation story. It explains how humans were created. I memorized a lot of it as a child," Mr. Chan said. "My father taught me."

"I only know some of the creation myths of the Eastern tradition. I teach Eastern philosophies and religions. Well—I did."

"I thought you sold your uncle's ceramic pieces in his gallery in Santa Fe. He loves to paint the mythological scenes from the murals at San Bartolo in Northern Guatemala. Of course you know that. Did you notice the bowl on the mantelshelf? Your uncle made that piece. It's very special. He used several vegetal and mineral colorants and even mixed the paint with mica so that it would glitter in the sunlight…. I love your uncle. I'm sure you're very proud of him," Mr. Chan said. "By the way, we're approaching Belmopan. It's near the River Valley. We'll be going through much more fertile farmland as we near the foothills of the Maya Mountains."

Jessica peered out the window. She couldn't make out a thing. "Like I said, I *used to* teach Eastern religions. Now I work in my uncle's studio." *Change the subject.* "I'd love to hear the Maya creation myth."

"Wonderful. It goes like this: In the beginning, there was Heart-of-Sky alone. There was no one to speak His name, no one to praise His glory. Heart-of-Sky said the word 'Earth,' and the earth rose. He thought of it, and there it was. He thought of mountains, and great mountains came to be. He thought of trees, and trees grew on the land. Heart-of-Sky said, 'Our work is going well.' He then made the creatures of the forest: the birds, deer, tigers, and snakes. And each was given a home. Then Heart-of-Sky said to the animals, 'Pray to us!' But the creatures could only squawk, they could only howl. They did not praise Heart-of-Sky. And so Heart-of-Sky tried again. His new creation was made of mud. But the mud people were crumbly and soft, lopsided and twisted. They only spoke nonsense. And so Heart-of-Sky let them dissolve away. Then Heart-of-Sky called our Grandfather and Grandmother, the Wisest Spirits, who said, 'It is good to make your people out of wood. They will speak your name.' And Heart-of-Sky replied, 'So it will be.' But the wooden doll-people had no blood. They had no sweat. They walked around with nothing in their hearts, nothing in their minds. Heart-of-Sky said, 'This is not what I had in mind.' He destroyed the doll-people by making it rain all night and day. The result was a terrible flood. The doll-people who were not destroyed by the floodwaters were visited by all of the animals of the earth, by all of the things of the earth that they had misused and mistreated. The creatures of the forest entered into their homes. 'You have chased us from *our* homes, so now we will take yours. You have abused us, so now we will eat you.' Even their cooking pots and grinding stones spoke, 'We will burn and pound on *you*, just as you have done to us.' The doll-people scattered into the forest, and their faces were crushed. They turned into monkeys, and that's why monkeys look so much like people. Finally, Heart-of-Sky created the True People, making them from four kinds of maize, each of a different color. This is how our first fathers, the Four Men, were created."[1]

"I love this story. There are so many creation myths across the globe that speak of humans being made from the earth, so many stories that speak of a great flood. I've never heard about humans being made from corn. Makes sense, though, given how important corn is to the Maya people," Jessica said.

"Indeed, maize is *sacred* to the Maya people," Mr. Chan explained.

As they traveled into the dense rainforest and rolling hills behind the pasturelands beyond Belmopan, they hit a pothole. The SUV began pulling to the right.

1. Based on a translation of the Popol Vuh by Dennis Tedlock. See also "Popol Vuh" at criscenzo.com.

"Feels like we might have a flat," Aapo said. "Best if we pull over and check." He stopped the Trooper. Mr. Chan grabbed a flashlight and a gun from the glove compartment.

"What's the gun for?" Jessica asked.

"The tigers are out. We can't be too careful," Mr. Chan said. The two men got out of the SUV.

Jessica listened to the howls of the monkeys in the background. And then she heard what sounded like a deep, chesty cough, followed by a bloodcurdling scream. Something was banging against the SUV, almost tipping it over. Maya squawked—twice. Jessica was afraid to look. She heard crunches, smacks, and purrs, and a loud belch—and then everything went quiet. She peered out the window only to find a big cat lounging against the front passenger door. He had Aapo's foot in his mouth. The rest of Aapo was desperately trying to stay under the SUV. The flashlight was on the ground, illuminating the grisly scene. All that was left of Mr. Chan was his straw fedora. Jessica opened her mouth to scream, but nothing came out. Then she spotted a thirty-foot long python as wide as a tree trunk. It wrapped itself around the SUV, wrapped itself around the big cat. And then she heard the cat speak one word: "Kaa…."

Kaa opened his mouth and began to speak in long hisses: "Ssssssso…."

And then Jessica saw a jungle boy running toward them, arms waving wildly.

"It'ssssssss Mowgli," hissed Kaa.

"Don't worry, Jessica, I'll save you!" yelled the boy. "And I've got twenty units of Botox to fix that forehead!"

Jessica awoke atop a white goose down comforter. She walked to the opened window and looked outside. She saw a courtyard with a large granite carving of a toucan in the center. She spotted Maya perched on a branch of a giant black mango tree. It was dotted with little pink flowers and what looked like tiny green mangoes. Aapo was stretched out on an oversized hammock, while Mr. Chan sat at a wrought iron table sipping a cup of coffee. She exited the room and found her way to the arch-shaped Honduran mahogany door opening to the courtyard.

"Good morning," Jessica began. "Where are we? How'd we get here?"

"Gud maanin, Jessica," Aapo said Kriol-style.

"Good morning, Miss Jessica," Mr. Chan said. "We're in San Ignacio…. Aapo, why don't you get Jessica a cup of coffee?" He extended his hand toward her. "Come over here and have a seat. The morning sun is quite lovely."

"I don't remember how we got here."

"You were asleep. When we finally changed the flat and got back into the SUV you were completely zonked out. We had to carry you inside when we arrived." Mr. Chan laughed. "No bother. Yesterday was exhausting. We'll rest here for most of the day and drive the last leg toward the Guatemalan border in the late afternoon. We've got about fifty more miles of pretty rough roads—rough enough to shake your fillings out. We're lucky we didn't break an axle last night."

Aapo walked back into the courtyard holding a fuchsia-painted wooden tray carrying a pot of coffee, two ceramic cups, a bowl of strange fruits, and a plate of chocolate-filled flaky pastries. He set it down on the table and pulled up a chair. He poured two cups (one for Jessica and one for himself) and then freshened Mr. Chan's coffee.

"Thank you," Jessica said. "What kind of fruit is this?" She motioned to the bowl. "I've never seen this kind of thing before."

"Breadfruit, sapote, soursop, guaya, dragon fruit," Aapo offered. "My gramma would make me soursop tea whenever I'd get a high fever. She'd use the leaves, of course…. You'll get to taste all kinds of wonderful fruit here. My favorite is craboo—especially craboo ice cream."

Maya flew down from the big branch and landed on the table. Jessica offered him a piece of fruit.

"I have something for you," Mr. Chan began. He extended a little box to Jessica. She looked into his dark eyes—so warm, so generous, she almost fell into them.

She opened the box. Inside was a necklace unlike anything she'd ever seen. It was made of red coral branch beads, interspersed with colorful clay beads and Spanish coins from the eighteenth century. A silver pendant of the Virgin of Guadalupe hung at the bottom.

"Just a little thank you. Of course you'll still get your share of the profits, but your uncle said you love jewelry."

Jessica pulled the necklace out of the box and began putting it on. Mr. Chan got up from his chair to help her.

"Do you like it?"

"I love it," Jessica said with a smile. "Thank you."

"Of course." He smiled back. "After we're through with breakfast, why don't you enjoy a dip in the pool. There's a closet full of women's clothing in the room where you slept. I'm sure you'll find some nice things to wear in just your size. Be sure to pack them for our trip," Mr. Chan began. "Don't forget to pick out a few of the fancy dresses and shoes. There's also some exquisite jewelry on the nightstand by the bed."

Why would I need such things at the camp?

Jessica needed to find out why they were here and what they'd be doing. She couldn't just ask, since her "uncle" had supposedly filled her in. She tried to come up with a clever way to get the answers.

"Tell me more about that banana heist, Aapo," she said, and then took a bite of the pastry.

"I left the peel on," Aapo said with a mock-frown.

"The man says he left the peel on," Mr. Chan said through laughter.

"I gave up that line of work long ago, Jessica. Now I work exclusively for Mr. Chan."

Well, that was perfectly unhelpful. Maybe we really are going on an archeological dig. But that still doesn't explain the fancy dresses.

Jessica didn't know what to do. She decided to keep playing along. *How bad can it get, really?* She'd find out soon enough.

While they were flying to Belize City, the *real* Jessica Kraus phoned her uncle after waiting two and a half hours at baggage claim. She told him that nobody showed to pick her up. Her uncle gave her Mr. Chan's number, and when he didn't answer, she called her uncle back and asked for Chan's address. She took a taxi to his estate in Rolling Hills. In the thirty-three minutes it took to get there, her blood started to boil. She buzzed the gate and demanded that the housekeeper let her in. When the house-keeper refused, Jessica Kraus scaled the eight-foot tall wrought iron fence, bruising her knee when she fell on the other side. She ran up to the door and pounded. A gorilla-sized man answered, while the much smaller housekeeper stood behind him.

"Where's Chan?"

"Who are *you*?" the man asked.

"Jessica Kraus." Impatiently, she pulled a wallet from her purse and handed him her driver's license.

The man studied it. "Jessica Kraus? …. Wait here."

The man closed the front door and pulled out his cellphone to call Mr. Chan. Of course Mr. Chan wouldn't answer. The man returned to the door.

"Please … come inside Miss Kraus." He motioned her to the sitting area, to the same wingback chair that Jessica Kraut had sat on.

"I don't have time for this," she huffed. "Where's Chan? Why wasn't anyone there to pick me up?"

"Mr. Chan is not here right now."

"When will he be back?"

"Six weeks."

"*SIX WEEKS*? What do you mean *six weeks*? I've got an assignment with him. My uncle arranged it."

"Please settle down, Miss Kraus. I'm sure there's an explanation. Once I'm able to reach Mr. Chan I'll have some answers for you…. Would you like a drink?"

"No, I would not like a drink. This mistake cost me *one million dollars*! This better be straightened out! … *Yes*, I would like that drink."

The man stood up and walked out of the room to get a bottle of wine. While he was gone, Jessica searched around for a bathroom. She found one down the hall, on the left. She noticed a card on the floor and picked it up.

"Finn Lauder, huh? Malibu…. I just might need to pay him a visit."

Jessica Kraus walked out of the bathroom and returned to the sitting area with the wingback chairs. The man had poured two glasses of red wine and was waiting for her return. He stood up and handed her a glass.

"You found the bathroom…. Please, sit down. I poured some Monfortino. Ever try it?"

"Got anything stronger? —Never mind." Maybe she could press this guy for more information. He wasn't forthcoming until sexual favors were put on the table, whereupon the man told her that a woman *claiming* to be Jessica Kraus left with Mr. Chan for Belize almost an hour ago. Jessica Kraus thanked the large man, downed her drink, fulfilled her "obligation," and went out to the taxi, still waiting for her outside.

Meantime local TV broke the news that a $25,000 scarlet macaw had gone missing from the Los Angeles Zoo. Someone thought he had spotted it with a woman at the LAX baggage claim, a sighting which was confirmed by security video. Police were working good leads and were certain both bird and woman would be found. Updates tonight at 11.

As for Finn Lauder, he wasn't missing his fiancée at all, since she wasn't due for a week. Jessica had taken an early flight to try to catch him in the act with his masseuse, who was being just a little too friendly with him on the table.

And now Jessica Kraut alias Kraus was at a villa in San Ignacio sipping her second piña colada while lounging on a float recliner in the pool.

She started thinking about Finn.

Two weeks earlier, Malibu, California

Finn Lauder III, complete with wavy dark hair, chiseled chin, and high cheek-bones, looking every bit the model he never was, sat with his good friend Edward Cox III (not nearly as pleasing) on the deck of Geoffrey's restaurant overlooking the ocean. Finn was picking at his Ahi tuna tartar, colorfully presented on a little white ceramic plate. He was on his third Gin Rickey. Edward his fourth. Well-deserved libations after a morning round of golf. Finn was just about to tell Edward about en-rolling his fiancée, Jessica Kraut, in cooking classes when an overly friendly Morkie jumped on his red and green plaid pant leg. Finn looked over at the dog's owner, who gave an entirely plastic smile—not a fake smile, mind you, but a *genuinely plastic one*, due to her propensity for going under the knife.

"Would you mind keeping your dog away from me? *I'm deeply allergic*," Finn said to the woman with equal measure of irritation and disdain. Then while looking at Edward from behind his Gucci sunglasses, he grumbled, "She's shitting all over my sunshine." He sneered.

Edward, far more jovial than his friend and a sucker for gossip, changed topics: "Just ran into Maggie yesterday at Duke's. She was asking about you. Said you left something at her place the other night." He gave a sly grin.

Finn smiled widely and then said, "What a rattle-brained angel…. Yeah, she tex-ted me about that. It's hard to get away now, obviously. I'll likely see her next week at Jasper's thirtieth, after Jess has gone back to Charlotte to pack more of her things."

Just then a seagull landed by Finn's feet which were snuggled inside his Italian designer golf shoes ($485). He kicked it away as it grabbed a wonton crisp. "Fucking bird."

Edward tried to lighten his friend's disagreeable mood, which one might think was due to a lousy round of golf. But Finn was just being his usual asshole self. Ed-ward tolerated Finn's disposition since their families had been friends for three gen-erations. "So you're actually going through with this? Giving up Maggie, and all those other Maggie-types, to marry a woman you barely know?"

Finn made a constipated face. Finally, he offered: "You know, Colin gave me good advice: Be sure to keep your wives and girlfriends separate…. In any case, I've got to go through with it. My old man keeps dangling the Donnelly 'carrot' (you know how much I want that account) and he's got Father Brennan chasing me around with the marriage 'stick.'"

"Don't you mean 'whip' rather than 'stick'?" Edward smirked. "At least your priest recognizes that marriage is *punishment*…. So Colin gave you that advice? You're sure-ly not going to listen to a man who pays over 50K a month in alimony to three ex-wives…."

"Good point." Finn grinned.

"So old man Finn won't just give you the Donnelly account?" Edward asked through a mouthful of puffed pastry. He licked some melted Brie off his fingertips.

"Not unless I marry a respectable woman who will turn me into a respectable…."

Edward cut him off, "And of course every respectable woman around here knows enough to leave you a bachelor…. Good for your old man. Manipulative. Conniving. I respect those qualities in him. Cheers to Old Man Finn—and to you."

"And to Maggie…." Finn smiled broadly and waggled his eyebrows.

"And to Maggie." Edward waggled back.

Without warning, Jessica Kraut appeared on the deck of Geoffrey's restaurant in a pale lavender sundress, her long dark hair pulled back in a loose ponytail. She looked around through her Walgreens sunglasses ($19.99) and spotted Finn and Edward raising their glasses in a toast. Finn finally noticed her as she approached.

"What brings *you* here? I thought you had your Brazilian Booty session with Carlos today," Finn said accusingly.

"I canceled," Jessica said and turned away.

"What do you mean *you canceled*? Our wedding is in seven weeks. You don't want a flabby ass for our honeymoon, do you?"

"Be easy on her, Finn. She looks great." Edward smiled.

"Thanks, Edward." Jessica tried to smile back.

"So why are you here, Jess?" He let the question hang there before he continued. "Checking up on me?" He scowled.

"Of course not. Don't be ridiculous. I was supposed to meet Maggie for lunch, but she just texted that she had to schedule an emergency session with her therapist. Something about Erickson's psychosocial crisis of intimacy versus isolation…. I thought I'd grab a bite to eat since I'm here anyway, then I spotted you."

Edward kept smiling. "I love that dress on you. Very nice."

Finn grimaced. "I've told Jess a thousand times that pastels just don't flatter her. They wash her out." Then to Jessica, he said: "But you insist, don't you?" He turned again to Edward: "Maybe you can get Caroline to take Jess shopping. She has terrific taste." And then once more to Jessica: "You say you were going to meet up with Maggie?" He gave a wholly fake smile.

"She said she wants to talk with me. Probably something about the designer cupcakes for the bridal shower she's throwing for me next month."

"Oh, of course…. That's probably it."

Present day

At 5 o'clock in the evening, deep within the Chiquibul Forest Reserve, at the ruins of Caracol dating from around 1200 BCE, in a little-excavated part, keel-billed toucans made their frog-like croaking calls while sitting atop the remnants of a small stone temple, watching the goings-on atop a crumbling ceremonial limestone platform below. King K'uk Mo, twenty-eighth generation priest-king of the black howler monkeys, was peering into the water of a freshly cracked coconut from a nearby palm. The "King's Palm," it was called. It was planted especially there, and especially for this purpose, in 1652. He carefully placed one black and one white feather from a harpy eagle, and stirred with a branch from a nearby ceiba tree before adding a handful of petals from a yellow orchid. Monkeys sat atop nearby temples and treetops, howling, shrieking, and chattering. Sometimes they would throw a shower of sticks or nuts (just for fun), as they jumped high in the air among the smaller branches. King K'uk Mo ignored them as he proceeded to add the skin molt of a Middle American indigo snake and the web of a wolf spider. He pulled a tuft of his own hair from above his heart, plopped it into the watery mix and stirred a final time. Then he lifted his offering heavenward and chanted for seven minutes. Finally, he stepped down from the platform as the sky glittered like specks of gold. All of the monkeys jumped from their places and gathered around him.

"She's about to arrive," King K'uk Mo said to them in monkey-ese—after all, they didn't understand human. But he would be talking to one particular human soon enough.

Scarlet macaw

Kinkajou

Motmot

Tapir

TWO

"We've still got a little over an hour to go," Mr. Chan said to Jessica, who was looking out the window.

They were driving through high-canopy rainforests. Lianas and other vines snaked from tree to tree. Orchids dangled precariously from the branches. Streaks of sunlight stretched down to the younger trees and ferns, like light filtering through the stained glass windows of a cathedral. The loud, guttural screams of the black howler monkeys could be heard from a few miles away, as well as the trills and shrieks, croaks and cheeps, whistles and whoops of the other denizens of the forest. A veritable cacophony of sounds. It was a religious experience.

Jessica spotted a flock of keel-billed toucans roosting in a breadfruit tree. "What'd you say?"

"I said we've still got about an hour's drive before we reach the camp."

"At least it's still light out so I can see." Jessica smiled.

"It'll be light for a few more hours. It's really dangerous to drive this stretch at night. The roads are very unpredictable. The red clay can be especially slick after a heavy downpour of rain. You really don't want to veer off the road in these parts. You never know what you'll encounter," Aapo explained.

"Jaguars and snakes." Jessica laughed.

"We'll be finishing this job just before the wet season, which runs from June through December," Mr. Chan explained. "We usually do two six-week jobs a year. We really shouldn't have too much heavy rain."

Jessica wanted to be more curious about Mr. Chan's comment, but she was so taken in by the surroundings. As they rounded a bend, a large peck of pickles—sorry, *pack of peccaries*—stood on the road. They were eating some of the nuts and fruits that had fallen from the trees. A baby peccary yawned, while her mother busily pulled at a stubborn root. Soon they had surrounded the Trooper. Aapo inched along, honking the horn, but since the peccaries were not interested in cooperating (they were there first, after all), he finally stopped the SUV and turned off the engine.

"Wild pigs," Jessica said. "Cool."

"Peccaries," Mr. Chan corrected. "We might be stuck here for a while. It looks like we've got some time to kill. Why don't you share an Eastern creation myth with us?"

"Yes, I'd love to hear that too," Aapo said. "I love creation myths." He turned the key in the ignition and honked again.

"Sure, OK. How about the Hindu myth of the sacrifice of Purusha?" She paused a few moments to consider how she'd begin. "First, it's important to note that what we call 'Hinduism' covers a wide range of beliefs representing an array of spiritual and philosophical traditions originating in South Asia. It's one of the most pluralistic religions in the world. And so Hindu texts do not present a single canonical account of creation, but offer many accounts, some of them contradictory.[2] The Purusha story, called 'The Hymn of Man,' is historically important because it was used to justify the Indian caste system and social inequality. It comes from the *Rig Veda*, the oldest of the four *Vedas* which were composed between about 1500 and 500 BCE, and considered Hindu's most sacred scripture. It's also the oldest literary record in the Indo-Europe-

2. Their discussion is based on Chapter 2, "Hindu Traditions," in *World Religions: Eastern Traditions*, Willard Oxtoby, et al., eds., Oxford University Press.

an languages."

"There are four main castes in Indian society, right?" Mr. Chan asked.

"Right. Four main castes (or *varnas*) plus the so-called untouchables or outcastes. Many Hindus believe that whatever caste you're born into is the most telling sign of your *karma*—of your past moral (or immoral) deeds. Hinduism, like other Eastern religions, teaches birth, death, and rebirth (*samsara*) according to karma."

"So who is Purusha?" Aapo asked, as he looked out the window for some additional entertainment. "Look at the coati up in the tree." He pointed at a raccoon-like creature with a longish weird nose. It was eating a bird egg, or an egg-shaped piece of fruit—too difficult to discern from such a distance.

"How cool!" Jessica exclaimed. Maya looked out the window too. Jessica swore she saw him smile. "Hey, it looks like the peccaries are starting to clear out." She noted a few of them moving off the road and disappearing into the dense underbrush. "Purusha is known as 'Primal Man' or the 'Cosmic Person,' sacrificed by the gods to create the world. Various elements of the universe are said to have arisen from his sacrifice. Now comes the part that forever changed the social and religious makeup of Hindu society...." She paused for effect. "From Purusha's mouth came the priestly caste (the *Brahmins*); from his arms, the rulers and warriors (the *Kshatriyas*). The artisans, merchants, and farmers came from his legs (the *Vaishyas*). And from his feet came the *Shudras* (the laborers and servant caste). And so we have the origin of the four varnas of Hindu society traced to the initial sacrifice of the cosmic giant, according to sacred scripture."

"What about the untouchables?" Aapo asked.

"The *Dalits* or 'outcastes.' This is the name they choose to call themselves, from the Sanskrit word *dalita,* which means 'oppressed.' Historically, they're called *Chandalas,* which is a Sanskrit word for someone who handles corpses. They're so despised they didn't even warrant a place in the sacrifice of Purusha."

"Aapo, honk your horn again and start moving," Mr. Chan said. "Terrific story, Jessica." He turned his head and smiled. The last few peccaries moved to the side of the road.

"You know, Gandhi denounced high-caste discrimination towards others, calling the concept of untouchability a blight on Hindu society," Jessica began.[3] "Gandhi called the untouchables 'Harijans'—children of Vishnu or God. Through Gandhi's efforts, the Indian constitution, adopted in 1950, outlawed untouchability. Unfortunately, that didn't end discrimination against this oppressed caste. Gandhi was, of course, the preeminent leader of the independence movement to free India from British rule. But I'm sure you know that."

As they continued on their way, they spotted two tapirs on the side of the road just ahead. One was drinking from the creek. Another stood knee-deep in the water.

"Aapo, pull over so Jessica can get a good look." Mr. Chan turned around and addressed her. "This is really a treat. Mountain cows are very shy. It's rare to see them out. Rarer still to see more than one at a time."

After a couple of minutes the tapirs discovered that they weren't alone. They ran up a path and disappeared.

"See that path?" Mr. Chan asked, pointing out the window. "Telltale sign we're in tapir country."

"This is great! I never imagined seeing so much wildlife. They look so weird com-

3. See Chapter 3, "Hinduism, Jainism, and Sikhism," in *Religions of Asia Today*, John Esposito, et al., eds., Oxford University Press.

pared to what I'm used to…. You know, tapirs remind me of Baku in Chinese and Japanese mythology. Baku is the dream eater. He eats bad dreams. He kind of resembles a tapir. Indeed, the kanji for Baku and tapir is the same. Baku has an elephant-like trunk, eyes of a rhino, tail of a cow, and paws of a tiger. If a child is having a nightmare, she's supposed to repeat 'Baku, come eat my dream' three times. Some children even have a Baku talisman at their bedside, to ward off bad dreams. But if Baku's not satisfied after eating your bad dream, he will eat your hopes and desires, leaving you with an empty life."[4]

As Jessica was talking, Aapo started the SUV and they were on their way again. Soon, Mr. Chan was snoozing, which left Jessica to find other ways to occupy her time. She opened her backpack, pulled out a notebook and pen, and began to write:

Amanda …. Amanda …? (She looked at Maya for inspiration.) *Amanda Macaw knew just what she wanted. The problem was how to find it. This was true of men too. They were always too…. Too….* (*Some string of adjectives to describe all those obnoxious character traits of all those obnoxious men I've dated.*)

As Jessica was trying to find just that string of adjectives to describe all those obnoxious character traits of all those obnoxious men she dated, Mr. Chan awoke and said, "Aapo, why don't you entertain us with a Kriol song." To Jessica, he said, "Aapo is Kriol, but his parents confused him by giving him a Maya name." He laughed.

"OK, let's do 'Palmer William.' You know it!" Aapo said to Mr. Chan, eyes bright.

"Sure I know it." Mr. Chan smiled widely and began tapping his thighs to set the tempo.

Aapo's right hand tapped along on the steering wheel as he began: "Titie grass di grow…."

"Palmer William, Palmer William," Mr. Chan sang out.

"Show me how you mommy walk…."

"Palmer William, Palmer William."

"Show me how you grampa dance…."

"Come on, Jessica!" Mr. Chan looked back at her and grinned.

"Palmer William, Palmer William!" Jessica smiled.

"Show me how you auntie run…."

"Palmer William, Palmer William."

Even Maya squawked, "Palmer William!" causing them to laugh.

"Usually we all break into dance, acting out each of the people named," Aapo explained. "Wait till we're a few bottles of rum in with all the guys at the camp! It's a riot."

"Aapo does a great 'kissing gramma,'" Mr. Chan said with a smile. Aapo turned to him and puckered his lips while batting his eyelashes. Mr. Chan puckered back.

Jessica giggled.

"'Palmer William' is a 'fattening' song," Aapo explained. "Fattening songs interrupt a storytelling. My grampa used to do this with us all the time. We would just laugh and laugh."

After they settled down from their merrymaking, Jessica asked, "So what was it like growing up in British Honduras?"

"It was already named 'Belize' by the time I was born in '74," Aapo began. "I was seven years old when we gained independence, so I don't really remember much—except the parades. We'd all be waving our Union Jack flags."

"We'd often have parades for the governor's visit. He'd stay at the Governor's

4. See http://www.ancient-origins.net/myths-legends-asia/baku-legend-dream-eater-002383.

House in Belize City. He was the Queen's representative. We'd all go to the pier and decorate it with coconut palms and Union Jack flags to prepare for his visit. He was a white man, all dressed in white and wearing a white helmet, looking very important and official," Mr. Chan said.

"And very white!" Aapo said through laughter.

"I was a boy then," Mr. Chan continued. "In '64 we gained self-governance, and power transferred from the Queen to the Premier. Only thirty people voted in our first election.[5] My father was one of them." He smiled.

"So Honduras was like the Caribbean version of England…." Jessica said.

"I suppose you could say that. All of our paper money had the Queen's face on it. Coins had King George and Prince Phillip…. And we'd even sing 'God save the Queen.'" Mr. Chan broke out into song: "God save the Queen. Long live our Noble Queen. God save the Queen…."

"If you listen to him go on, I'd say Mr. Chan most remembers the fútbol matches." Aapo laughed.

"And sneaking in to see the horse racing…. I was damned good at picking horses."

"Still are." Aapo smirked.

"Oh, and I'll never forget when Muhammad Ali did that exhibition at the Palace Theater in '65. I was eleven years old." Mr. Chan smiled, memories bobbing in his head.

After some silence, Jessica said, "You know, I always get riled up thinking about the history of colonialism." She wrinkled her forehead. "Take India: The British took control in 1858 (calling it 'The Jewel of the Crown') until India's independence in 1947. But even a few centuries before that, when they started trading for spices, silk, indigo, and cotton goods as the East India Company, British officials believed it was their duty as 'more enlightened' White Europeans to spread their civilization to the so-called backward people. It was happening all over the globe…."

"Including right here," Mr. Chan piped in. "But don't forget, Jessica, Americans were also masterful colonizers. Think about what they did to the American Indians— what they're still doing."

"You've got a point." Jessica continued, "Anyway, British missionaries would preach the Gospel to the 'Infidel Barbarians,' demanding they convert and be saved. Colonized people across the globe faced ideological challenges of the Enlightenment's scientific worldview, humanistic critiques of religion, and theories about European racial superiority…. This had to have been very distressing to the colonized, since conquest suggested that their own gods had lost to the almighty Christian God. And of course the Brits played into this narrative by suggesting that their conquest showed that their god had judged the local gods to be idolatrous—demonic even. Consider too the tremendous impact of having traditional beliefs, practices, and cultures completely undermined."[6]

Maya squawked in agreement. Mr. Chan and Aapo joined in with nodding heads.

"You're right, of course," Mr. Chan said. "And don't forget the British introduced slavery here too. I mentioned this before."

"Right," Jessica said with a sour face. "Another thing that they have in common with Americans."

"So what got you interested in Eastern religions, Jessica?" Aapo asked.

5. See Angel Nuñez, "What It Felt Like to Live in British Honduras," at ambergriscaye.com.
6. See Esposito, Chapter 3.

"I guess I'm syncretic: Christian Buddhist." Jessica chuckled. "My Aunt Jacqueline was a New Age Hindu of sorts. She even had her own guru. I moved in with her when I was fifteen, after I left my grandparents. She loved James Redfield's *The Celestine Prophecy*. She called it her 'New Age soul candy.'" She chuckled again.

"This aunt must be on your mother's side," Mr. Chan began. "since your Uncle Nick only has one sibling—your father." But Jessica didn't hear him. She had closed her eyes and was thinking about her Auntie Jack.

Fifteen years earlier

After three knocks went unanswered, fifteen-year-old Jessica Kraut cautiously opened the front door, hot pink suitcase in hand. Her aunt, wearing a pale blue tee that read 'Namaste,' was sitting on a meditation pillow in Quarter Lotus position in the middle of the floor, eyes closed. Next to her sat a red- and gold-painted wooden Chakra singing bowl. Dozens of mini candles in pink, blue, yellow, and white illuminated the room, which smelled like white sage, lemon, and lavender. Jessica ever so quietly entered, set down her suitcase, plopped on an orange upholstered accent chair—and waited. She looked on a nearby table. There sat a bottle of Kuan Yin spray (the $22.95 price tag still affixed to the label), a Mythical Goddess tarot deck, a stack of meditation CDs, and a tattered copy of *The Celestine Prophecy*. On the wall behind her aunt, left to right: a poster with the Hindu spelling of 'Om' (ॐ), a chart showing the seven main chakras, a poster of a blue cartoon bear in Lotus position against an orange background, and a print of a white unicorn illumined in emerald green.

Her aunt opened one eye and said, "Hello Jessica." She picked up a wooden stick and struck the bowl three times and then ran it around the rim. "I'm balancing my chakras…." She opened her other eye and unfolded her legs. "I can do this later." She stood up, walked to the kitchen, and opened the fridge. She pulled out a pitcher. "Want some Chai iced tea? I make it myself. I use organic milk and honey." She grabbed two glasses from the cabinet, poured, and extended one to Jessica.

"Thanks, Auntie Jack," Jessica began. "And thanks for rescuing me from that hell hole."

Aunt Jacqueline motioned Jessica to the kitchen table. "Have a seat." Then more seriously: "I know how dad can get, especially when he drinks."

Jessica sat down and took a sip of tea. "He would hit me and Grandma."

"I know—I'm sorry. You can stay here as long as you'd like." She looked at Jessica from across a single white daisy sitting in a hand-carved, soapstone vase.

"It's OK with mom?"

"Absolutely. I just talked with her this morning."

"They don't want me to come back home?" Jessica gulped, choking back some tears. "I didn't mean to, Auntie Jack. I didn't mean to. I was only twelve years old." Her voice cracked. "Will they ever forgive me?"

"They've got a lot on their plate right now—I know it hurts." Jacqueline nervously grasped her amethyst pendant. After some silence, she said, "Here, let's go to my dragon altar."

They walked back into the living room to a little table draped in red, burgundy, and orange silk. All kinds of dragon totems and blood red candles were scattered atop it. Red, burgundy, and orange gemstones of various shapes and sizes were placed in small crystal bowls. Jacqueline grabbed a lighter and lit all of the candles. She held Jessica's hand.

"We need to reawaken your life force, deep within your body. Here…." She pointed at Jessica's pelvis. "Now, visualize your Fire Dragon. See it swirling, glowing, growling, waiting to be released to come to your rescue, to protect and defend you."

Jessica looked at her aunt curiously, but played along. She closed her eyes.

Jacqueline smiled. "Good…. Now, imagine it moving up your body from deep within. The screaming power of your Fire Dragon, made of flames, moving up through your throat…."[7]

Jessica gulped.

"Good…. Now SCREAM!"

Jessica let out a roar, causing Jacqueline's blue and white parakeet to drop dizzily from her perch in a nearby cage.

"Great! Do you feel better?"

Jessica looked at her aunt, who was still holding her hand. "I really do," she said, surprising herself. She gave a warm smile.

"We have a few hours to kill before my guru, Sri Gambhīrā, shows up. What would you like to do?" Brief pause, then: "Oh, I haven't shown you my Lord Krishna altar. It's in my bedroom. Bring your suitcase with you. You'll be sleeping in the other twin bed."

They walked into the bedroom. Same kind of stuff, same kind of New Age feel.

"You have the bed by the window," Jacqueline said. A blue-painted table separated the two beds each draped with purple nebula duvet covers. A copy of the *Bhagavad Gita* sat atop it, next to an orange salt lamp and a glass elephant pipe.

Atop a small wooden bookshelf, on a swath of white silk, sat a framed print of a beautiful bluish *Krishna* playing the flute against a sapphire background. To the left was placed a small cup filled with water. To the right, a white candle in a holder, a little bell, and incense in a hand-carved stone elephant holder. In front was placed a blue ceramic plate with three oranges and a handful of jasmine flowers thoughtfully arranged and smelling sweet—exotic even.

"Lord Krishna is to be approached with *bhakti*—devotion," Jacqueline said as she plopped on her bed. Jessica sat across from her. "Krishna teaches bhakti yoga in the *Bhagavad Gita*. You should read it sometime while you're here. It's a spiritual treasure and part of the Hindu epic *Mahabharata*. Krishna can extend his grace, absorb our karma, and liberate us from suffering and samsara."

"Samsara?"

"The cycle of birth, death, and rebirth, determined by our karma—our actions."

"What's with the fruit?" Jessica pointed at the altar.

"It's an offering…. Did you know when Lord Krishna was a boy, he heard a woman in the street selling fruit. He wanted to buy some but didn't have any money. So he gathered a handful of grains and ran to the woman. He asked her whether he could exchange the grains for some fruit. But when he opened his little hand, he had just a few pieces of grain left. The rest had fallen to the ground as he ran to her in his excitement. The woman noticed this, but told Lord Krishna to take whatever fruits he liked. He placed the few grains in her basket, and she filled his hands with as much fruit as he could carry. When she got home, she looked into her basket, which was overflowing with gold and jewels. She never had to sell fruit again." Jacqueline smiled.

"That's a cute story. Who is Krishna? Is he that blue guy?"

Jessica pointed at the print.

"Yes. Krishna is the most important *avatar* of *Vishnu*."

"Why's he blue?"

7. See "How to Build a Dragon Altar," at old-earth.com.

"'Krishna' means 'dark one.' He's usually colored blue in Indian art, perhaps because blue is more alluring and irresistible to look at than say brown, black, or white. Also, think about it: things that are vast, things that are beyond our perception, tend to be blue: the ocean, the sky, the cosmos. Krishna is so much larger than our perception, so much larger than our understanding. It makes sense that he'd be blue."

"So what's an avatar anyway—and who is Vishnu?"

"Lord Vishnu is the Supreme God. He lies on his cosmic serpent, and from his navel grows a lotus plant. From the lotus, the creator god *Brahma* is born—the first of all creation. Life evolves over countless years, out of the divine energy at the center of the universe. Eventually all things return into Vishnu, and there everything lies dormant while he sleeps, until the process starts all over again—a renewal of creation....[8] The whole cycle repeats itself over and again in an endless process of creation and destruction. Each cosmic cycle has four ages or *yugas*. The worst and last age, the morally dark age, is called *Kali Yuga*, which began at the end of the Mahabharata War. This is our current age. At the end of Kali Yuga, *Kalki*, the final incarnation of Vishnu, will appear as the harbinger of the end of time.... An avatar is an incarnation of Vishnu, and Sri Krishna is the most revered of Vishnu's avatars."

"This sounds like Jesus. Jesus is the Incarnation of God. That's what Grandma says—and I guess I believe that too."

"There are many similarities between Sri Krishna and Jesus, Jessica.[9] Like Jesus, Krishna was born of human parents. He's both man and God. Like Jesus, Krishna shows grace and compassion, and rewards his *bhaktas*—followers. The *Purānas*, ancient Hindu tales, tell many wonderful stories about Krishna's playful childhood. In the *Bhagavata Purana*, we find the story of Sri Krishna and the woman fruit vendor. Because Vishnu loved the world, he descended into the womb of Devakī. Like Jesus' mother, Devakī was chosen because she was exceptionally pure. When Krishna was born, moonlight shone over the whole earth, heavenly nymphs sang, and the gods dropped flowers from the heavens. Like Jesus, Krishna was born under the rule of an evil king—Kamsa. Kamsa wanted to kill Krishna because a celestial voice prophesied his death at the hands of Devakī's eighth child. Like Jesus' father, Joseph, Krishna's father was told in a dream to take baby Krishna to safety. Like the evil King Herod, Kamsa also ordered the massacre of all male babies. Like Jesus, Krishna had special powers...."

Jacqueline stood up, walked to the altar, grabbed the print of Krishna, and brought it to her heart. "Lord Krishna died at the hands of a hunter who mistook his foot for a deer, shooting him with an arrow while he was meditating. He abandoned his mortal body, and his imperishable spirit ascended back to his eternal abode—heaven—to preside over paradise, where his faithful followers hope someday to join him." She smiled.

Jessica smiled back. "That does sound a lot like Jesus. The spirit of God conceived him in Mary's womb. Of course Mary was a virgin. Since Krishna was Devakī's eighth child, she obviously wasn't. Instead of moonlight shining over the whole earth, the Star of Bethlehem brightened up the sky when Jesus was born. The star shone so brightly that magi from the East were able to follow it to bring gifts of gold, frankincense, and myrrh to the special child."

"Right...." Jacqueline carefully placed the print back on the altar and returned

8. See Chapter 1, "About Religion," in Oxtoby.
9. Ibid. See also Geoffrey Parrinder, *Avatar and Incarnation: The Divine in Human Form in the World's Religions.*

to her bed. "Many Hindus have no problem accepting Jesus as an avatar of Vishnu. We're syncretic. We can easily incorporate all of these disparate teachers. You know, Gandhi, who loved the *Gita*, rejected the historicity of Krishna. And there's certainly plenty of evidence in the *Gita* to suggest that it *should* be understood allegorically—symbolizing life in the body as a constant warfare between good and evil forces. In my mind, though, we should understand it historically *and* allegorically."

"What about the differences between Jesus and Krishna, Auntie Jack? I can think of one. You said that Krishna was the most revered of Vishnu's avatars. Vishnu had more than one avatar, whereas Jesus was God's only Incarnation."

"You're right. Krishna clearly states, 'I come into being age after age.' Most agree that there have been nine avatars of Vishnu. Krishna's usually considered to be the eighth, and Gautama Buddha, the ninth. (That reminds me: do you know my girlfriend Noel? You've met her, right? We lead a queer Dharma group at the Buddhist Center. You should come!) The tenth will be Kalki. There are other significant differences too. Foremost the two understandings of their deaths. After all, Jesus died on the cross for our sins. Krishna, on the other hand, *chose* to die to fulfill a sage's words. Krishna offended the sage when he failed to wipe his feet. In his outrage, the sage announced that the whole of Krishna's body would be invulnerable, except for his feet. This was *literally* Krishna's Achilles heel. Sin also doesn't have the same weight for us as it does in Christianity. We don't understand samsara to be the result of a 'Fall' of our nature. Krishna liberates us from samsara if we seek him with unswerving devotion. As Lord Krishna says in Chapter 8 of the *Gita*, 'Remember me at all times *and fight on*. With your heart and mind intent on me, you will surely come to me.'"

Jessica settled back into her pillow, closed her eyes, and smiled.

Present day, sunset, arriving at the camp

Jessica stepped out of the SUV. Maya flew up to a branch of a nearby gumbo-limbo tree and started eating the deep red fruit. Golden-leaved bromeliads grew on the copper-colored bark of the trunk, which peeled like strips of paper.

The camp was on a mostly clear forest floor, under a canopy one hundred feet high. Past logging and hurricane damage had left their signatures, making the forest feel—*vulnerable*. Nine big tents sat roughly in a circle. Jessica could hear the babbles of a nearby stream and the wee-yoo calls of the pauraque. Several fluttered about, their greyish-brown variegated plumage standing out against the pinkish-violet sky. They were nabbing at the passing insects. As Jessica watched them, a couple mongrels raced past her.

"We're trying not to leave a big footprint, and obviously we don't want to draw attention, so we keep it pretty simple," Mr. Chan explained.

Jessica looked around, all too aware of her white American face. About two dozen brown and black men, she guessed. Five of them sat together playing instruments. They were all dressed roughly the same way: tan pants, short-sleeved, button-down cotton shirts, and donning straw fedoras. One man stood out in a black top hat and vest. Another stopped playing his instrument, took a swig from a rum bottle, and started up again.

Mr. Chan noticed her looking. "They're quite good, aren't they? That's Henry playing the conch shell. Edouard's on the cowbell, Obi, the jigsaw, and Marcos plays the maracas. The guy in the top hat playing the bongo is Prosper. Their favorite is reggae. They also play funk. You can't help but get up and move your feet."

"They're really great!" Jessica smiled broadly.

They wandered around the camp. Aapo stayed a few feet behind them.

"Most of us share a common faith—Catholic—or syncretic Catholic.

"My gramma practiced Obeah—" Aapo interrupted, "I don't put much stock in that superstitious stuff anymore."

"I'd love to hear about Obeah sometime," Jessica said.

"Sure…." He grinned.

Mr. Chan continued, "There's a stream over there for bathing, washing clothes and dishes, and for cooking—just make sure you boil the water first before you drink it. If you walk upstream about five minutes or so, you'll find a waterfall and pool for swimming. We have a couple of inner tubes over there, next to the supply tent, if you'd ever like to use one. Just let someone know where you're going first. And be sure to keep a lookout for pugmarks. There are tigers around…. Oh, the nearest village is about eighteen kilometers away, if you ever need anything. Someone can take you there. They know me, and you can get whatever you want on credit."

"OK."

"Most of these guys have been here the past couple weeks, setting up," Mr. Chan explained. "They cleared a dump over there. Just be sure to bury your garbage, to keep the animals away. We've got firewood next to the supply tent which has everything you could possibly need, including cooking utensils, hats, rain jackets, towels, binoculars, flashlights, lanterns, jugs for water, a machete…."

"Great …"

"STOP!" A towering man with chocolate brown skin and coarse black hair, moustache, and beard approached. He was wearing a butter-colored tunic. A jade amulet hung from his neck.

"What? What's wrong? Do I have a big bug on me or something?" Jessica asked, circling around.

"Give me your palm," the man said. He looked at her with dark, penetrating eyes.

"There's no escaping it, Jessica," Mr. Chan said through laughter. Aapo just shook his head.

The man took her right hand and caressed it. "So soft. You don't work with your hands much, do you?"

"No, not really."

"Not much gardening? You really should try it. Cabbage, tomatoes, maybe some peppers…. Perhaps some eggplant? You know, you can make a lot of great dishes with eggplant. You're a good cook, I hope."

Jessica gave no response.

"I hope? …" He ran his fingers along her own. "You're one of those intellectual types—like a teacher. Or creative. An artist, maybe."

Jessica studied the man, whose hand felt strong and imposing.

"She's a bit of both," Mr. Chan offered. "She works in Nick Kraus' gallery. This is his niece, Jessica. She's also a professor."

"Nick Kraus' niece?" He looked at her suspiciously.

"Glad to meet you." She tried to release her hand.

"Don't pull away—I need to do a reading." He ran his finger across her palm. "You're very passionate…." He gave a sly smile. "But see how these two lines touch? You're also vulnerable. I can see that your heart's been broken many times." He traced a line to the bottom of her palm. "This is a sign of good health." He grinned. "But see here? How these lines cross? You're in emotional crisis." He gently kissed her palm and released her hand. "Am I right?"

Jessica smiled uncomfortably.

"My name's Chicken Eyes." He paused for several seconds before he added, "Well, don't you want to know *why*?"

"Sure…. Why?"

"Because I can see into the future." His face brightened. He had a pleasant smile, if you didn't notice the pain behind his eyes.

"The only future he can see is which chicken will become tonight's dinner," Aapo interjected with a laugh. "More like Ojos de Pollo Loco."

Jessica laughed along.

"Entiendes el Español?" Aapo asked.

"*Crazy Chicken Eyes*—Un poco."

"Aapo only says these things because he can't stand how popular I am with the pretty ladies," Chicken Eyes said.

Aapo rolled his eyes at the nonsense. "Mout seh anyting."

Chicken Eyes grinned widely.

"Chicken Eyes will be staying behind to help you, while the others are out on the job. Whatever you need—including slaughtering the meat du jour," Mr. Chan said, chuckling at his choice of words.

I'm going to be Snow White—to two dozen men?

Suddenly Malibu seemed the sweeter deal.

She looked over at a man sleeping in a nearby hammock. *There's Sleepy.* And then another man trying desperately to drink from a corked bottle of rum. *—And Dopey.*

"Chicken Eyes has prepared dinner for us tonight." Mr. Chan took Jessica's hand.

"Great," she said with all the enthusiasm she could muster. *Better enjoy it.* She'll be the one cooking dinner for the next forty nights. "So what's on the menu?"

"Agouti ragouti!" Chicken Eyes blurt out.

"Agouti ragout," Mr. Chan said.

"What's agouti?"

"It's like a wild guinea pig," Aapo explained.

Jessica wrinkled her nose at the thought. Images of her childhood pet disturbed her appetite.

"Plantain no eat like rice," Aapo jested. He loved throwing out Kriol phrases.

"You eat what's available…" Mr. Chan translated. "Now, let's go over to the table. Don't mind Padre, he tends to turn grace into a sermon." He chuckled.

"Is he a real priest?"

"No, but he plays one on TV—Well he did, on a Mexican soap opera back in the nineties."

She smiled.

"I've arranged to have you sit next to B'alam. He knows all the medicinal plants to treat whatever might ail you."

Jessica sighed. "*Doc….*"

Meanwhile, back in Malibu

A lime green tree frog with bulging red eyes and a cute smile, weighing in at a whopping 0.35 ounces and a mere 2 inches long, stood in the taxi line at LAX behind a big sweaty woman in pink flowered sweatpants. He was donning a hot pink plastic ten-gallon hat and carrying a hot pink plastic suitcase, both made especially for

Malibu Barbie, left behind by a little girl as she boarded a minivan. She had been on a daytrip with her parents from San Ignacio to Caracol, the largest Maya archeological site in Belize, and the largest metropolis in the Maya lowlands during the Classic period. She had accidentally left behind other travel accessories too: a hot pink plastic golf bag and guitar—and the little frog's favorite, an electric purple plastic boom box with two matching speakers—but alas, they were too much for his little red webbed hands to carry. The little red-eyed tree frog had received these gifts for his third birthday from a Keel-billed toucan ("bill birds" the Belizeans call them), whose name was none other than *Mr. Bill.*

The little frog's reason for his visit? He had been inspired, by Mr. Bill's telling of how these accessories were for a *Malibu* Barbie, to go to Malibu to try to meet none other than the Coen Brothers—his favorite directors. The little frog had it in his mind that once the two brothers heard him sing, they would most assuredly cast him in their next movie. He wanted to be in a singing scene like the one with the dancing sailors in *Hail, Caesar!* And so when the opportunity arose to find his way into the suitcase of an American tourist—a suitcase with one of those baggage tags from LAX—he simply couldn't resist.

When the little frog entered the taxi, he told the driver to go to the Ralphs supermarket at the Malibu Colony Plaza. Every director, indeed every movie star, had to buy groceries at some point. After all, they had to eat. The taxi driver wondered what *he* had eaten to make him believe that he was conversing with a talking frog. But his little green passenger paid his fare when the driver dropped him off in the Ralphs parking lot—and money is money, whether coming from a talking frog or otherwise.

The red-eyed tree frog made his way to the produce section and hopped onto a pile of mouth-watering peaches. As he bit into a piece of the succulent fruit, he spotted none other than Pamela Anderson, most striking even without her face made up, in cutoff jeans and white tee, carefully inspecting a head of cabbage. Satisfied, Miss Anderson put the vegetable into her basket and walked to the cashier.

Just then a man, complete with wavy dark hair, chiseled chin, and high cheekbones, looking every bit the model he never was, and clothed in a black cotton tee (only $110) and army twill trousers ($225), showed up at the produce section. As he grabbed for a nearby peach, the little frog cried out with nectar dripping from his little mouth, "Excuse me, sir, I was wondering, may I trouble you for a favor?"

"Huh? What?" Finn Lauder looked around to try to find the source of the squeaky little voice.

The little frog waved his little red webbed hands to get the man's attention. "I'm right here!"

Finally, Finn noticed him. He rubbed his eyes in disbelief and then looked at the peaches once again—but the frog was still there.

What was in that chicken vindaloo I ate last night?

Finn decided to play along. "Shouldn't your legs be over in the meat section—on ice?"

The little frog ignored the man's impolite question. "I need to meet the Coen Brothers. Can you introduce me?"

Finn studied the frog before offering, "You're on the wrong coast, little buddy." He grabbed a couple of peaches, put them in his shopping basket, and turned to walk away.

As Finn was doing so, the little frog hopped into his basket. He looked up at him with bright red, bulging, round, *imploring* eyes and said, "Where are you going? Can't you help me?"

"To the pharmaceutical aisle. I think I need an antacid…." Finn shook his head before adding, "You seem so *real*."

The little frog continued, "I'm trying to be discovered. My friends tell me I have a beautiful singing voice…. Let me demonstrate." He cleared his little throat and began, "*As a shorty playing in the front yard of the crib, fell down, and I bumped my head….*"

"Impressive, but I really can't help you…."

The little red-eyed tree frog beseeched him, "Isn't this Malibu? Don't you have contacts?"

"I've only met Kevin Costner at Blockbuster Video. We were both grabbing for *Mad Max: Fury Road*. It's better than most of the Mad Max movies. Of course nothing can beat the original. But what would a little frog know about such things?" Finn was wondering why he was carrying on a conversation with so obvious a figment of his imagination.

The little frog responded, "You'd be surprised."

"Look—I think you should get an agent. You won't get anywhere without an agent."

"How much does *that* cost?" The little frog saw his dreams begin to dash before his little red bulging eyes.

"Best go back to where you came from." Finn paid the cashier and walked out into the parking lot. "Good luck, little guy. No matter what you do, stay away from the chefs at Mélisse's.…" Finn waved goodbye to the little red-eyed tree frog left standing in his emptied basket, got into his metallic silver Porsche, pulled out his phone, and texted Maggie: *OMG! Friend having nervous BD. Can u share contact info of ur shrink?* — And then he sped away.

Later in the evening, at the camp

While Jessica was unpacking, Aapo appeared at the entrance to her tent.

"Want to go for a walk?"

"Oh, hi." Jessica gave a warm smile. "It's very dark out. Is it safe?"

Jaguars and snakes…

Aapo held up his lantern and then tapped the thigh pocket of his sand-colored cargo pants. "I've got a pistol…. But we won't be venturing off too far, in any case. I just wanted to step away from all the noise."

Aapo was right. It was still noisy. The guys had resumed playing their music. There seemed to be some kind of card game going on in a nearby tent. Chicken Eyes was doing a tarot reading for Dopey (whose name she did not know, but she swore that when she did, she would remember not to call him that). Twenty-four drunken men making the most of their night, before they'd start their job in the morning.

"It's all a bit overwhelming." She set down her things and walked up to him.

They managed to sneak out of the camp, unnoticed. As they were walking, Jessica noted that the ground sparkled. Little did she know that it sparkled with the eyes of hundreds of spiders creeping about.

"So where're we going?" Jessica asked. As she was walking just behind Aapo on a slightly worn path, she almost tripped over a moss-covered root of a mahogany tree.

"There's a place I like to go to escape. Nobody else knows about it. It looks like the remnants of some limestone steps—probably Maya. We're almost there."

Towering trees tangled in vines surrounded the steps leading to…more stone crumbles. Aapo sat down and placed the lantern by his side.

"Why don't you sit down, Jessica, beside the lantern."

Jessica thought how romantic this might be: under a full moon and with Mr. Chan.

"When did you find this place?"

"About three years ago." Aapo looked at her with friendly eyes.

"Is that how long you've been coming here? Three years?"

"Yes. It seems to work well for us—better than the last place. The villagers keep their eyes and ears open for anything suspicious. They've got our backs."

"Is this a Maya village?"

"Yes, Q'eqchi'."

"Mr. Chan's family?"

"Mr. Chan has no family. Well, we're his family."

Just then Jessica heard a rustling in the underbrush, and then a whining, ghost-like sound: "Ah—oowah." She reached for Aapo's arm.

"What's that?" she asked, heart racing.

"The Lords of Xibalba are calling for you." Aapo couldn't help but tease. He tried to hide his smile.

"Xibalba?" She knocked over the lantern as she tried to hug Aapo.

"The Maya underworld…. They're coming to get you."

"Ah—oowah. Ah—oowah. Ah—oowah."

"What is it? What is it, really?" She was now cradled in Aapo's arms. She looked into his eyes, but it was too dark to see anything with a tipped-over lantern.

Aapo burst out laughing. "It's a bird, Jessica—a slaty-breasted tinamou, likely calling for his mate." He picked up the lantern. "Good thing this isn't kerosene."

Jessica released her embrace. "A bird…." She shook her head. After a pause, she said, "Don't tease me like that. This place freaks me out, especially at night."

"Sorry," Aapo smiled. "It was just too hard to resist." But Jessica wasn't amused.

He tried to lighten the mood. "Did you know that Chicken Eyes claims he hit Big Foot with his motorcycle?"

"What? What do you mean? Big Foot?"

"He was a physicist, you know. At Columbia University. He's quite brilliant…."

"No way."

"He was…. But then he couldn't stop talking about Big Foot. They laughed him right out of the department."

"Is that why he's into all this psychic stuff now?"

"Yep. He thinks there're many things that just can't be explained, that are beyond our scientific understanding. Whenever he opens his mouth, I swear I feel like I'm standing neck-deep in crazy. But he's a great guy—Really. You'll really like him."

"And what about Mr. Chan?"

"Mr. Chan mostly keeps to himself in his tent. Sometimes he'll meet us on the job, to see how things are going…. In a few days, he'll make a trip to Argentina, to meet with the brokers."

How can I ask Aapo what's going on? Why we are here. But then maybe the jig will be up. What should I do?

"So who're all these guys? Where'd they come from?" She absent-mindedly rubbed her hand against the coarse, weathered stone of the step.

"Kriol, Mestizo, Maya, and Garifuna. You know, many Garifuna live in LA. We all speak English, Spanish, and Kriol. We're like brothers. We'd *never* let each other down. Never turn our backs on each other. Despite the diversity of the Belizean people, there's a lot of racism and bigotry. *But not here.* Not between us. Mr. Chan's really made us one big family."

"Mr. Chan seems like an amazing man. I mean he's got everything going for him: looks, charisma, good taste, money...."

"Don't get all lovesick over Mr. Chan. He makes a point of not getting involved with the women who oversee the camp."

"I'm not. Don't be silly...." She tried to stop smiling. "So tell me about racism in Belize."

"The darker your skin, the more racist people are towards you," Aapo said, a little self-consciously.

"That's true pretty much everywhere," Jessica responded, a little self-consciously.

"Right. And if you really want to see the racism come out, just add alcohol. Sometimes it'll sneak out in the camp, but like I said, we're all like brothers.... The Maya are generally despised across the board. Well, the Garifuna tend to stand up for them. But a lot of people think the Maya should just check in their identities, learn English, forget their traditions, forget their communal lands."

"Is that what happened with Mr. Chan? Did he decide to check in his identity?" Once Jessica realized that Aapo wasn't going to answer, she said, "Can't we find better solutions? Indigenous traditions and lands are crucial for their survival. Discriminating against Indigenous peoples by taking their lands and robbing them of their traditions has gone on for centuries. It really pisses me off."

"I'll give you a recent example of all this," Aapo began, "of racism between groups.[10] Last summer, Maya leaders and some of the villagers of Santa Cruz were arrested for unlawful imprisonment of a Kriol man who had been trying to build a house on their land. For months the Maya tried to get help from the national police, who never responded. Finally, the village police arrested the man. After his release, he pressed charges against the Maya, accusing them of racism for not allowing him to build a house on their land. The man said he wasn't welcome because he's black. The Garifuna supported the Maya, saying that they also face threats to their land rights and autonomy in their own communities."

"This seems like a no-win situation all around," Jessica began, adding her two bits. "Of course with the national police refusing to get involved, they were just pitting groups against each other."

"The government only gets involved when it benefits them, when it suits their purposes.... I guess it's truly amazing that we all get along so well in the camp."

Just then they heard footsteps—distinctly *human* footsteps—or so at least it seemed to Aapo's trained ear. He reached for his gun.

"There you two are," Mr. Chan said. "I see you find this spot as peaceful as I do." He held up his lantern and smiled.

"How did *you* find out about this place?" Aapo asked, feeling robbed of a treasure.

"Like you, I sneak away for a little peace and quiet, now and again." He looked at Jessica and said, "Would you like to join me for a glass of homemade wine outside my tent? Chicken Eyes made it with some wild berries."

"Sure, I'd love to." Jessica simpered, clearly pleased with the turn of events. She rose and stood straight in front of him as he held out his hand.

10. Aapo's story, and much of their discussion, comes from "Racism, Indigeneity, and Land in Belize: A National Debate," at https://www.culturalsurvival.org (7-6-2015).

"We were just getting ready to leave anyway," Aapo said somewhat pathetically, and frowned.

"Did you know the Maya were stargazers? Great astronomers," Mr. Chan said as he poured Jessica a glass of wine. They were sitting on two chairs outside of Mr. Chan's tent, looking at the stars. Maya had settled in a nearby ceiba tree. She began preening her feathers.

Mr. Chan looked up into the branches. "You've got your bird really trained. I'm surprised he doesn't just fly away."

"I wouldn't mind if he did. He'd be free."

"Best keep your eye on him here. We wouldn't want anything to happen to him."

"But macaws are native to Belize. What could possibly happen to him?"

"Sure, *but you know what I mean*…. As I was saying, the Maya priest-astronomers would study the heavens. Given their knowledge of the patterns of the sky, they could predict the future: the time the sun would rise and set, the planting season, and so much more. They were also astrologers. The movements of constellations across the sky revealed a connection between these celestial events and human affairs."[11]

Jessica hung on his every word. "Fascinating…."

"Do you know anything about the ceiba tree?"

"What do you mean?"

Mr. Chan pointed up at the tree where Maya was perched. "This is a ceiba tree. You'll get a better look at it in the morning. This is a younger tree. Its trunk is still covered with thick, conical thorns. Once the tree matures, the thorns will fall off. Right now it lacks a fully developed root system. The thorns are there to prevent animals from damaging it…. The Maya honor the ceiba tree. They consider it to be sacred. They call it 'the Tree of Life.' It connects the Earth to the underworld and heavens."

"Aapo teased me about Xibalba." Jessica couldn't help but smile.

"Aapo likes to poke fun…." Mr. Chan gave a pleasant laugh. "The ceiba tree is where the Maya gods abide—both the celestial gods and the gods of Xibalba. The Maya believe that the souls of the dead ascend to the treetops to go to heaven."

"Do you believe that, Mr. Chan? I believe in souls, celestial beings, and beings of the so-called underworld." She put her hand to her breast. "Do you?"

"Without question I believe that the cosmos influences our lives. Beyond that, I'm not really sure…. Did you know that the ancient Maya gods were worshipped in sacred ceremonies that included human sacrifices? I guess most everyone knows this. Maya rulers and nobles were believed to be descendants of the gods. They thought that their own blood (through bloodletting), or the blood of the royal captives, was an ideal offering. Of course Maya priests today don't perform blood sacrifices to the gods. Instead, they use the sacred elements of fire, wind, water, and earth, as well as maize, honey, sea salt, and essential oils. And today, Maya religious practices often incorporate elements of Roman Catholicism."[12]

Mr. Chan freshened Jessica's wine glass and then asked, "So what do you do, besides work for your uncle? Since you no longer teach, do other activities occupy your time?"

"I'm writing a romance novel," Jessica said proudly. Her fingers ran along the necklace that Mr. Chan had given her, finally resting on the Virgin of Guadalupe. She

11. See "The Astronomy of the Mayas," at starteachastronomy.com.
12. See "Ancient Maya Civilization," at yucatanadventure.com.

smiled.

Mr. Chan pursed his lips. "A romance novel? You know, men really don't like romance novels. Steamy sex with strangers sporting washboard abs and chiseled chins." He laughed, clearly amused with himself. "You're cutting your potential readership in half by writing a romance novel."

"I'm not writing for Harlequin—I meant to say that I'm writing a novel that includes romance. About two strangers who fall in love."

"If I were you, I'd put an end to the romantic element of your story. Make the man detestable in some way. Of course women often go for those bad-boy types. In any case, I'd kill him off. Whatever it takes. Otherwise you'll lose your male audience…. This is just my advice."

"I guess I could do that. I've only started the first chapter."

"This is really the way to go…. Good. Now to the business at hand."

He smiled. "I'm sure your uncle filled you in, but just to reassure you, you'll get twenty percent of the profits for running the camp. I can't promise you exactly how much that'll be, since we can lose up to sixty percent of the animals in transport, but if we're lucky (and this really does depend on luck) you could get about one million. Certainly 650 to 700."

"Oh," she said, not quite understanding.

"In case you're wondering, all the men are paid well, too. Certainly by Belizean standards. And of course Chicken Eyes gets a big cut. Aapo is like a son to me, so he's always well-cared for. Don't forget, you'll be making a short trip with me to Argentina toward the end of the job."

It was clear that Jessica was struggling with feelings of fascination and revulsion. *What exactly is he saying?* But she couldn't quite bring herself to ask. All her words got stuck in her throat.

Noting Jessica had no response, Mr. Chan continued, "You would be amazed that some clients will pay upwards of 25K for the larger birds and monkeys, but the average is about 5 to 8."

"Who are your clients?" A chill came to her voice. Jessica wanted to get up and run—all the way to the Guatemalan border.

"Most of them are private: exotic animal collectors, or wealthy fathers of ten-year-old boys wanting an unusual pet—some zoos," he said matter-of-factly.

"How did you get into this business?" So many thoughts swirled in her head. Maybe if she stuck around, she could make sure that the animals were properly cared for in transit. *I mean if this is their fate anyway.* She often thought about what she would do for a million bucks. *Maybe* she could do this—*Sure* she could. *Or could she?* She smiled with a twitching mouth.

"My father…." Mr. Chan said in a low voice.

"Huh?" Jessica had checked out of the conversation.

"My father got me into this business." His eyes looked vacant.

Forty-nine years earlier, Belize City

Thirteen-year-old Edin Chan stood before his kneeling father, the pant legs of his baggy chinos rolled up to his thighs. His father grabbed one of the eight juvenile, olive-throated parakeets from the wooden cage and gave it about 2 cc's of Valium. Then he took a strip of duct tape and attached the bird by its belly to Edin's leg. His father repeated this seven times until Edin's legs were completely taped up—four birds per limb. His father carefully rolled down his son's pant legs, stood up, patted him on the back, and smiled.

His mother, Lucia, a striking beauty, and daughter of refugees of the Caste War of Yucatán, which lasted from 1847 until 1901, appeared at the doorway. She looked at her son with pained eyes, straightened her apron, and then turned and walked back into the kitchen.

Edin looked away in shame as a small wet spot appeared at the front of his trousers, which became a bigger wet spot, eventually reaching down his inner thigh.

"In my village, boys your age would meet their fathers at the *milpa* right after breakfast. They'd work the land from dawn to dusk." He handed Edin a towel. "Now, if anyone asks, you're meeting your uncle. There will be a man at airport baggage holding a sign which will read 'Sr. Canul.' Go to him. The flight time is just over thirty minutes. He'll put you back on the plane and the whole thing will be over in a matter of hours. Then I'll take you to a fútbol match tonight. Doesn't that sound like fun? Don't worry, son. It'll all be OK. These birds will be going to good homes with boys just like you." He smiled. "Now, let's get you to the airport."

"Fútbol match," Mr. Chan mumbled.

"Football match, Mr. Chan?"

"Nothing…. We need to get some rest, Jessica." Mr. Chan set down his glass and stood up from his chair. "Goodnight."

"Goodnight." Jessica studied Mr. Chan. He looked—*empty*. She started walking back to her tent, literally bumping into Aapo along the way.

"Sorry…" Jessica said with downcast eyes. She continued walking. Maya flew from the branch and landed on her shoulder. Jessica hardly even noticed.

"Are you OK?" Aapo asked.

Jessica turned to look at Aapo. He was still standing at the place where she had bumped into him.

"Oh, hi," she said flatly. "Yes, I'm OK. Have a goodnight."

"Goodnight, Jessica."

She opened the tent and plopped down on her cot. She felt hollow inside.

If only I hadn't been so stupid. I'd still have my job. I'd certainly never have accepted Finn's proposal (being the absolute ass that he is) and I wouldn't be here, caught up in all this!

Jessica lay back and thought about *him*.

One month earlier

Jessica Kraut sat in the grandstand of the Atlanta Motor Speedway. She was watching a NASCAR race, lap 162. She had driven 3½ hours from Charlotte to meet her best girlfriend, Izzie, who was at a conference. Only Izzie never showed—*like she always never does*—having bailed on Jessica, yet again, for a *man*. Jessica had no interest in a NASCAR race, but Izzie thought this would be oh-so-much-drunken-fun and convinced her to make the trip.

So there she sat next to an empty seat on her left, and a big haired, bleach-blonde lady donning an American flag tank top on her right. Jessica had already had three beers—three being her absolute limit. She was listening to redneck talk, at least as she had imagined it: Lady Big Hair was telling her big-haired friend that their other friend "can't carry a tune in a bucket," speaking of their recent outing at a karaoke bar. The big man behind her, proudly wearing his red-white-and-blue Atlanta Motor Speedway baseball cap, announced that his chicken wings were "granny-slappin' good," and that he was "happy as a puppy with two peckers." This was followed by an exaggerated belch. Jessica was *bored out of her gourd*, but she had the ticket, and there was nothing better to do on a Saturday afternoon 3½ hours from home. Besides, this redneck talk was *sort of* entertaining….

But then things got violent—well, perhaps not by NASCAR fan standards, but nonetheless…. Jessica got bopped in the back of the head with a greasy chicken bone. Now ordinarily she wouldn't have done this (the alcohol getting the better of her), but Jessica found herself turning around and saying, "Watch what you're fucking doing!" This caused the big man's big girlfriend to stand up and pour a big plastic cup of cold beer over Jessica's head while saying, "Fucking bitch…."

Jessica got up from her seat and pushed her way past four oversized racecar fans to reach the aisle. She tried to find her way to the ladies' room. She walked past a souvenir stand and there she spotted her deliciously hot student, Jansen, selling American flag can coolers.

Jansen saw her at the same time. "Hey, Dr. Kraut. What brings you here?" He smiled a deliciously hot smile, which sent deliciously hot streaks through her body.

"My friend…." Then she realized that she was standing before him with beer-soaked, greasy chicken wing hair—definitely not the sexiest of looks. "Where's the bathroom? I got clobbered by some bitch in the stands." She smiled. Jansen smiled back, then pointed behind him, to the right.

"Thanks, Jansen. So why are *you* here?"

"My brother lives here in Atlanta. He runs this stand. But he broke his hand a couple days ago and asked me to help out…. Hey, our friend will be taking over in about ten. Why don't you wait for me? You can clean up at my brother's place."

"Sure, OK."

"Great! We'll take my truck. It looks like you're not in the best shape to drive."

Jansen drove them to his older brother's apartment, about fifteen minutes away. He opened the door. Nobody seemed to be home.

"The bathroom's right over there. I'll get us a couple beers."

"Mind if I shower?"

"Go ahead."

Jessica took a shower, used the blow dryer under the sink, and reapplied mascara and lipstick, which she always kept handy in her purse. She found one of his t-shirts hanging on the towel rack. She slipped it over her head and walked back into the living room. Jansen was on the couch watching the NASCAR race on TV. Jessica sat next to him. He handed her a beer.

"Thanks."

Now, what comes next is a lesson to all of you whose brain cells go out to lunch when you drink too much. Jessica's brain cells were dining at the nearby Benihana Japanese Steakhouse watching the chefs do death-defying tricks with their fancy knives.

After about ten minutes, Jessica snuggled into Jansen and said, "You're adorable."

Jansen, who for his part had always had a hot professor fantasy, immediately replied, "You are too"—whereupon her lips landed on his.

Jessica might have stopped after their ten-minute make-out session, but her brain cells were on their third fancy umbrella drink and fumbling with their chopsticks.

"Let's go to the bedroom," Jansen said. He took her hand and led the way.

"What if your brother comes home?"

"We always knock if the door's shut."

THREE

Jessica gathered up the last of the breakfast dishes. Chicken Eyes had helped her prepare the plantain-, beans-, and sweet potato-stuffed tortillas, and now he was off somewhere catching tonight's dinner. The men had left for their first day on the job, and Mr. Chan was cloistered in his tent. She would have to walk to the stream and fill a big bucket of water to wash the plates and forks. She hated doing the dishes—even with a dishwasher. She was pissed. Mostly pissed at herself for getting into this situation in the first place. If she could see her reflection in one of the plates, it would reveal eyes as hard as jade. The thought of what the men were doing out there sickened her—*but did it sicken her enough to actually do something about it*? Could she look away for a million bucks? It'd all be over in six weeks anyway. Finn would never consider marrying her again (that's for sure), and a million bucks would hold her over until she figured out what she wanted to do with her life.

As Jessica pondered all this, visitors observed her from fifty feet above. Suddenly a shower of fruits and nuts fell down from the branches. As she was just about to look up, she heard the sound of hands clapping in applause, followed by ear-covering chatters and howls. Before she could even think *What on Earth is going on?* twelve howler monkeys climbed down from the various branches and surrounded her, making the funniest faces they could think of. They couldn't help but laugh at themselves.

A mix of excitement and fear washed over her. She called out to Mr. Chan. If he could hear her shouts (he couldn't through the monkeys' drowning voices), it would be too late to come to her rescue anyway, for just then she was swooped up into the monkeys' arms and swinging through the treetops. Was this a dream? She wasn't quite sure, but she was determined to enjoy the adventure. Did that thin topmost branch just now crackle and snap beneath them—or had she fallen asleep sometime between gathering up the dishes and going to the stream? As she pondered the thought, the monkeys flung her down to the lower limb of an adjacent tree and resumed their journey. A branch whacked her unforgivingly, smarting her right cheek. She looked skyward through the treetops and glimpsed Maya flying above, seemingly observing all the goings-on. Then she looked downward and saw a heap of ruins, vines growing in and out of the stones. The monkeys quickly jumped down, plopping her onto the forest floor. They boasted in loud chatters about their absolutely masterful achievement, until an ancient howler monkey appeared from a small temple and raised his hand to silence them. He slowly approached Jessica, hopped upon a limestone slab, and looked at her with eyes revealing a kind soul. He addressed her in perfect English—not the slightest hint of howler monkey accent. Of course the twelve heard only gibberish, having never mastered the fine art of human-speak.

"Miss Jessica, please sit down beside me," the ancient one said good-naturedly, as he tapped his hand upon the stone.

Jessica looked at him curiously. "What am I doing here?" she finally managed to say. She looked up at the twelve, who had returned to the branches above.

"Let me tell you a story. You'll recognize it, I'm sure. It's a Hindu fable, adapted for our forest." The ancient one smiled—or at least Jessica thought he did.

He extended his hand and she took it. "The story involves a baboon, a crocodile and a jaguar, though the characters don't really matter in the telling of the story. Instead of a jaguar, it could have been an ocelot—or even a *woolly mammoth*!"

Jessica laughed at this.

The ancient one continued, "There was a baboon who took a walk through the rainforest. He happened upon a crocodile in a small pool of water. The crocodile called out to him, 'Please help me. I'm injured, separated from my family, and I don't know my way back. Can you take me to the great river?' The baboon, whose heart filled with compassion at seeing the crocodile's plight, told him to crawl into the big sack that he was carrying. After he did so, the baboon dragged him to the river. When he opened the sack, the crocodile crawled out and said, 'Now I will eat you!' The baboon looked at him with pity and said, 'How ungrateful.' The crocodile responded, 'I'm not ungrateful. I just follow the way of the rainforest: 'You can eat anything when you're hungry.' The baboon studied the crocodile for a minute, and then said, 'That's not the way of the rainforest. Tell you what, if we can find three judges who agree with you, then not only can you eat me, but my entire troop!' The crocodile grinned at this. They first approached a mango tree. The baboon asked, 'Is it fair to eat anything when you're hungry?' The mango tree thought for a few moments and then said, 'Humans sit in my shade and eat all of my fruit. Finally, they cut me down and use my wood as tinder, consuming me in their fires—Yes, it's fair to eat anything when you're hungry.' At hearing this, the crocodile grinned widely. Next they came upon a cow. The baboon asked her, 'Is it fair to eat anything when you're hungry?' The cow said, 'Yes. Humans let me graze in their meadows. I provide milk and butter, but then they kill and eat me!' The crocodile laughed from deep within the grumblings of his belly. He said to the baboon, 'Two judges agree with me. Hurry! Let's find a third judge, for my stomach is growling.' They came upon a jaguar. The crocodile asked him, 'Is it fair to eat anything when you're hungry?' The jaguar studied the crocodile, whose drooling revealed his excitement at the thought of eating a troop of baboons. The jaguar said, 'Before I answer you, tell me: how did such a large crocodile like yourself get into such a small sack?' The crocodile, whose arrogance would soon get the better of him, replied, 'Let me show you!' whereupon he crawled into the sack…. The jaguar would have a meal for many days."[13]

"Why are you telling me this?" Jessica asked. She looked beyond the ancient one and spotted a little ferruginous pygmy owl with bright yellow eyes sitting in the hollow of a tree just beyond a big bush with pouty red flowers. She smiled.

"It'll all make sense soon enough." His eyes twinkled in the sunlight. Then more seriously he said, "Mr. Chan has lost his way. He no longer lives by the heart. He no longer walks in the light."

"But what can I do?"

"Walk in the light…." The ancient one stood up and pulled a large, green, prickly, egg-shaped fruit from a nearby tree, thanking it as he did so. Then he took a big stick and pierced it, finally breaking it open. He sat back down and offered half to Jessica.

He bit into the white flesh and said, "Since the earliest days of the European Enlightenment, Western people have sought to remove themselves from nature and from the non-European 'savages.' They separated what they called 'culture' from 'nature,' valuing the one and exploiting the other. They equated 'culture' with 'civilized' European society, and they brought that society to our enchanted places." He pointed around as he spoke. Jessica's eyes followed his hand. "Nature is the abode of the gods. The Christian God is not a nature god. He *transcends* the natural world. Christianity banished the nature gods, bringing about a desacralization of the natural world. The

13. See http://www.kidsgen.com/stories/folk_tales/the_brahmin_the_crocodile_the_fox.htm.

result was *dis*-enchantment: a severing of culture, nature, and the divine. Since the natural world is now devoid of the holy, Western people celebrate their control and domination of the desacralized world. Without a deep-seated reverence for nature and her creatures, the natural world has become a passive ground for human destruction. Indigenous people like the Maya, on the other hand, are deeply connected to nature (physically, emotionally, and spiritually) and they revere her as the seat of sacred and mysterious forces. They give to nature abundantly, investing their whole being, and they receive her bountiful fruits. Everything is connected, Jessica: animals, people, stars, the gods. And this has been true since the beginning of creation. This intimate connection repudiates world-renouncing Christianity and Western desacralization. We must heal the divide caused by Western 'civilized' society."[14]

As Jessica watched her new companion, she took a bite of her fruit, spitting out the seeds.

The ancient one continued, "Your light is dimming, too, Jessica. Like Mr. Chan, you know better. Think about some of the Eastern religions and philosophies you teach. Hinduism instructs us to respect the Divine Self in all creatures—human and nonhuman. Remember that in the *Bhagavad Gita* Krishna teaches that those who possess wisdom of the Self have equal regard for all. They see the same Self in a spiritual aspirant, an outcaste, an elephant, a cow, and a dog. We should follow Krishna and be a friend to *all creatures.*

"You're right of course." Jessica's heart sank a bit. "Who are you?"

"I'm King K'uk Mo, king of the baboons in these parts for many generations."

"I'm honored."

"You know the truth in your heart, Jessica, but you've been living in your head. It's time to return to your heart." He smiled. "Remember Krishna also teaches that whatever occupies the mind at the time of death determines the destination of the dying. He suggests that whatever occupies the mind reflects the values that one holds in one's heart. Are these the values that you want to hold?"

Jessica rested her hand on her chest. "Of course not." Her heart sank a bit more.

"Remember the huipil that Mr. Chan gave you to wear?"

"Of course. It's beautiful."

"The embroidery depicts the day keeper, Imox, or crocodile, of the Tzolk'in calendar. The 260-day Maya calendar consists of twenty day keepers (animal guardians or *nahuales*) each one counted thirteen times in a cycle. The Tzolk'in is a sacred calendar, and the oldest one known in Mesoamerica, dating to at least 600 BCE. The day on which you're born defines your soul, character and destiny. Each person has a nahual—an animal counterpart who shares your soul, and hence your fate. Nahuales accompany a person through her life's journey. In this way, human and nonhuman natures are intimately connected, revealing the mystic unity of all creation. In Mesoamerican religion, a nahual is also a person who has the power to transform either spiritually or physically into her animal form."[15]

"So is the Imox *my* day keeper—my nahual? Is that why I was wearing it?"

"No…. The Imox is Mr. Chan's day keeper. The Imox symbolizes the dark hidden forces of the universe. The Imox also teaches us about evil and good."

"So what's my day keeper?"

14. See Jay T. Johnson and Brian Murton, "Re/placing Native Science: Indigenous Voices in Contemporary Constructions of Nature," *Geographical Research* 45(2), June 2007. See also Ellen M. Chen, *The Tao Te Ching: A New Translation with Commentary* (St. Paul, MN: Paragon House).
15. See "Mayan Calendar Tzolkin—The K'iche' Count," at mysticomaya.com.

"The I'x, the jaguar or tiger."

"And what does the jaguar symbolize?"

"The I'x symbolizes patience, strength, responsibility, respect, and kindheartedness."

Jessica hesitated, "So the story..." but then she finished more confidently: "is about you, me, and Mr. Chan."

"Something like that." King K'uk Mo rested his hand on Jessica's back and smiled. "But what can I do?"

"Walk in the light. Follow Krishna and strive constantly to serve the welfare of the world and all creatures." He looked at her with tender eyes. "Time to get you back to the camp, Jessica."

"Will I be seeing you again?"

"Without a doubt."

Jessica kept staring at the thirty-pound blue catfish—Chicken Eyes' morning catch. He had already gutted and skinned it for her, but only after he had presented it eyeballs, whiskers, and all—and she cringed. The guys would be back in a matter of hours. Chicken Eyes suggested a Kriol-style stew. *Finally*, she started cutting the fish into bite-sized pieces, setting the chunks to one side. High above, a gray-headed kite watched intently, making hunger-induced mewling cries. After perching patiently for thirteen seconds, it swooshed down and grabbed two talons-full for a light meal. Chicken Eyes watched from a few feet away and chuckled. He walked up to her.

"Here, let me help you with that." He grabbed another knife. "Why don't you cut up some onions and sweet potatoes?" Jessica would soon discover that *whatever* the dish of the day, and no matter how creative the cooking, it would always include onions and sweet potatoes.

Jessica smiled. "Thanks." She looked at Chicken Eyes curiously, and after a few minutes of trying to figure out exactly how she would put it, she said, "Have you ever, um, *talked* with a howler monkey?"

Chicken Eyes looked at her with concealed amusement. "The baboons? ... Sure, I can talk to the baboons." He cleared his throat and then boomed in slow motion, "Wow-ah-woo." Pause. "Wow-ah-woo." He looked up into the trees and then said, "Wa-oo. Wa-oo. Wa-oo."

Jessica couldn't help but smile.

Suddenly Chicken Eyes said, "Did you hear that? Did you hear that?"

"Hear what?"

"THAT...."

She played along, "You mean the 'Wa-oo. Wa-oo'—off in the distance?"

"YES! The baboon just asked, 'Who is that pretty lady?'" He touched her shoulder playfully.

Jessica chuckled at that and then said, "In the Hindu epic, *Ramayana*, Prince Rama, the seventh avatar of the god Vishnu, was banished from his kingdom by his father. His beloved wife, Sīta, who is an avatar of the goddess Lakshmi (Vishnu's consort) follows Rama into exile in the forest. There, she's abducted by the demon king, Ravana." Jessica wondered why she was thinking about this at all, let alone *aloud*. She looked at Chicken Eyes who seemed attentive enough for her to continue.

"Anyway, Ravana imprisons Sīta on an island, but Rama rescues her and kills Ravana in a ferocious battle—a battle carried out with help from the monkey king

Sugrīva's army of monkeys, including the monkey god, Hanuman. You know, Rama's alliance with Hanuman symbolizes the intended harmony between people and animals, and the divine and the natural world."

Chicken Eyes beamed, clearly enjoying her tale.

Jessica continued, "The demon king, Ravana, had a fatal flaw, though: his hubris. The creator god, Brahma, born from a lotus growing out of Vishnu's navel, had granted Ravana a boon: bestowing invulnerability against the gods and other demons. But Ravana didn't ask for protection against people and animals. And so Vishnu became a human (Rama) and with the help of the monkeys, he liberates his beloved Sītá. When Rama met Ravana in battle, he aimed for his heart. Although Ravana had ten heads and twenty arms (which he could replace whenever they got injured), he didn't think to safeguard his heart." Jessica looked at her companion with imploring eyes, willing him to understand, and then with a cracking voice, she repeated, "He didn't think to safeguard his heart."[16]

For his part, Chicken Eyes couldn't figure out what in the story was bringing Jessica to tears. After all, it seemed like it'd make a really great action film—certainly as good as his all-time favorite: *Jason and the Argonauts*. He wasn't sure he wanted to press her (having never mastered the fine art of "exploring feelings"), and so he decided to change the subject:

"Let's do a reading."

"A reading?" Jessica wiped a tear.

"I'll go grab my tarot deck." Chicken Eyes got up and walked to his tent.

"OK," she said reluctantly.

As Jessica continued to chop the sweet potatoes, a high-pitched buzzy sounding *Jeeeee-Jeeeee* followed by a stretched-out *Wooooo* caught her attention. She spotted a tiny white-crowned manakin juddering along one of the lower branches of a nearby breadnut tree. Soon his mate flew down and joined him. Jessica set down her knife and watched with some girlish delight as she seemed to be feeding him a piece of the reddish-orange fruit. She recovered a bit from her dispirited mood. Chicken Eyes arrived and smiled.

"Let's clear off some room on the table," he began.

Jessica interrupted, "But what about dinner?"

Chicken Eyes could hear the anxiety straining her voice. "This won't take long…. Don't worry, I'll help you."

He shuffled the deck three times and then handed it to her. "Shuffle."

"I don't know how to shuffle."

Jessica wasn't kidding. Her "shuffle" sent three cards flying to the ground. She hastily picked them up and put them back into the middle of the deck. "Sorry." She grimaced. "Will it still work?"

Chicken Eyes nodded and said, "Now, divide the deck into three piles…."

"Do they have to be equal piles?"

He rolled his hand, letting his palm rest impatiently in the air. "Can we get on with this already?" She was beginning to get on his nerves.

"Oh, sorry." Jessica divided the deck into three near-perfectly-equal piles, even moving a few cards from one pile to the other so that they were just so.

"Now put the piles back together…."

Before Jessica had a chance to ask "Does it matter what order?" Chicken Eyes said louder than he thought he should, "And it doesn't matter the order." He paused and

16. See "Ravana," at sscnet.ucla.edu. See also Oxtoby, Chapter 2, and Esposito, Chapter 3.

then chirped, "Now, ready to be dazzled?" She responded with a broad smile.

He drew the first card and laid it down: The Lovers—reversed. He touched Jessica's hand and said very seriously, "You're feeling ambivalent about a relationship or a situation that you currently find yourself in." Pause, then, "Pay attention to what your gut tells you."

"Or my heart," Jessica said. "You're right. Or I should say *the card is right.*"

Chicken Eyes drew another card: The Tower. "This card means 'change.'" He drew another card, the Eight of Cups, and said, "I definitely see change. You will choose to leave a situation that's no longer working for you. Or you will do something about it."

Jessica looked away.

Chicken Eyes drew two more: Death and the Devil. Jessica looked down at the cards lying on the table. Her stomach turned inside out. She got up and ran away, scraping her arms on some of the branches in her haste.

Not quite knowing what to do, Chicken Eyes finally stood up and called out, "Jessica, come back! It's not what you think. It's not what you think…. *Please come back.*" When he saw her disappear deeper into the forest, he sat back down and, imagining her sitting there, said somewhat dejectedly, "It means change, Jessica. Change followed by a new beginning. Take action. Be in control. Free yourself from whatever holds you back, whatever holds you in bondage." He frowned and then drew one more card: The Fool. "See? New path…."

Somehow Jessica managed to wander to the same limestone steps that Aapo had taken her to the night before. She sat down and watched several iridescent green hummingbirds whizzing around and drinking in the sweet nectar from the red tubular flowers of an oversized butterfly bush. The high speed hum of their tiny wings buzzed in her ears, offering messages of healing and joy. It was magical.

What was she doing? She knew what she *should* be doing. After all, she lived it (at least she thought she did) and she taught it: we cannot isolate ourselves from the plight of animals, as we ourselves have, in some past life, experienced it—just as animals have experienced our plight in previous lives. Every living being we come across—down to the tiniest of insects—has been, at some time or another, a dear family member or friend who has treated us well. That being so, we should return the kindness in the present.[17]

Jessica thought about King K'uk Mo. And then she thought about Maya. She hadn't seen him since this morning. She feared that he'd flown off. Maybe he'd been caught by one of the guys from the camp, to be sold to some zoo or private collector. The thought sickened her, and so she dismissed it as soon as it came to mind and resumed contemplating the wisdom of the hummingbirds.

She thought about some of the *Upanishads*, the philosophical tracts that were appended to the *Vedas* (the sacred texts of Hinduism) after 1000 BCE. The Katha Upanishad, for example, teaches that hidden in the hearts of all living beings is the Self or *Atman*, the divine in all of us and identical with *Brahman*, the Ultimate Unmanifested Reality. In the Brihadaranyaka Upanishad, Yajnavalkya tells his beloved wife in a parting dialogue before he is about to leave home to pursue Self-realization, that all creatures are loved, not for their own sake, but because of the Self that lives in each of them. Indeed, *everything* is loved, not for its own sake, but because the Self lives in it. When we love another, we are responding to the Self within that person or

17. See Peter Harvey, *An Introduction to Buddhist Ethics.*

creature. The Brihadaranyaka ends with this injunction: *Be compassionate.* Respect the divine in all, both human and nonhuman.

After musing on all this, Jessica got up and found her way back to the camp.

Meanwhile, back in Malibu

The real Jessica Kraus took a taxi up a winding road opposite the ocean side of Pacific Coast Highway. She walked up the twenty stone steps to a 3.875-million-dollar Pagoda-style house, nestled in an eclectic garden, which included many native ferns that had somehow survived the drought-ridden climes of Southern California. The house's style was inspired by the architect Frank Lloyd Wright who had a fascination with Japanese culture. Of course Jessica Kraus did not know this, nor would she be impressed if she did, not being much of a learned type. She took a deep breath and knocked on the door. A man with wavy dark hair, chiseled chin, and high cheekbones, looking every bit the model he never was, answered the door.

"May I help you?"

Jessica looked him up and down. He was dressed in a black and gray plaid shirt ($265), and black pants ($385) spun especially in Portugal from premium wool.

"Yes, I…"

Finn leaned into her, cutting her off. "You're not selling something are you? … Not interested."

Jessica rolled her eyes. "Do I *look* like I'm selling something? Please, give me a break." She tried to sound offended.

It was Finn's turn to look *Jessica* up and down. She was in the habit of wearing stylish expensive clothing. Her Uncle Nick insisted that she look nice for the high-end clients who would visit his gallery. She wore a black and white, wavy striped dress with big pink and red flower appliqués geometrically arranged across the stripes. She accented her look with short black leather boots and Bohemian red hoop earrings.

Finn finally said, "Of course not. I'm sorry. You must have gotten the wrong address. Who're you looking for? The Brooks live next door. Are you looking for the Brooks?"

"Finn Lauder?" Jessica blurted out.

He felt himself flush. "Do I know you? Don't tell me we hooked up at Durango's party." He ran his fingers through his hair. "I was completely wasted…. If we did, I'm sorry but I've forgotten your name. Please come inside." He motioned her to the living space which featured a twenty-foot-long ceiling to floor window offering a panoramic view of the ocean.

"We've never met." She wanted to be angry. She wanted to touch his shirt.

"If we've never met, and you're not selling anything, then why're you here?" He looked her up and down again. "Don't tell me it's about the Kravitz account? I swear, I knew nothing about it." He walked up to the bar. "You're an attorney, aren't you? Would you like a drink?"

"Sure, I'll have a drink. Do you have cognac?"

"Exquisite taste…." Finn smiled appreciatively, grabbed an opened bottle of Martell's Cordon Bleu and two tulip glasses. "So who did you say you are?" He looked out the window and imagined himself sailing on the sun-kissed water.

"I didn't…." She looked around the room, looked at his signed and numbered print by Japanese artist Shohei Otomo hanging above the mantelpiece. She grimaced at the rawness of it. Finally, she offered, "Do you happen to know a Mr. Chan?" It was time to get to the matter at hand, to the reason she was here in the first place.

He turned around to look at her. "What? What are you talking about? Look, I don't want to be impolite, but you're starting to sound a bit…." He struggled for the right word, settling on "*unhinged.*"

"Cut the cute stuff. My name's Jessica, and I found your card at…."

"Jessica…that's my fiancée's name. You look a lot like her." He handed her a tulip glass of dark copper colored liquid. He gently swirled the cognac in his own glass, put his nose up to the opening, and savored the warm buttery caramel, pear, peach, and apple notes. He took a sip, keeping the spirits in his mouth for two full seconds, and then swallowed. While he was doing this, Jessica Kraus drained her drink.

"*Of course!*" Jessica's faced brightened at her epiphany. "Your *fiancée* seems to have robbed me of one million dollars."

Finn laughed derisively, then shook his head, his face contorted. "Give me a break…. Jessica doesn't have a mean bone in her body. Nor is she clever enough to steal one million dollars. Not yours, not anybody's." He extended his hand. "Look—may I have your glass? I think you should go now."

But Jessica Kraus kept a tight grip. "Your *clever* fiancée pretended to be me—and now she's in Belize."

Finn took a deep breath. "Belize? What for? Besides, she hates Belize. I wanted to take her there for our honeymoon for a scuba trip, but she refused."

Jessica set down her glass and crossed her arms. "Call her. Try calling her right now. I guarantee she won't answer."

Finn picked up his cell and phoned his fiancée's number. After four rings he said, "She's not picking up…."

"She won't…."

Finn walked back to the bar, grabbed the bottle of Martell's, freshened his drink, and took a big gulp. "So what if you're right? —I'm not saying that you are. This doesn't sound like her, doesn't sound like her at all. And she'd never go to Belize, certainly never go without me…. But what if she did? She'll be back. She has to. We're getting married in five weeks."

Jessica threw her head back with a laugh. "Is that right? Well she'll be gone for *six* weeks. She's standing you up at the altar, Finn. And with my money!"

With shaky hands, Finn tried his fiancée's phone number again, this time leaving a message. "Jess, where are you? You'd better f—ing call me. Where are you?" He hung up and with squinty eyes he said, "Are you *f—ing serious*?" (Portions of Finn's outburst have been redacted so as not to give offense to those with more Victorian sensibilities.)

"Yes, I'm fucking serious. She ran out on you—with *my* money."

Finn slammed his glass down on the table, breaking it. A small sliver cut his hand. "God dammit! F—. What can we f—ing do?" He looked down on the bamboo floor, noting that a few crimson drops had landed on his white sheepskin accent rug. "F—!"

"Where's your bathroom? I'll get you a towel."

Finn grabbed his hand. "It's down the hall, to the left…. F—!"

Jessica returned and handed him a fingertip towel made of plush Egyptian cotton. "I know where she is, Finn. All you need to do is get us two tickets to Belize."

Finn forced a smile. "OK. OK, I'll go online. Probably too late to get out tonight. We'll see what good comes out of this mother-f—ing mess. Some good has to come out of it. It'll all work out. It has to. It damn well better."

Jessica smiled back. "Can I crash at your place? I don't have anywhere to go."

Finn looked her up and down again and, turning up his charm, gave a disarming smile. "Sure, beautiful. Sure, you can stay here with me tonight." He grinned wolfishly. "Want another drink? We can soak in my hot tub. I can always get the tickets in the morning."

He walked back to the bar and grabbed the bottle of Martell's.

"I'd love to…." She plopped into a black cowhide and chrome chaise lounge. For her part, Jessica Kraus was delighted at the thought of stealing the man from the woman who stole her promised million. For his part, Finn Lauder just wanted to get laid.

Back at the camp

Jessica Kraut alias Kraus looked around. Chicken Eyes was nowhere to be found, but the cast iron pot was hanging over the campfire. She closed her eyes and took in the smells of cayenne, black and white pepper, as well as paprika, garlic, and onion. The guys would be back any time, and Chicken Eyes had already warned her that they'd be tired and irritable, all the more so if they weren't greeted with a fresh pot of coffee. He'd already written down his "Eight Steps to Making a Great Pot of Campfire Coffee." Now she just needed to find the grounds. As she made her way to the supply tent, she looked up into the trees hoping to spot Maya. No such luck. She hadn't seen him since that morning, when she was carried off by a troop of howler monkeys. When Jessica looked back down, she noted the trunk of a rainbow eucalyptus tree. The pastel colors—yellows, greens, oranges, and reds—had painted something of a picture: an image of a woman who resembled herself. It could have been a portrait made by second graders a little overzealous with the paint palette. It could have been a Picasso. She admired it for a short while and then walked into the tent where she found a big can of coffee grounds and a five-gallon bucket. She set the can on the table and made her way to the stream. As she approached, she spotted a beautiful woman bathing in the knee-deep water. Her long dark hair fell past her rounded hips. She looked at Jessica and smiled sweetly. And then she began to sing. Her voice was so inviting, her body so sensuous, her eyes so alluring, Jessica all but forgot what she was doing there in the first place. The woman slowly stepped out of the water and onto the opposite bank. Glistening droplets clung to her brown body. She ran behind a ceiba tree, giggling along the way—and then disappeared. Jessica looked down at the bucket which had dropped at her feet. She bent to pick it up, drew some water, and walked back to the camp. Her heart sang a bit from the encounter.

Chicken Eyes walked up to Jessica. She had burnt the coffee. That was all right, though. Burnt coffee was better than no coffee, and it didn't smell nearly as burnt as the coffee Dean Gallegos was in the habit of making in his office. Chicken Eyes sat down, closed his eyes, and found himself thrown into a 1940s-era noir novel:[18]

I peered through the opened door. Dean Gallegos was sipping his second cup of joe, dressed in his green-label suit, back to the window, scowling at the telephone. The smell of burnt coffee was godawful bad. A plate of cake crumbs sat atop his cheap office desk. He looked up, then spun his back to me with his swivel chair. But he knew that I still

18. Inspired by Dashiell Hammett, *The Maltese Falcon*, and Jim Thompson, *The Killer Inside Me*.

stood there watching him. I put my hand on the doorknob and cleared my throat. I liked the guy—as much as I like most people, anyway. Polite, intelligent. He was what most men would like to be: confident, able to handle himself in any situation. He spun around again to face me. His black hair and thickish brows made him look almost devilish. The smile on his face was strained, like he wanted to smack me in the beezer.

Finally, I said, "How are you, Dean Gallegos?"

"I got no kick," he said in a voice as empty of expression as his face.

Then I said, "Do you have time to talk about this again?"

Gallegos' shoes squeaked as he squirmed. Sure I'd been in his office one too many times. Sometimes we'd just bump gums, but lately I'd insisted that he take me seriously. This WAS serious research. I slid my hands into my overcoat pockets in the manner of Sam Spade.

"Don't be a bunny, Nathaniel. Oxford debunked it," he said, kind of running his words together. "Sure," I said, "but they'd only tested samples at the museums and in private collections." I had my experience and a banged up motorbike to prove it.

"How about this heatwave?" he said. I knew he wanted to change the subject.

"It's not the heat that makes it so hot. It's the humidity. A lot of people think it's the heat. But it's not. I bet you didn't know that." I wondered why I offered such drivel. If there's anything worse than a bore, it's a bore who talks about the weather.

Dean Gallegos brushed a cake crumb off his shirt and spoke in a tone one might use with a child on the verge of tears: "I can't keep defending you, Nathaniel. Just—stop it already."

"But, I...." I hated how pathetic I sounded.

"You sure know how to hash things up," he said irritably. "Just try to keep your nose clean...."

My throat tightened. I hardly knew what to say next. This whole place was lousy with people saying how batty I was, saying I belonged in some booby-hatch. All because I had showed the photos of my banged up bike, told them that I saw what I saw. I wanted to take a long slow draw on a cigarette, even though I'd given up smoking five years before.

"Another thing about the weather...." I found I was repeating myself.

Dean Gallegos spun his chair again. With back turned he said, "I'm busy, Nathaniel. Come up with a new research plan."

"Nuts to you," I heard myself say (well, not exactly those words). I pounded my fist on the door.

"I've heard enough of your wisecracks...." Dean Gallegos shook his head and spun around one last time.

I didn't really regret the words, but a few minutes later I found myself on my bike. I never went back, never went back to that godforsaken place again. I'm a man—a man and a gentleman—and if a gentleman has anything, it's integrity.

I got home and stepped onto the porch. The door opened an inch or two. Then it opened all the way, and Anastasia stood there looking at me. She was a real looker, with gams up to her elbows. She wore her favorite sleeping shorts and a tight pullover sweatshirt. Her dark wavy hair was tousled from sleep. Her face still unpainted. But it didn't matter. She could have crawled out of a hog wallow wearing a gunny sack. That's how dizzy I was for this dame. I gave her a smile, but she didn't give it back. She stopped smiling long ago. Once she swore she loved me because I told such fascinating stories. But she grew tired of my stories. I leaned in to kiss her.

"Don't say you're sorry. I'm tired of hearing you're sorry," she said.

I followed her into the house and shut the door. She fumbled with my shirt, fumbled with my belt, and kissed me. At that moment, I couldn't have loved her more. But I knew it was over. I opened my mouth, then closed it without having said anything. I didn't want to tell her, didn't want to worry her pretty little head, and so I stuffed a backpack full of clothes, and some cabbage in my wallet. I got on my bike and road south to Georgia, then west to Texas, before turning south again to Mexico. I lived in the back of an orange VW van with a free spirit named Angel who sold Virgin Mary pendants at the local mercado. One day, out of the clear blue sky, Angel looked at me and said, "I don't like moochers, and even if I did, I wouldn't like crazy moochers. And even if I liked crazy moochers, I could never like you."

Angel gave me the bounce, and I headed to Belize. It was there that my bike broke down and I had to abandon her. I became a boozehound.

Jessica had been studying Chicken Eyes. An assortment of expressions passed over his features: anger, despair, joy, apprehension, hope. She couldn't tell whether he was dreaming, or maybe he was having another one of his visions.

Just then he opened his eyes, looked at her, and said, "I was dead without being dead. That's the best I can describe it." His voice choked. "It wasn't long before Mr. Chan found me bent over in an alleyway. I owe him my life, Jessica—*my life*." He stared off into space.

Jessica wasn't sure what to say to Chicken Eye's cryptic words. She finally asked, "When are the guys expected back?"

"Any time now. An hour ago. Something must be holding them up." Pause, then "I'm sorry about earlier today."

"It's OK. I'm sorry I freaked out…. Oh, I saw a woman bathing at the stream. Do you know who she might be?"

"What? A woman? Impossible, Jessica. The nearest village is about eighteen kilometers away."

"She was a beautiful brown woman with wide set eyes and long black hair."

"That describes about eighty percent of the women I know. Are you sure you didn't get into some Jimsonweed?" He cracked a smile.

"Jimsonweed?"

"A weedy looking plant with white tubular flowers. Famous for causing hallucinations. Never use it as a condiment in your cooking—though it might be fun at a party."

"No, I'm serious. I know what I saw, I…" Jessica was interrupted by sounds of merrymaking. The guys had just arrived at the camp.

Meantime, back in Malibu, Finn Lauder and the real Jessica Kraus sat under his luxurious white satin sheets and goose down comforter, all of which sat atop his $13,000 Swedish ergonomic mattress. After a frustratingly futile hour, Finn stopped trying and flipped on the 6:30 news. Jessica couldn't figure out why—given her unquestionable beauty, never mind her talent—this guy was having so much trouble with *you know what*. Finn wondered that himself. Maybe it was the booze, or the hot tub, or how completely fucking pissed he was. His blood boiled over in a hundred different directions. Finn kept trying to watch the news, and Jessica kept trying to distract him. Finally, at exactly the moment the anchorwoman announced an update to the story of the missing macaw, Jessica's efforts were paying off. And so they both missed the report that the woman, now facing felony charges and identified as Jessica Kraut, and the bird were last seen getting into an old white Isuzu Trooper with two men at the parking lot of the Philip S.W. Goldson International Airport just outside of Belize City at half past midnight two nights before. The LAPD were now working with Belizean authorities, and were confident the case would be solved in a matter of days and the bird safely returned to the LA Zoo. The anchorwoman promised to bring viewers any new developments as soon as they happened.

The woman in question—this very woman now *sans bird*—smiled widely when the guys arrived. Chicken Eyes was already dishing out the stew.

"Can I get you some coffee? Stew's being served up right now. You wouldn't believe the size of the catfish Chicken Eyes caught." Jessica's smile turned to a grimace when she saw a hobbling Aapo leaning against Doc. She pushed through a few of the guys to reach them.

"Are you OK? What happened?"

"It was quite brilliant, really. Aapo slipped down a ridge. If it weren't for me, he would've broken his neck," Doc said.

"E tauk big, but e shit small," Aapo said through laughter.

Just then Mr. Chan emerged from his tent and joined the scene.

"Are you OK?" Mr. Chan asked.

"I will be after a few swigs of rum."

"Anything broken?"

"Probably just a bad sprain," Doc offered. "He'll be OK, though it looks like you'll have another hand at the camp, Jessica. Aapo will have to rest his foot for a good week or more. I'll go grab some monkey fiddle from my bag. The swelling should be gone in no time."

After they emptied the stew pot, they retired to their tents—all but Jessica, Chicken Eyes, and Aapo who were already on their second bottle of rum. Somebody would have to do the dishes to keep the tigers away, but the mongrels were doing their part licking the bowls and spoons clean.

FOUR

As Jessica returned from the stream with her bucket of water to do the morning dishes, she heard the clicks, grunts, whistles, and barks of sixteen female coatis sitting atop the tables eating the leftover rice and beans from breakfast. Of course Jessica hadn't seen them yet and her heart jumped at the noise. She let out a scream, which caused the coatis to leap into the trees and Aapo to spring off his cot and run out of his tent. Then *he* screamed from the pain in his foot. This caused Mr. Chan to poke his head out of his tent and shout, "What's going on?!" By now Jessica had spotted the coatis looking down at her from their long snouts. She yelled back, "Nothing!" and then noted Aapo's pained grimace. "Sorry—I'm so sorry." She put down the bucket and helped Aapo to the table. Chicken Eyes had missed the commotion, as he was busy somewhere catching dinner.

"Sorry for freaking out," Jessica said. Aapo tried to smile through the pain, to which she repeated "Sorry," and then frowned.

"It's OK…. Did the coatis leave anything to eat? I'm hungry."

"Oh, that's right. You slept through breakfast." She looked around. "They didn't tip over the pot. I'll bet there's some rice and beans still in there." She walked over to the pot, opened the lid and smiled cheerfully. "Rest your foot and I'll dish some out."

"Thanks." Aapo watched Jessica while she prepared his food: long dark hair in a loose ponytail, white tee and sleeping shorts, the silver pendant of the Virgin Mary that Mr. Chan had given her dangling from her neck. "You know, you're really beautiful" he wanted to say. But he couldn't quite get the nerve to say it. Instead he said, "I can't really do much to help you today, but I promise to be great company while you do all these dishes."

"Sure, that'd be nice." Jessica glanced about the tall trees that formed a barricade around the camp. The coatis had cleared out.

"Could I possibly have a cup of cinnamon tea?" Aapo asked with a smile.

"Cinnamon tea?" She gave a quizzical look.

"It'll help with the pain. Too early to start on the rum. Maybe in a couple hours. Doc left some cinnamon along with the monkey fiddle. You do know what cinnamon looks like, right? You can identify it by its smell." Then he thought, "What a stupid thing to say." He grinned sheepishly and then took a spoonful of the rice and beans.

Jessica hated the smell of cinnamon. It reminded her of her grandmother's kitchen. That damnable smell would mingle with the stench of her grandfather's dime-store cologne. She tried not to be put off by the unpleasant memory. "Of course," she finally said. "But I'll have to get some more water. Can you wait?"

Aapo tried to rescue himself from his embarrassment with something of a joke. "I don't think I'll be going anywhere soon, unless I'm able to hop away on one foot." He smiled.

"True…." After a pause, Jessica said, "Hey, yesterday I saw a beautiful woman bathing in the stream. Know who she might be?"

"Beautiful woman? You have quite an imagination. Have you been getting into the Jimsonweed? The only beautiful woman around here is you," Aapo heard himself say out loud. He looked away. He wanted to crawl under the table.

"Thanks." Jessica found herself blushing. She shook her head. "No. No Jimson-weed. I saw a beautiful brown woman with wide set eyes and long black hair bathing in the stream yesterday. I'm not kidding."

"That describes about eighty percent of the women I know." Aapo laughed. The conversation was going better now.

"Have you been talking with Chicken Eyes?"

"Huh?" Aapo raised an eyebrow. "Honestly, Jessica, the only women we've ever had around the camp are the ones charged to oversee it."

"I'll go get some more water—I know what I saw, though."

Jessica returned with a jug of water. She had hoped she would spot the woman at the stream again. Instead, her eyes lit up when she saw Maya sitting with Aapo. He was petting him. Jessica set down the water and Maya flew to her. "You're back." She scratched Maya's head. "I thought you'd never return."

"Had he been missing?"

"Since yesterday morning…. I'll go grab the cinnamon." Maya flew up to a nearby branch and watched Jessica prepare the tea. Jessica poured two cups and sat down. "The dishes can wait."

"So you never really told me how you got interested in Eastern religions." Aapo wanted to show Jessica that he was capable of carrying on with an intelligent woman.

Jessica took a sip of tea. "This is surprisingly good…." Perhaps she could create better memories of this spice. "I've always been interested in religions. My parents got me a world religions book when I was a girl. I already told you about my Aunt Jacqueline. I call her 'Auntie Jack.'" She smiled broadly. "She's my favorite person on Earth."

"Auntie Jack. That's cute."

"I've always been fascinated with the purpose of religion, and its evolution. I'm particularly interested in religions of the Axial Age. Eastern religions, especially Buddhism and Hinduism, have always been attractive to me. But I'm a Christian too. You might say that Jesus is my Barong from Balinese mythology. Barong is the lion-like king of the good spirits who fights evil." She hesitated and then offered, "I've had to battle a lot of demons in my lifetime. Mostly of my own creation. But I won't trouble you with any of that." Jessica looked down and spotted a furry tarantula. She lifted up her feet and shrieked.

Aapo chuckled. "You've got no reason to worry about the tarantulas, Jessica. Now if you come across a brown recluse, that's a different story. Always be sure to look inside your shoes and blankets. They have flesh-eating venom."

"Flesh-eating venom?! This place freaks me out."

"Living in the rainforest is great—that is, if you don't mind the deadly snakes, killer bees, and blood-sucking bugs." He laughed out loud. But Jessica wasn't amused.

"Oh and the tigers too. But tarantulas? Tarantulas are our friends." Aapo extended his hand to the ground, welcoming the spider for a pet. The spider wasn't in the least interested in his offer. It walked away. Aapo looked up at Jessica and said, "So tell me about religions of the Axial Age."

"But the dishes …"

"… can wait. You said so yourself. Besides, I'll help you." He winked conspiratorially.

Jessica couldn't help but smile. "OK. The term 'Axial Age' was coined by philosopher Karl Jaspers. It refers to the eighth through third centuries BCE when similar ways of thinking about religion and philosophy appeared simultaneously across many parts of the world. This was the age of great thinkers like Zoroaster, Buddha, Laozi, Confucius, and Socrates. It's important to understand what happened *before* the Axial Age to really appreciate the important developments that happened during the Axial Age."[19]

"So what happened before?" As Aapo was speaking, Maya flew down with a little round green fruit and dropped it on the table in front of Jessica.

"Guaya." Aapo smiled. "Try it. It's great." They watched with delight as Maya would pull a piece of fruit from the tree, fly it down to Jessica, then fly back up to grab another piece. Maya busied herself flying back and forth depositing piece after piece as Jessica and Aapo were talking. She seemed to be making a game of it, building a pyramid in miniature.

By now Mr. Chan was sitting outside his tent watching the scene with a certain amusement.

"In early religions, the natural world was populated with souls, spirits, and demons, which later became the nature gods of the early peoples. During the Axial Age, these nature gods were replaced by a more transcendent entity, no longer confined to any particular place. Since this entity, whether it was called 'God,' 'Heaven,' or 'Dharmakaya,' transcended the Earth, people found security, comfort, and happiness looking beyond this world. These religions offered a way to escape from Earth's bondage."

Aapo, for whom everything Jessica was saying was a complete novelty, listened attentively, fixing on her with gentle eyes. She continued:

"The nature gods were driven out—banished by these so-called high religions. The Earth, now emptied of its gods, was completely devoid of any spiritual value. In early religions, fear of the powers of the natural world led people to ally themselves with the nature gods. But in high religions, this gave way to a dissatisfaction (even disdain) for this world. Our familiar binaries were introduced during this time—heaven and earth, soul and body, eternality and temporality, and culture and nature. The first of each binary is overvalued at the expense of the second. During this time, the Earth loses its reality."

"What's that mean?"

"The idea that the phenomenal world (the world in which we live) is a mere illusion. Socrates expressed a similar idea that this world is a mere shadow of the true reality, which he called the Realm of Forms. In the *Phaedo*, Socrates even teaches that philosophers are 'almost dead' insofar as they withdraw from their bodies and bodily pleasures in order to access this true reality, since the body serves as an obstacle to Truth. Hinduism is similar. It distinguishes two paths. The so-called pleasurable path leads to death and rebirth, to being thrown back into samsara. The preferable path leads to wisdom and liberation from samsara (called *moksha*) through denial of earthly pleasures—indeed, through withdrawing from the world. In Buddhism, liberation (freedom from suffering) is called *nirvana*. For both Buddhism and Hinduism, this world of samara, and all the suffering in it, is mere illusion. A notable exception to these world-negating religions of the Axial Age is Taoism, which has always been Earth- and life-affirming. High religions also led to people's secret desire to become godlike. For example, Hinduism teaches 'Thou art That.' That is, the soul or Self (the divine part in each of us) is identical to the one Underlying Unmanifested Reality—the only thing that exists. *The Lotus Sutra* of Buddhism teaches that we all have a Buddha-nature, that we'll all eventually become Buddhas—even the evilest among us. The world-negating religions of the Axial Age continued in the Christian West, which teaches that the Earth and our earthly bodies are obstacles to salvation. This view prepared for the conquest and destruction of the natural world, all in the name

19. This discussion is based on Chapter 2, "The Tao Te Ching as a Religious Treatise," in Chen, *The Tao Te Ching*.

of scientific exploration (or rather, *exploitation*) and 'progress.'" She scratched the air with quoting fingers.

When Jessica finished talking, she looked over at Mr. Chan, who was smiling broadly. Her brains, never mind her raw beauty, pleased him a great deal. He walked back into his tent. Jessica looked at Aapo, stood up, and began busying herself with the dishes. "Sorry, I got caught up in my lecture. I didn't mean to bore you."

But Aapo wasn't bored in the least. He gave a cheerful smile. "You miss it, don't you?"

"Miss what?"

"Lecturing. I can't imagine you're happy working in your Uncle Nick's gallery. You must be bored silly. Aapo extended his hand to Jessica, who began washing off the dishes in the bucket of water. "Here, give me a towel. I'll help you dry."

She handed him a towel and then said, "I do miss it. But I really screwed up. I can never go back."

"Did you hurt anybody? If you didn't hurt anybody, you can always go back."

"Only myself. I have a great fondness, it seems, for screwing up my life." She decided to redirect the conversation away from herself: "How did *you* get mixed up in all of this, Aapo? I don't know you very well, but you don't seem the type."

"We're not hurting anybody."

"Are you kidding me?!" she said in a loud voice.

"Sleep wit yo own eye." Aapo reached across the table to grab a bottle of rum which sat next to a jar of pickled herring and a small pile of serrano peppers. He opened the bottle and took a swig. Then he opened the jar and speared three pieces of herring with his fork. He took a big bite.

Jessica twisted up her face at his choice of snack. "Huh?"

"It's best to leave this alone, Jessica. You don't understand. *You can't understand*," Aapo said irritably. He was trying to be polite, but she was beginning to strain his nerves.

Jessica saw how protective Aapo was of Mr. Chan. She decided to push anyway. "Help me understand…. What about the banana heist?"

"I had to. To take care of Lottie."

"Your little sister?"

"Yes. After our grandparents died—I was only fifteen—it was just me and Lottie. I tried to make a legitimate living, I really did, but it was hard. I was lucky to work as a porter at a fancy hotel, until some rich white lady accused me of stealing and I lost my job. Then I became a dockworker. But waterfront work isn't all that reliable. I helped the neighbors sell produce, but that wasn't enough to take care of Lottie—especially after she got so sick. Mr. Chan…"

Jessica cut him off, "Why'd you get mixed up with Mr. Chan? Can't you understand what…." She immediately regretted it.

Aapo interrupted her with a shaking head. Her incessant line of questioning was getting to him. "Fisherman nevva seh e fish stink…. As I was trying to say, Jessica, Mr. Chan had already moved to the States by then. He was on business in Belize City when he found me. He brought Lottie and me back to California. He became like a father to us. I owe him a lot."

Aapo smiled as he thought about the first time he met Mr. Chan.

Twenty-seven years earlier, 2 pm at the fish market
on the Swing Bridge, Belize City

Several small fishing boats dotted the water around the Swing Bridge, which divides the city north and south and spans the mouth of Haulover Creek where the Belize River meets the Caribbean. A few fishermen sat in their vessels, lazing away the afternoon. The water was so still one could clearly see the picture-perfect reflection of the open-air fish market on the pier and the nearby wooden buildings, all painted in pastel colors. The fish market was a gathering place for locals and tourists alike. Its yellow and white wooden beams were topped with a flat tin roof which shielded the customers from the oppressive sun. Several weigh-scales hung from the rafters, and fish of various colors, shapes, and sizes were piled high on the countertops. Customers, many donning colorful tees and baseball caps, carried big plastic buckets or coolers, negotiating with the sellers in a lively fashion.

On the opposite side of the bridge was a street lined with small wooden houses, most of them painted white, some displaying brightly colored shutters. From one of those houses there emerged Aapo, a few days shy of his sixteenth birthday, and looking stocky in a blue faded tee, burgundy denim shorts, and yellow baseball cap. He walked across the bridge's pedestrian path, passing a few men walking their bicycles. Faded, peeling paint revealed that the bridge was once painted a bright yellow. Aapo entered the fish market and smiled when he noted a well-dressed man, mid-thirties, wearing white twill pants and a grey button-down cotton shirt, buying a 20-pound red snapper.

Aapo approached the man and asked, "Can you help me, mister? Mister, can you help me?"

The man tried to ignore him, but the boy persisted. "Please, mister. I need your help."

When it became clear that the boy was not going to leave, the man said, "What do you want, kid? I don't have any money."

"Please help my sister. My sister is sick," Aapo pleaded as he tugged on the man's shirt.

"Where are your parents?"

"They're dead."

"Where do you live?"

"At my grandparents' house, not far from here. Just across the bridge. Please help me, mister."

"Go back to your grandparents. I'm sure they'd be disappointed to learn that their grandson has been begging on the streets."

"My grandparents are dead. It's just me and my sister. Please help, mister."

The man felt a swell of compassion for the boy and agreed to follow him across the pedestrian bridge to his grandparents' house. They entered the main living area where ten-year old Lottie, thin with sunken features, was asleep in a bed. The room was dark; hardly a detail could be seen, except for a streak of light which filtered through the yellowed lace curtains.

Aapo leaned over and whispered to the man, "She can't get out of bed. She's so tayad and weak. She won't eat. She says she's cold, but I think she has a fever."

"How long has she been like this?"

"Awhile now. She's in pain. She says her bones hurt. Please, mister. Please you've got to help."

"You've got no one?"

"No, sir, no one but me and Lottie."

"I spend most of my time in Los Angeles now. I'm leaving tomorrow morning. Why don't you and Lottie come back with me? We've got great medical care. I'm sure UCLA Medical Center can help your sister."

Aapo beamed. "Los Angeles? I've never been to California. Thank you. Thank you so much, mister." He tried to hug the man who clearly felt awkward with the boy's affectionate gesture.

"Of course, kid."

"Is Lottie still there? In California?" Jessica asked.

"No, she died about twenty years ago—leukemia. Let's turn to something a little happier."

"I'm sorry, Aapo. I had no idea." Jessica was sorry that she had pushed so hard. She touched his shoulder. "Would you like to learn some more about Hinduism?" She wasn't sure how a discussion of Hinduism would help turn things around, but she didn't have anything else to offer.

"Sure, I'd love that." He forced a smile.

"I'll be focusing on the *Advaita Vedanta* school, one of the major schools of Hinduism. This tradition is monistic. They follow the teachings of the *Upanishads* and believe that there is a singular reality, an impersonal spirit called Brahman—and that Atman, the Self or soul, just *is* Brahman. The most influential philosopher of this school was Shankara, who lived between 788 and 820 CE." Jessica touched Aapo's shoulder again and then said, "I'm really sorry."

"It's OK. It was a long time ago."

Introduction to Hinduism

Jessica glanced at Aapo. His eyes were still a bit clouded. She felt awful for the way she had pressed him. She was hoping she could brighten him up somehow. And so she began:

"Hinduism is the third largest religion today, with over 800 million followers. 'Hindu,' a Persian word, comes from the Sanskrit word 'Sindhu,' meaning the Indus River. The Indus Valley civilization originated around 3500 BCE. India is the seat of Hinduism. The region has a long history of migrations and invasions. First came the Aryan people from the northwest in about 1500 BCE, who brought their festivals, sacrifices, and the early Vedic deities (we get this word from the *Vedas*). The northern region was conquered by the Muslims in the twelfth century CE. This resulted in over 500 years of Muslim rule, first by the Delhi Sultanate in 1192, followed by the Mughal Empire in 1526. The sultanate mostly allowed Hindu traditions to continue. That all changed with the arrival of the Europeans. The first Europeans to have settled in South Asia were the Portuguese in the late fifteenth century, mostly Roman Catholic missionaries. They were followed by the Dutch, French, and British, who came as merchants trading for spices, silks, indigos, and cotton goods. It was the British, under the East India Company, who established themselves permanently. The region was subjected to British colonial rule from about 1800 to India's independence in 1947. Before the British had assumed control, most Hindu rulers under the sultanate accepted a great degree of local autonomy, but the British felt a moral, religious, and political obligation to impose sweeping changes, without any regard to local traditions and practices."[20]

Aapo loved learning about history and other cultures. He had all but forgotten their ruffled conversation just minutes before. He leaned into Jessica and asked, "Tell me: how were the British able to oust the Muslims? After all, they had been ruling the region for over 500 years."

Jessica smiled at Aapo's enthusiasm and so continued in her long-winded way: "By the early eighteenth century, the Mughal Empire had slowly disintegrated, and the weakened rulers were incapable of exercising any control over the region. So much so that the Hindu vassal states had begun asserting their independence. Civil disorder increased which caused trade to decline. It was then that the British introduced military detachments. Soon Indian subjects lived under British rule. British schools were established to train young Indians to serve in the lower ranks of colonial bureaucracy, English became the lingua franca, and Christian missionaries vigorously challenged Hindu beliefs and practices, including the caste system and sati, the practice whereby a widow throws herself onto her husband's funeral pyre. Some Hindu intellectuals accepted these challenges, which mobilized them to institute various reforms. The nineteenth century saw many Hindu reform movements."

"You had mentioned that Hinduism is one of the most diverse religions in the world." Aapo speared another piece of herring and extended it to Jessica. "Want a bite?"

She wrinkled her nose. "No way. You can have the whole jar to yourself.... What did you say?"

"That Hinduism is the most diverse religion in the world." Aapo smiled. This time it was genuine. He ate the piece of herring, and then grabbed one of the serrano peppers and bit it to the stem.

"Keep eating like that and you're going to need an IV and a psychiatrist," Jessica said with a laugh.

Aapo chuckled. 'I said that Hinduism is one of the most diverse religions in the world...."

"Oh, right. Yes, there's no agreed upon definition of what Hinduism really is. It's the most pluralistic and least centrally organized religion in all the world. The Classical Era of Hinduism (from 180 BCE to 900 CE) boasted 330 million gods and goddesses, including the early Vedic deities, although by about 100 CE they had assumed a minor role. By 1200 CE, Hinduism had even absorbed Buddha into their system of gods. Today, some even incorporate Jesus."

"I've always wondered: what is that dot on their foreheads?"

"Their forehead mark is called a *tilaka*. You're probably most familiar with the red dot or *bindi* traditionally worn by married women. But even male ascetics and temple priests can be seen wearing forehead markings. It can be interpreted in all sorts of ways. In many cases, it's just decorative rather than associated with religion or marital status. Unmarried women and Christians will often wear bindis. Other forehead markings indicate the god or goddess the person worships, as well as the community to which the person belongs. Followers of Vishnu, Krishna, and Lakshmi (the consort of Vishnu), who call themselves *Vaishnavites*, wear vertical marks. Followers of Shiva, who call themselves *Shaivites*, wear horizontal or crescent marks with a red dot in the middle. A combination of dots and crescents are worn by followers of the Great Goddess. They call themselves *Shaktas*."

20. This discussion is based largely on material from Chapter 3, "Hinduism, Jainism, and Sikhism," in Esposito. See also See Chapter 2, "Hindu Traditions," in Oxtoby.

Aapo was thoroughly enjoying their conversation. Jessica was unlike any woman he'd ever met. She frustrated the hell out of him. But he was drawn to her. This frightened him. The last time he fell hard for a woman, he freaked out and ran away. "You no know di use ah di wata till di well run dry," he said out loud, not realizing that he had done so.

"What's that?"

"Huh?"

"I was talking about the forehead markings and you said something about water in a well...."

"Sorry. Not sure why I said that. I guess I'm distracted with other things."

"Lottie?"

He shook his head and then said, "Nothing really. Go on." He felt himself flush.

Jessica was confused about their exchange. She was hoping that he was no longer upset about her not letting things go. She continued anyway: "Since the Classical Era, the most common practice is bhakti, where each devotee (or bhakta) chooses a personal god to be the center of her religious life. Most commonly, and especially since the Gupta Period (320-647 CE), these are Shiva and Vishnu—or one of Vishnu's avatars like Krishna or Rama. Many Hindus also worship Shiva's consort, variously known as Parvati, Durga, or Devi—or simply 'the Great Goddess.'"

"The Gupta Period?" Aapo was trying desperately to regain his concentration.

"The period of time in which cultural expressions of devotional Hinduism flourished in all the fine arts."

"Are there sacred texts that teach a person to be a good bhakta? You'd mentioned that the *Vedas* are the sacred texts of Hinduism. Are there others?" *I'm just having a conversation with her about Hinduism for crying out loud. Get your head on straight.*

"Yes—the *Puranas*, written during the first millennium CE and often called the 'Fifth Veda.' These stories were composed to glorify the gods, communicate their form of worship, and celebrate models of exemplary devotional faith—the bhaktas. Also, the *Bhagavad Gita* (the best known of all Hindu scripture and part of the great Hindu epic, *The Mahabharata*) provides a wonderful example of bhakti faith. Here Krishna, in dialogue with the warrior Arjuna, promises grace to the person seeking wisdom and liberation from samsara."

"So what're some of the core teachings of Hinduism? How is one liberated from samsara? That's the cycle of birth, death, and rebirth, right? You mentioned the preferable path as the way to achieve liberation. What exactly is the preferable path?"

Jessica loved that Aapo was so engaged in the conversation. Finn had no patience with her when she went on like this. "*What good are book smarts?*" he'd often say. "*You care about all the wrong things.*" She continued:

"We find most of the core teachings in the *Upanishads*, the philosophical tracts that were added to the *Vedas* after about 1000 CE. One of their central beliefs is *samsara*, the cycle of birth, death, and rebirth, subject to the law of *karma*, which is the idea that our actions (good and bad) condition our future. We are stuck in this cycle until we fully grasp the ultimate underlying reality, Brahman. Everything in this world is just a manifestation of Brahman, including the gods. The individual soul, Atman, travels through samsara until it achieves liberation (*moksha*) by realizing that it is nothing other than Brahman. This realization, this awareness that Atman just is Brahman, is called *samadhi* and is accomplished by achieving a trance state through advanced yoga practice. All of the world religions that emerged from Hinduism (Buddhism, Jainism, and Sikhism) accept the reality of samsara and karma, but they hold different doctrines about the existence and nature of the soul, as well as karma and liberation. They each advocate specific yoga practices to help one realize the highest truth and achieve liberation. For the Advaita Vedanta school of Hinduism, as I mentioned, the highest truth is that there is only one non-dual Unmanifested Reality, Brahman, and Atman just is Brahman — 'Thou art That.'"

"And the preferable path?"

"The *Upanishads* teach two paths: the path of renunciation and detachment from this material world and worldly desires (the so-called preferable path) and the path of attachment (the so-called pleasurable path). The goal for those who pursue the preferable path is moksha—liberation. When a person achieves moksha he becomes one with the universal soul or consciousness, Brahman. Those who are on the preferable path must eventually renounce 'son, wealth, and world.' This proves so difficult that they often defer pursuing moksha to a future life, instead choosing to stay with their families. One begins the preferable path by entering the four stages of life, available only to twice-born males...."

"Twice-born males?"

"*Dvija*, males of the three upper castes—Brahmins, Kshatriyas, and Vaishyas. Their second birth is spiritual: a rite of passage into Vedic studies. The four stages include: first, the student stage (in which the male learns the *Vedas* appropriate to his caste from his guru); and second, the householder stage (in which he marries and has children). Few go on to the third and fourth stages, since they're very difficult, requiring that the man not only leave his wife and family, but live a life of extreme asceticism. In the third stage, after the man's hair turns white, and he 'sees his sons' sons,' he leaves his household to the care of his sons and becomes a forest dweller. He detaches from the world and focuses on rituals and meditation. The fourth stage builds on the third. Once he has achieved samadhi, he becomes a wanderer, devoting himself to pilgrimages and yoga practice, attaining moksha at death."

Aapo shook his head. "So only twice-born males can achieve liberation from samsara? If you're not a twice-born male (or if you're a woman), it sounds like you have to be reborn a twice-born male in some future life to even have a shot at moksha."

"Right," Jessica began. "And as I mentioned, most twice-born married males defer moksha to a future life, since it's so difficult to leave one's wife, family, and all material possessions. You know, I once had a Hindu student from Nepal tell me that we need people to be on both paths (the preferable and pleasurable paths), and so that's why humans are so susceptible to worldly desires. Not everyone can be on the preferable path and have society function properly. We must each play our respective roles in society."

"So what can they hope for—I'm talking about those who do not go through the four stages of life—since they can't achieve moksha?"

"Heaven of their chosen god, by being a good bhakta. Of course, heaven is only a temporary abode. They hope to eventually be reborn a twice-born male. This leads us to the pleasurable path. There are different ways to be on this path—better and worse ways. The pleasurable path is so called because one remains attached to this world. If you lead an exceptionally depraved life on the pleasurable path, you might be reborn an oyster—or even a clump of grass, at least according to some scholars. The person on the pleasurable path does not pursue the Self (Atman). In the *Bhagavad Gita*, Krishna introduces a new way of being on the pleasurable path: *karma yoga*. This is acting for the benefit of others, without being attached to the fruits of action. One pursues the Self *in the world* for the welfare of others. It's almost as if the practitioner of karma yoga has a foot on both paths. This is what Krishna commands the warrior Arjuna to do. In Chapter 3, verse 19, he tells him, 'Strive constantly to serve the welfare of the world. By devotion to selfless work one attains the supreme goal of life.' Krishna also teaches moderation rather than extreme asceticism. He even adds that the karma yoga path is no less preferable than the so-called preferable path, and may even be *more* preferable, especially in special circumstances such as facing a war against evil, as the warrior prince Arjuna was facing. Krishna notes that both the renunciation of action (on the preferable path) and the selfless performance of action (the karma yoga path) lead to the supreme goal. The supreme goal is, of course, moksha. And in chapter 5, verse 6, Krishna teaches that the wise, following the path of selfless service, quickly reach Brahman. Brahman here means moksha—Atman becoming one with Brahman. Krishna is really trying to be inclusive. He even seems to suggest that bhakti yoga leads to moksha, so long as the fruits of one's actions are offered to god. That is, Krishna seems to wed bhakti to karma yoga. Krishna also suggests that bhakti is open to everyone. In chapter 9, verse 32, Krishna teaches that women, Shudras, even men born from the wombs of evil women can attain the supreme goal. Of course it's up for debate whether they attain moksha in that lifetime or have to wait for a more auspicious rebirth."

"The *Bhagavad Gita* seems like a text for the everyday Hindu: staying attached to this world, practicing moderation and selfless service to others, worshipping their chosen god," Aapo offered.

"Indeed it is. And it's also the most beloved text." Jessica smiled. "In the *Gita* we also find a hint at the injustice of the caste system, and an ethic that includes human and nonhuman creatures. Chapter 5, verse 18 states 'Those who possess wisdom have equal regard for all. They see the same Self in a spiritual aspirant and an outcaste, in an elephant, a cow, and a dog.'"

"The cow is sacred in Hinduism, right? Don't Hindus worship the cow?"

"Yes. The worship of the cow has deep historical roots. India has many pastoral, cattle-tending communities. Since children are typically given cow's milk after being weaned from their mothers' breasts, the cow is considered to be a second mother. Some say that the cow is an incarnation of the goddess Devi. And worshipping the cow is an expression of respect for all creatures. All creatures are sacred, but the cow holds a special place in Hindu society."

Jessica continued, "In Chapter 6, verse 29, Krishna similarly notes that those who possess wisdom, 'see the Self in every creature and all creation in the Self...they see everything with an equal eye.'"

"So now I think I understand your reaction to my earlier comment that we're not hurting anybody. We should respect Atman, the divine Self, in all creatures both human and nonhuman."

"Precisely." Jessica grinned at Aapo's epiphany.

"That seems like a good ethic to live by, but Mr. Chan has done a lot of good for a lot of people. I doubt he'd be able to help as much as he does, if he were in a different line of work. You said it yourself: selfless service for the welfare of others." Aapo smiled at the thought of all that Mr. Chan had done for him and Lottie.

"You've got a point, but I'm not so sure that Mr. Chan engages in *selfless* service. I've seen his fancy home."

"True. But Mr. Chan is a good man, Jessica—Anyway, I like Hinduism's ethic."

"I guess you're right, Aapo. Mr. Chan *is* a good man." She wondered whether she actually believed her words. "You know Hinduism also has a not-so-good ethic. Remember that Hinduism has the caste system. Hinduism teaches that each caste has its own *dharma*, or duty. Living according to one's place in society, determined by one's caste and gender, allows one to make good karma and move upward in samsara. Hindu ethics also revolve around dharma and caste."

As Jessica was finishing her sentence— "dharma and caste" —she spotted Mr. Chan stepping out of his tent and holding up another one of the bottles of wine that Chicken Eyes had made. He gestured Jessica to join him. She smiled and then turned to Aapo and said, "Keep resting that foot. Be back soon." Aapo sighed at Mr. Chan's interruption, *yet again.*

Inside Mr. Chan's tent, early afternoon

Jessica sat across the little table. Mr. Chan was pouring their wine. She studied the angles of his face. A face she'd love to photograph. Maybe that's what she could do with the million dollars—open a photography studio. Photography had become something of a serious hobby. And novel writing. Forget Mr. Chan's advice, she wanted to write a romance novel. She smiled. Then her face grew dark as she started thinking about what the guys were doing. How did they catch the animals? How did they house them? In a crowded holding pen? In small cages? How would they be transported? She imagined that the guys had cleared out some of the rainforest and made something of a road. She imagined camouflaged military trucks, the ones with the big covered cargo beds, hauling the animals across the Guatemalan border. They'd probably have to be tranquilized to go unnoticed. All of this imagining was so distressing that she put these thoughts out of her mind, took a sip of wine, and continued to look at Mr. Chan. He was smiling at her. A gentle smile. A smile at odds with what she now knew about him.

Maybe he isn't that bad after all. Actually he seemed like a good man. Jessica thought more about his smile. He was *definitely* a good man. She smiled back. *What a gentle smile.* Of course Jessica knew better than anyone that smiles can be deceptive. Finn Lauder was proof enough of that. Edin Chan's smile turned to fascination—if fascination had a look. Jessica was definitely familiar with his expression. His head was tilted, his eyes lingered on her own. *Why isn't he saying anything?*

Edin Chan *was* fascinated. It was hard to say exactly what made him so smitten. He had been since Jessica first showed up at his door. He tried to keep these feelings hidden. He knew better than to get involved with the women who ran the camp. And Jessica was half his age. In any case, his whole life was a string of relationships gone sour. Why should he think this one would be any different? Never mind that his line of business just wasn't suitable for romance. *What was he thinking?* Why couldn't he take his eyes off her? Why wasn't he saying anything? He frowned.

Jessica wondered why Mr. Chan was frowning all of a sudden. Maybe he too was thinking about what the guys were doing. Nah, such thoughts didn't bother him— *couldn't bother him.* He was probably like those Auschwitz doctors that Robert Lifton wrote about.[21] Lifton introduced the concept of *doubling* to explain how doctors, who were devoted to saving lives, could participate in the evil of Auschwitz. Psychological doubling allowed the doctors to compartmentalize their lives, leading to a dual existence: their Auschwitz self and their 'normal' self. Maybe Mr. Chan also had two selves. Maybe that's how he could live with (what should she call it?) his *Trafficking* self. Finally, she decided to say something: "Have you ever considered another career,

21. See Robert Lifton, *Nazi Doctors*, Basic Books, 1988.

Mr. Chan?"

Mr. Chan's eyes twinkled when he answered, "I would love to live in the highlands of Peru, rearing sheep."

Jessica wasn't sure whether he was joking. She smiled. "I'd rather live in the lowlands rearing alligators—but that's just a personal preference." And then she winked.

Mr. Chan laughed and then said more seriously, "You know, I was listening to your conversation with Aapo earlier. About the evolution of religion, and religion during the Axial Age."

Jessica found herself blushing. "Yes, I saw you watching. Do you know about this subject?"

"I read books…." He gave a playful smirk.

"Do tell, Professor Chan." She returned his smirk with a teasing smile.

"OK, I will do just that, Professor Kraus. You noted that religion initially arose as a human response to the difficulties of the world, a fear-driven response in which people sought alliances with the gods of the natural world. During the Axial Age, people turned away from the world and sought deliverance by a *transcendent entity*— is this what you called it?"

"It was. You were paying attention." She smiled broadly and took another sip of wine.

He smiled back. "You mentioned our control and domination of the now desacralized world. But you didn't mention the most powerful religion that has emerged in the twentieth century as a result of this desacralization: Capitalism."

"N-i-c-e." Jessica drew out the word. She was pleased with his clever response, with his ability to carry on such a conversation. She seemed to have forgotten that Aapo too held his own with her.

"Thank you." Mr. Chan's eyes brightened and he playfully waggled his eyebrows. *This is going well.* "Capitalism, a secular religion, has now all but replaced Christianity—at least in the West. We might call capitalism 'Christianity turned worldly.' Remember, Christianity condemns the rich to bless the poor.[22] Luke 6:20 says, 'Blessed be ye poor, for yours is the Kingdom of God.' And Luke 18:25 notes, 'It is easier for a camel to go through a needle's eye, than for a rich man to enter into the Kingdom of God.'"

"You know your Bible…."

"*Religiously.*" He chuckled at his wit. "Capitalism turns the Christian idea on its head. Salvation is now measured by a person's success in *worldly* endeavors. Wealth and power assure the capitalist that he's among God's elect, as contrasted with the lazy masses. Christianity has the saved and the damned, capitalism winners and losers."

"Is this what you believe, Mr. Chan?"

"It doesn't matter what I believe. But don't you find this fascinating?"

"Sure. But capitalism is founded on greed and aggression. It doesn't bring about peace, justice, or prosperity to humans. Capitalism breeds slums outside the cities. Capitalism creates a new class of poor. Not to mention the devastation to the environment and nonhuman creation," Jessica said.

"No more devastating and destructive than any other religion. Many religions have warrior gods. The Hebrew or Old Testament god is a perfect example. Think about it. Every religion claims to hold *the key* to salvation, and wages unending warfare in the face of conflicting doctrines. Religion teaches the faithful to love their neighbors, right? But by 'neighbors,' it means only those of the same faith, sect, or

22. The following conversation is based on Chen, *The Tao Te Ching*.

tribe. Every religion excludes outsiders from salvation. This hardly brings about peace or justice for humankind." Mr. Chan's exasperation fueled his every word.

"Not all religions are like this. Eastern religions tend to be more peaceful, gentle, and inclusive. Religions that elevate humans above the rest of nature lead to devastation, destruction, and war. But Eastern religions aren't like this. They are modeled on the life of a plant: tender and yielding. Western religions, on the other hand, are modeled on some fiction about animal life, characterized by never ending struggle, domination, and survival of the fittest. Indigenous people don't elevate humans above the rest of nature either...." Jessica shook her head. "*You're Maya*, Mr. Chan. Have you forgotten that? I shouldn't have to remind you of this."

After a few moments of silence, Mr. Chan's good judgment began to crumble and he said, "You're not like most of the women I bring here. There's something different about you. I like it.... I like *you*, Jessica." Mr. Chan rested his hand on Jessica's arm.

Jessica no longer knew what to think. A couple of days ago she would have welcomed Mr. Chan's intimate gesture. But now it just didn't feel right. A couple of days ago she was thinking entirely too much about his captivating smile. Now she wanted to slap that smile right off his face. She was growing increasingly impatient. She downed her wine, stood up, and said, "Chicken Eyes should be back by now and I have to prepare dinner. Aapo might need some more cinnamon tea."

"I'll be leaving for Buenos Aires tomorrow, Jessica." He had already said more than he should. He decided to go all-in: "Why don't you come with me? It'll be just you and me." He sounded pathetic, even to himself.

"I can't, Mr. Chan. I have to oversee the camp."

"Aapo can help Chicken Eyes. I can't imagine that his foot will be healed enough for *this* job. Ten-plus hours a day running around on his feet? No way.... *Come with me*." He didn't like how pleading he sounded, how desperate. His smile tightened and he looked away.

"Thank you, Mr. Chan, but I'll stay behind at the camp. This is what you hired me to do."

He chanced to look at her again long enough to say, "You're right Jessica. Get back to your tasks. Of course I still expect you to join me on my second trip to Argentina." *What was I thinking?* He began fussing with some papers. "I've got work to do to prepare for my trip," he said—but not to Jessica.

Jessica exited the tent and took off the necklace that Mr. Chan had given her. She dropped it. It sizzled and melted into the ground. The event was witnessed by a spider monkey sitting overhead on a lower limb of a gumbo-limbo tree. He had been looking for the perfect gift for his wife when he spotted the shiny object and smiled. Imagine his disappointment when it disappeared before his very eyes. Jessica walked past the rainbow eucalyptus tree. Its bark dripped globs of rancid yellow, like wallpaper glue. She approached Aapo and Chicken Eyes who seemed to be caught up in some private joke: "Yu si mi crass!" Aapo said with a guffaw, as he slapped Chicken Eyes' back.

"What's up guys?" Jessica asked and smiled. But then she grimaced when she saw the catch *du jour*. "I don't want to know."

"Don't worry Jessica. I'll clean it up for you. You'll just need to throw it in the pot with some onions and sweet potatoes," Chicken Eyes said with a snicker.

After sunset at the camp

The sun had set and Jessica was clearing off the dinner dishes. Prosper, donning his trademark top hat and vest, had broken out his fiddle. The men were gathering around him as he started plucking at the strings. Henry joined in with the harmonica. Soon the guys were on their feet dancing. Chicken Eyes grabbed the dirty plate from Jessica's hand and set it back down on the table. He took her other hand and twirled her around in ballroom fashion. She was all smiles. Aapo was beaming too. His *good* foot was tapping to the music. Suddenly Chicken Eyes looked at Aapo and yelled "Crick!" Aapo responded, "Crack!" The music stopped and all eyes were fixed on the two men.

Then Chicken Eyes sang out, "You gramma coat string pop." At that, Aapo stood up, only to bend down and do his best impression of a wobbly kneed gramma pulling up her underpants which had just dropped to the floor. All the guys burst out laughing. For her part, Jessica was having a difficult time trying to figure out what was going on. Aapo sat back down and said, "Dis da wahn time when time was time, when monkey chew tobacco and spit out lime!" After Aapo was done speaking Prosper drew his bow across the strings in dramatic fashion. All the guys yelled out, "Crick Crack! Twelve o' clock. Monkey sit down pon a rock!"

Chicken Eyes swigged from a bottle of rum. He passed the booze to Aapo, who took a swig as Chicken Eyes yelled out, "You mi di deh?"

Aapo yelled back, "Right deh, man!"

And then Chicken Eyes responded with "You mi see?"

Aapo called back, "Sure, I was *right deh*."

"Beautiful!" Chicken Eyes said and then laughed.

Prosper drew his bow across the strings once more. Jessica looked around. She still wasn't sure what the guys were up to, but she was clearly enjoying herself. Then Aapo yelled out, "Titie grass di grow!" He turned to Jessica and egged her on with a grin: "You know this...."

Jessica's face brightened. She shouted, "Palmer William! Palmer William!"

Aapo broke out into song—"Show me how you mommy walk"—at which point all of the guys began walking about in womanly fashion, hands daintily on display, mock curtseying, and all the other things they imagined women do, while yelling out, "Palmer William! Palmer William!"

When Aapo got to "Show me how you gramma kiss," Chicken Eyes pulled Jessica close to himself and kissed her smack dab on the lips. He smiled, eyes wide. Jessica laughed. Then Prosper and Henry started playing their instruments again and everyone danced away for the better part of an hour. Finally, the guys retreated to their tents, leaving Jessica, Chicken Eyes, and Aapo to polish off the last opened bottle of rum and finish up the dishes.

It wasn't long before Aapo rose to his feet and said, "Mi tayad." He rested his hand on Jessica's upper back. "Gud night."

"Goodnight," Jessica said and smiled as Aapo walked to his tent.

Chicken Eyes said, "Night, man." Once he knew that Aapo was out of earshot, he said, "Can I tell you something?"

"Sure, anything."

"It's heavy."

"I don't mind heavy." She wasn't quite sure what to expect.

He cleared his throat a couple times before saying, "I'm cursed."

The two words dangled in the air.

What could I possibly say to a man who spoke like that?

Jessica finally said, "What? Cursed? Don't be silly."

"No, I mean it. A witch. She accused me of killing her father." Chicken Eyes willed her to believe his story. *Why won't anyone believe my stories?*

Jessica caught herself laughing at the ridiculous turn the conversation was taking. But then she realized that Chicken Eyes was serious. "Did you kill her father?"

"No, of course not. She was just some crazy witch. She told me that everyone I care about would die."

"That sounds crazy. Of course you don't believe her, do you?"

Chicken Eyes was silent.

"Do you?"

"My wife Anastasia died. We were estranged, but I never stopped loving her. I called her a few years ago, and when nobody answered, I called her mother. That's when she told me."

"What happened?"

"Car accident." Chicken Eyes choked on the words.

"I'm so sorry, Chicken Eyes. Car accidents happen. It was just a coincidence, I'm sure. You're not cursed." She extended her hand to touch him.

But Chicken Eyes stopped her. He was becoming more than a little impatient with Jessica's failure to grasp the gravity of the situation. He looked at her straight-faced and said, "Mr. Chan is next—I can feel it." He became a bit teary-eyed. In a low voice, he continued, "Something bad is going to happen here. Something bad is going to happen to all of us. I feel it."

"Don't talk like that. You're scaring me." *Would you please please please please please stop talking.* At this point Jessica was truly becoming frightened. She wasn't sure what to make of his story. After all, she had been experiencing some strange things ever since they had arrived at the camp. She didn't know what to believe any-more.

"That's why you can't fall in love with me, Jessica," Chicken Eyes whispered anx-iously.

She wasn't sure whether he was being serious, or whether he was trying to recover some of his playfulness.

He looked Jessica straight in the eyes. Finally, he said. "There's only one way the curse can be broken: I must drink a vial of tears from a woman who's lost her own father." He produced a small vial from a deerskin pouch. "Did you lose your father, Jessica? I sense that you have."

"No—my father is still alive." Jessica's words were empty. She tried to smile at Chicken Eyes, but she couldn't. He looked like a little puppy tethered in the rain.

As Chicken Eyes watched Jessica looking at him—as he watched her look *into* him—he dared to wonder: What does she see? Madness? Had he always been mad?

He willed his mind to burst—to release his mind.

Gibnut (paca)

Pauraque

Black howler monkey

Coati

FIVE

Mr. Chan left for Argentina to meet the brokers. Chicken Eyes was off somewhere catching dinner, and Jessica and Aapo found themselves once again at Aapo's "secret" limestone steps. Jessica smiled as she saw Maya fly overhead. Aapo's foot was feeling a bit better (he convinced himself) and he had set out to take a short walk. Jessica insisted on joining him in case he needed some help along the way. They had just sat down when Jessica spotted what looked to be an ancient stone carving resembling a jaguar no more than a dozen feet away. She stood up and walked over to it.

"This is incredible!" She moved her hand along the smooth, rounded edges. "It looks like a jaguar, but with human-like features."

Aapo walked over to Jessica. He shook his head and smiled broadly. "I can't believe I've never noticed this before." He joined her in caressing the stone. "I've been coming here for three years. How could I have missed this?"

"Sometimes it just takes a fresh pair of eyes." She touched his back affectionately.

"Maya respect the tiger," Aapo explained. "They call the tiger 'B'alam.' They appear in many Maya carvings and statues. Their pelts were a chief adornment among the Maya royalty."

"B'alam—that's Doc's name."

"He's also known as Thaddeus, Teddy, Tadeo—Sweet Talking Ted to the ladies." Aapo chuckled. "He goes by many aliases."

Jessica crossed her arms and looked away. Aapo wondered what might have distracted her. He tried to draw her back into the conversation, "You know, the tiger is God of the Underworld, the Night Sun, one of the major deities of the Maya pantheon. Maya believe that the universe is divided into three levels: the celestial world of stars, planets, sun, and moon, the terrestrial world (Earth), and the underworld (Xibalba). The Earth was often depicted as a gigantic crocodile. In the center was the sacred ceiba tree, which connects the three levels of the universe. Each level has its own gods. This carving looks like the Jaguar god."

Jessica looked at the carving again. "I wonder how old it is."

"It looks like it's from the Classic Era, between the years 300 and 900 CE. Probably before 700, since after that time most of the major Maya cities were abandoned and left to crumble. The collapse of the Maya civilization is still a mystery...." Aapo looked up, wondering if the Sky God might offer up an answer to the puzzle. He finally added, "Jessica, despite Mr. Chan and I teasing you, tigers rarely attack people. Of course it's always best to be safe. That's why we carry guns. But a tiger's roar will surely liven up a night! In any case, if they get too close to the camp the dogs will bark."

"I feel safe around you." Jessica touched Aapo's arm and smiled sweetly.

"Even with Belize's best conservation efforts, the tiger is threatened with illegal hunting and loss of habitat," Aapo said with a frown.

"You guys don't...?" Suddenly Jessica's stomach turned inside out.

"Of course not. We never trade in threatened species."

Jessica walked back to the limestone steps, sat down, and lowered her head. Aapo sat by her side. He could tell that she was upset. Was she this bothered by what they were doing? Then why accept the job to oversee the camp in the first place? Her Uncle Nick had to have told her stories. Jessica's face suddenly brightened when she heard the familiar buzzing of dozens of colorful hummingbirds. She looked up and smiled.

"The hummingbirds were here a couple days ago," she exclaimed.

"You came out here on your own? —Or were you with Mr. Chan?" Aapo didn't really want to know the answer.

"I stumbled upon it when I was…." She wasn't sure that she wanted to tell him about the tarot reading with Chicken Eyes, and so she finally just said, "I was on my own."

Aapo smiled. "Mr. Chan once shared a Maya story with me about how the hummingbird became so colorful. Want to hear it?"

"I'd love to."

"When Tzunuum, the hummingbird, was created by Great Spirit, she was very plain. Although her feathers lacked bright colors, she didn't seem to mind. When it was time for Tzunuum to get married, she had neither a wedding gown nor a necklace to wear, and she became very sad. And so some of her friends decided to make a wedding dress and necklace to surprise her. Back in those days, Ya, the vermillion-crowned flycatcher, wore a crimson ring of feathers around his neck. He decided to use some of them for a gift. He tucked a few of his red feathers in his crown and gave the rest to Tzunuum for a necklace. Uchilchil, the bluebird, donated several of her azure feathers for Tzunuum's wedding dress. The vain motmot (not to be outdone) offered some of his turquoise blue and emerald green feathers. The cardinal offered some red ones. Then Yuyum, the oriole, sewed up all the plumage into a beautiful wedding gown. Ah-leum, the spider, brought an exquisite web woven of shiny gossamer threads for Tzunuum's veil. Ah-leum helped Yuyum weave intricate designs into the dress. The Azar tree dropped a carpet of petals over the ground where the ceremony would take place. Pakal, the orange tree, put out sweet smelling blossoms, and a kaleidoscope of colorful butterflies arrived to dance about during the ceremony. On her wedding day, Tzunuum was so surprised and grateful that Great Spirit sent his messenger, Cozumel, the swallow, to tell Tzunuum that she could wear her wedding gown for the rest of her life. And so she did—and all of her descendants."[23]

"What a wonderful story. You know, Hinduism tells a story about a grateful little unassuming bird—a sparrow. It involves Garuda, an enormous bird-like creature that appears in both Hinduism and Buddhism. Garuda is the *vahana* of the god Vishnu."

"Vahana?" Aapo smiled as a shimmering, magenta-colored hummingbird hovered between them.

"'Vahana' means 'that which carries,' and refers to a Hindu deity's 'mount' or vehicle on which the god rides. Garuda has the head, beak, wings, and talons of an eagle, but the legs and torso of a human. Garuda represents birth and heaven and is the enemy of all snakes, which are symbols of death and the underworld. The *Mahabharata* recounts the stories of Garuda's birth and how he became Vishnu's mount, by the way. In the story, Garuda comes to the aid of a little sparrow who has been taken advantage of by Ocean. She laid her eggs on the beach, but Ocean carried them away with his waves. Sparrow begged Ocean to return them, but he ignored her. And so Sparrow decided that she would dry up the ocean. She began to scoop up the water in her little beak and deposit it on the sand. Of course everyone laughed at her. The news of her determination spread, and finally Garuda got word of her activity. He felt compassion for his little sister bird and promised to help. 'Return Sparrow's eggs,' he told Ocean, 'Otherwise I will take over her work.' Ocean was frightened by this, and he returned the eggs to the grateful little sparrow.[24] There are other Garuda stories. One involves

23. See http://www.firstpeople.us/FP-Html-Legends/Gift_To_The_Hummingbird-Mayan.html.
24. See http://www.harekrsna.de/garuda-e.htm. See also http://www.ancient.eu/Garuda/.

Yama, the god of death. This story doesn't turn out so well for the little bird."

"What happens?" Aapo's eyes followed the iridescent bird as it flew beyond the jaguar carving and disappeared into the dense forest.

"One day, Garuda stood at the entrance of the god Shiva's abode on Mount Kailasha, while Vishnu paid Shiva a visit. There Garuda's eyes fell upon a beautiful little bird. Just then Yama, the god of death (whose vahana is a buffalo) arrived at Mount Kailasha to pay Shiva a visit too. Yama's eyes passed over the little bird. He gave a quizzical look and then went inside. In ancient Indian thought, even a passing glance by Yama was said to be the harbinger of death. Garuda, noticing that Yama looked at the little bird, believed that it could only mean one thing. His heart filled with pity, and he decided to rescue the little bird from her imminent death. He swooped her up with his mighty talons, flew her to a forest, thousands of miles away, and set her down on a rock by a small brook. Then he flew back to Mount Kailasha and resumed his position at the entrance of Shiva's abode. Soon Yama emerged and Garuda asked: 'When you saw the little bird as you were going in to see Shiva, why did you look so pensive?' Yama replied, 'When my eyes fell upon the little bird, I saw that she was going to die within a few minutes, being swallowed by a python, thousands of miles from here in a forest by a brook. I wondered how it was possible that this tiny little creature could travel so far in such a short time. But surely it must have happened somehow to fulfill her destiny.' At that, Yama went away, leaving Garuda at a loss for words."[25]

"Sometimes our best intentions can cause tremendous harm," Aapo said with a frown. "Then again, Garuda's actions benefitted a hungry python."

"Not only that, but the story plays with cause and effect. I really love the story for this reason." Jessica smiled. "Think about it. Who caused the little bird's death? Had Garuda not seen Yama look at the bird, he would never have transported her thousands of miles away just to be python food. Had Yama not looked at the bird in the first place, Garuda would never have transported her. But Yama would not have looked at the bird in the first place except that Garuda *would* transport her—*because* Yama looked at her!"

"You can sure tangle up your thoughts thinking about it. But I wonder if the question 'who caused the little bird's death?' is really beside the point. It seems that the point is that the little bird was fated to die, as Yama himself told Garuda. I like the first story far better though—happy ending."

"You know, your comment raises an interesting question about Hinduism and freewill. It turns out that the answer is extraordinarily complicated. Let me tell you what I mean. Remember that our karma (good and bad) determines how we will be reborn in samsara. In Chapter 6 of the *Bhagavad Gita*,[26] the warrior Arjuna asks Krishna about the person who has attempted but failed his spiritual goal: Did he renounce the world for nothing? Krishna responds that when such people die, they go to other realms where the righteous live (heaven, of course) where they will dwell for countless years before being reborn into a home which is pure and prosperous. Or they will be reborn into a family that practices meditation and where the wisdom that they acquired in previous lives will be reawakened. That is, they will be reborn in a spirit-centered home which then offers them the best hope for Self-realization. So the good choices and actions that we make in a previous life set us up for spiritual enlightenment in the next. Of course we can still make poor choices in that next life.

25. See http://www.harekrsna.de/garuda-e.htm.

26. All references to the *Bhagavad Gita*, as well as to the *Upanishads*, are to translations by Eknath Easwaran.

We still have freewill, but the environment in which we are born strongly influences how we will live that new life. Indeed, in Chapter 17 of the *Gita*, Krishna teaches that everyone is born with faith of some kind. He identifies three main personality types, based on the three gunas or qualities in the material world: *sattvic, rajasic,* and *tamasic*, which are rooted in our nature according to the faith we are born with. And these personality types strongly condition our actions, even down to the food we eat. This chapter is really quite funny. For example, Krishna explains that tamasic people, those who live in complete ignorance and darkness, like overcooked, stale, leftover, and impure food, food that has lost its taste and all nutritional value—think cold French fries!" Jessica laughed. But then she frowned. "I guess it's really quite funny until you realize that these personality types align with the castes. For example, sattvic personalities, which are associated with wisdom, goodness, and light, tend to be found in the Brahmins. Tamasic personalities, on the other hand, are associated with the Shudras and the outcastes. As Krishna explains in Chapter 18, verse 40, no creature is free from the conditioning of the three gunas. 'The different responsibilities found in the social order—distinguishing Brahmin, Kshatriya, Vaishya, and Shudra—have their roots in this conditioning….' It seems that even though karma informs how we will be reborn and the type of nature we will have, we still have freewill, albeit extremely limited, though even this can be challenged. I'm thinking of a passage where Krishna tells Arjuna that the Lord makes all living beings 'revolve like puppets on a carousel.' This sounds like a death blow to any notion of freewill. But in Chapter 16, Krishna further complicates matters. He teaches about the so-called demonic personality who dooms himself to being reborn with a demonic nature into a demonic home. Such a person seems fated to an evil life, never to escape samsara. Krishna explains that 'Life after life I cast those who are malicious, hateful, cruel, and degraded into the wombs of those with similar demonic natures. Birth after birth they find themselves with demonic tendencies.' The demonic person is doomed to be reborn from the womb of a demonic woman. He cannot escape this destiny. This sounds like fatalism. Certain choices will lead us to a point where we put ourselves on an evil fatalistic path. We see a similar fatalistic strand when Krishna tells Arjuna that even if he says that he will not fight this battle, his resolve will be useless, since his own nature *will drive him into it*, will drive him to do even that which he doesn't want to do."

Aapo smiled and then said, "This whole topic concerning to what extent we are free really fascinates me. I still think that the Garuda story suggests that the little bird, at least, was fated to death. The story reminds me of an Arabic fable retold by Somerset Maugham called 'Appointment in Samarra.' It goes like this: There was a merchant in Bagdad who sent his servant to the market. Soon the servant returned trembling and afraid and said, 'Master, just now when I was in the marketplace I was jostled by a woman in the crowd. When I turned, I saw it was Death. Death looked at me and made a threatening gesture. Please, lend me your horse and I will ride to Samarra to save myself and avoid my fate. Death will not find me there.' The merchant lent his servant his horse, and the servant mounted it and rode as fast as the horse could gallop. Then the merchant went to the marketplace and there he spotted Death and asked, 'Why did you make a threatening gesture to my servant?' to which Death replied, 'It was not a threatening gesture, it was an expression of surprise. I was astonished to see him in Bagdad, for I have an appointment with him tonight in Samarra.'"

Jessica smiled widely. "Wow, that story is amazingly similar. I wonder if they're connected somehow in history? I wouldn't be surprised if they were. How'd you ever learn about this?"

"I read John O'Hara's novel of the same name. In his foreword of a later reprint, he explained how he came up with the title when Dorothy Parker showed him the story in Maugham's play, *Sheppey*. Mr. Chan really got me interested in literature. He really taught me a lot. Like I've said before, I owe him my life."

"I guess you do...."

"So back to Garuda." Aapo began. "You mentioned he appears in Buddhism too?"

"In Buddhism, we don't find Garuda, but *garudas*—a mythical species similar in appearance to Garuda. Their wingspan is several miles wide, and when they flap their wings they cause hurricane strength winds. They are the sworn enemy of the Naga serpent race."

"You called yourself a Christian Buddhist...."

"Right, I'm syncretic. I guess I'm a bit Hindu too in that I believe that we must respect the divine in all creatures." *This is why I'm so saddened by what's going on here, Aapo.* But she couldn't bring herself to say that just now.

"You've already explained how Jesus is your Barong—fighting evil in your life."

"Right. I sleep with a hand-carved olive wooden cross from Jerusalem. It keeps the spirits away."

"So tell me about Buddhism. What is it about Buddhism that you like?"

Introduction to Buddhism

"I love Buddha's teachings, especially that a human life should never be wasted. We should live with purpose, detached from hatred and cruelty, and work towards enlightenment. Buddhism grew out of Hinduism.[27] The founder of Buddhism is *Siddhartha Gautama* (also called Shakyamuni Buddha, from the Shakya clan), who lived in the late sixth century BCE. Siddhartha came from the Kshatriya or ruler-warrior caste. He was born during a time of spiritual questioning and asceticism unmatched in the history of religions. There were many ascetic seekers, called *shramanas*, who pursued yoga practices with the hope of achieving enlightenment. Shramanas rejected most of the Vedic teachings, especially the spiritual and social hierarchy established by the Brahmins or priestly caste. Siddhartha's parents ruled a small state in the Himalayan foothills. His birth was accompanied by celestial signs, and a wise man's prediction that Siddhartha would either become a universal monarch or a great ascetic. Siddhartha's mother died shortly after his birth, and his father did everything in his power to ensure that his son would become a great monarch. Siddhartha was pampered with all the princely pleasures, including a wife and a concubine, and he was confined within the palace walls. At twenty-nine years old, his life changed when he asked his chariot driver to take him outside the palace walls. It was then that he encountered a sick man, an old man, a dead man, and a shramana. Buddhists call this the *Four Passing Sights*."

"I can imagine the impact this had on a man who had been safeguarded from the grittier sides of life."

"Exactly.... Siddhartha had been seeing the world through rose-colored glasses. After this life-changing experience, he abandoned his family and palace life (including his newborn son) to search for a teacher among the forest-dwelling ascetics. Siddhartha found a guru who taught him advanced meditation, which he quickly mas-

27. This discussion is largely based on Chapter 4, "Buddhism: Paths Toward Nirvana," in Esposito. See also Chapter 5, "Buddhist Traditions," in Oxtoby, and Chapter 3, "Buddhism" in *Invitations to Asian Religions*, Jeffrey Brodd, et al., Oxford University Press.

tered. Siddhartha realized that the guru had nothing more to offer and so he moved on. Then he found another guru, but he quickly mastered everything *that* guru could teach him. At that point Siddhartha set off on his own. He soon found five men who were extreme ascetics, living on a few grains of rice a day. Siddhartha adopted that lifestyle for five years, but finally abandoned it as too extreme. Thoroughly weakened, he sat beneath a Bodhi tree where he was determined to find enlightenment. He began to meditate when he was disturbed by Mara, a personification of death, delusion, and temptation. Mara summoned his demons to tempt Siddhartha. Siddhartha resisted the temptation and resumed meditation. He finally reached *prajna*—spiritual awakening or insight into the true nature of reality called the *Three Marks of Existence.* 'Buddha' is a title meaning 'The Awakened One' or 'The Enlightened One.' Prajna is similar in experience to *samadhi* of Hinduism insofar as it's a mystical experience beyond intellectual understanding, beyond articulation. For seven weeks Gautama Buddha stayed under the Bodhi tree, entering the blissful state of nirvana. Mara returned to tempt Buddha to stay put and enjoy the experience. But one of the gods intervened and encouraged Buddha to teach others the path to enlightenment. Buddha then walked to a place called Deer Park where he found his five former ascetic companions. At first they treated him with disdain, until they were overcome with his radiance. The Buddha then sat down and taught them the *Dharma* (his teachings), including the *Four Noble Truths* and the *Eightfold Path.* These five ascetics became Buddha's enlightened followers, called *arhats*, and the first members of the *sangha*, the Buddhist monastic community. They were charged to teach enlightenment to all the people of the world. Buddhism is the first missionary religion, although it was the emperor Ashoka of the Maurya dynasty (a convert of Buddhism who lived from 273 to 232 BCE) who was the most instrumental in spreading Buddhism across his empire and beyond."

"What is the true nature of reality for Buddhists—these Three Marks of Existence that you mentioned? Hindus believe that this world is an illusion and there is only one non-dual reality (Brahman), and the soul or Self (Atman) just *is* Brahman—at least according to the Advaita Vedanta school."

"You're an excellent student, Aapo." Jessica smiled broadly.

"I love learning about religions, history, and other cultures." In the who-knows-how-many times that Jessica had seen Aapo smile, this was the first time that he twinkled, that he looked genuinely happy rather than masking some deep sorrow.

Just then a little spider monkey jumped down from a nearby branch right in front of Aapo's feet. He was the same little guy who saw Jessica's necklace melt into the ground. Aapo reached into one of the deep pockets of his khaki cargo pants (the one without the gun) and pulled out a lavender jade pendant in the shape of a crescent moon.

"What are you doing?" Jessica asked.

Aapo looked at Jessica and said "Watch..." as he dangled the pendant in front of the monkey who, for his part, was dancing in anticipation of finally finding the perfect gift for his wife. After an entirely too long eight seconds of dangling, Aapo finally tossed it to him. The monkey picked it up with his little hand, jumped up onto the branch and then disappeared into the darkness.

"Monkeys love jewelry. Of course he would prefer the silver chain from which this pendant might hang, but he didn't look like he was particularly disappointed. Aapo smiled sweetly. "I buy dozens of these little pendants every time I visit the village. They aren't expensive, and I help support the women's families. Aren't they pretty?"

Jessica smiled. "So you have more?"

Aapo reached into his pocket again and handed one to Jessica. "Hand-carved. Do you like it? ... It's yours."

"I love it. I'll have to get a chain for it…. Thank you." She gave him a hug. "OK, back to the lesson. The Three Marks of Existence are impermanence, suffering, and *Anatman* or No-Self or soul. Buddha's first mark of existence teaches that everything is in flux. Nothing remains the same (well, except the blissful experience of nirvana), not even for a single moment. The Buddha's second mark of existence is suffering. All life entails suffering. We shouldn't fight these inevitable experiences of human existence: birth, death, old age, and disease. Suffering is also caused by our desire to hold onto things, but everything is fleeting. We are uncomfortable with impermanence. Wanting is also suffering. For example, if I want some fancy new shoes but I don't have the money to pay for them, I feel dissatisfied. That dissatisfied feeling is suffering. But if I'm happy with what I have, that desire to buy the fancy new shoes never arises, and so that suffering would never arise. Fearing that you might lose something or someone is also suffering. Wanting things to stay the same is suffering. Wanting things to be different is suffering. Worry, hatred, anger, envy, desire, grief, loneliness, anxiety, and frustration: these are all suffering. But this should not cause us to be pessimistic. Rather, it should encourage the appropriate responses to suffering: compassion, gentleness, kindness, and understanding."

"So Buddhism encourages compassion, gentleness, and kindness to all living creatures? Buddhism shares this with Hinduism."

"It does." Jessica smiled. She was hoping that these lessons in Eastern religions would help him better see her perspective. "You know, religions of the Western tradition, such as Judaism and Christianity, give us the wrong kind of animal and environmental ethic—at least I think so. Most people are familiar with God's injunction in Genesis 1: 'Be fruitful and multiply, and fill the earth and subdue it, and have dominion over the fish of the sea and over the birds of the air and over every living thing that moves upon the earth.' They have a pretty lousy human ethic too. Consider 1 Samuel 15:3. God says through the prophet Samuel to Saul: 'Now go and attack Amalek (that is, the Amalekites), and utterly destroy all that they have. Do not spare them, but kill both man and woman, child and infant, ox and sheep, camel and donkey.' He does the same in Deuteronomy, when the Israelites are invading the promised land. Why would God command such a thing?"

"I don't know, Jessica. I think Christianity gives us a good ethic to live by. Consider Jesus' two greatest commandments: Love the Lord your God with all your heart, and with all your soul, and with all your mind, and love your neighbor as yourself. If you truly love God and your neighbor, it seems that you'd treat others with compassion, gentleness, and kindness. Take any religious text, and if you poke around it enough you'll find something disagreeable or offensive."

"I guess you're right. Sorry, I didn't mean to offend. But while Jesus taught compassion, tolerance, and respect (teachings that his brother, James, continued as head of the Jerusalem church), Paul and those writing in Paul's name perverted Jesus' teachings. Christianity would be a much different religion if James' teachings had become popularized rather than Paul's." She grimaced. "Sorry. I got carried away…."

But Aapo didn't seem to mind much. Instead, he responded, "James must not have had a good PR person." He chuckled.

Jessica smiled and continued, "We don't see anything like this in Eastern religions. As I told Mr. Chan, Eastern religions are modeled on the life of a plant—tender and yielding. Western religions, on the other hand, are modeled on some fiction about animal life, characterized by never ending struggle, domination, and survival of the fittest." She gave a heavy sigh. "Anyway, back to the Three Marks of Existence. The final mark of existence, Anatman, follows from the universal characteristic of impermanence. Of all the things we desire, our greatest attachment is to an unchanging and eternal soul or Self—Atman in Hinduism. But impermanence applies even to us. We don't have a changeless Self or soul. Indeed, holding onto this false idea of a Self which has no correspondence to reality, produces harmful thoughts of 'me' and 'mine,' resulting in selfish desires, cravings, attachments, hatred, ill will, conceit, pride, egoism, and other defilements. It's the source of most all the troubles in the world, from personal conflicts to wars between nations.[28] The Buddha teaches that *all things* are empty, devoid of an essence. Nothing is fixed, permanent, unchanging or independent. The only permanent changeless reality is the deathless reality of nirvana, called *parinirvana* (final nirvana, or nirvana without residue)—liberation from samsara, and a state of tranquility and abiding peace and joy. This is the Buddhist version of Hinduism's moksha. You know, Mahayana Buddhists believe that even parinirvana is empty. Parinirvana is nothing other than a way of experiencing samsara through an enlightened lens."

"So Buddhists, like Hindus, believe in samsara and liberation from samsara?"

"And they also believe in karma, which determines how one will be reborn in samsara."

"If there is no soul or Self, then what travels through samsara?" Aapo looked over at the jaguar carving who seemed to be smiling at how well he was following along.

"Great question. Buddha's answer is rooted in the *skandhas*, meaning 'bundles' or 'heaps,' which are the five basic components that make up a person: the body, perceptions, feelings, innate tendencies (or dispositions shaped by karma), and consciousness—all of which, like everything else (except nirvana) are in flux. It's our consciousness that travels through samsara."

"This idea is really difficult to wrap my head around—and it's even more difficult to accept. We're all very attached to the notion of a soul or self that persists through time and change."

"It's actually quite liberating, and it doesn't imply destruction of something that we love very much (namely, our *selves*), since our consciousness can experience parinirvana: the end of all suffering and the perfection of happiness." Jessica briefly rested her hand atop Aapo's and smiled.

"I can't help but compare the Buddhist conception of the self as a bundle of five skandhas to David Hume's claim that the self is a bundle of perceptions," Aapo said.

"How do you know about Hume?"

"Mr. Chan, of course. He persuaded me to take a philosophy class in college. He tried to ensure that I'd become something of a Renaissance man." Aapo smiled.

"You went to college?" She grinned. "To your point about the comparison: Sure, though Hume isn't making a metaphysical claim about the self, whereas Buddhism *is* making a metaphysical claim. Hume is making an epistemic claim. He denies that we have any real *idea* of the self. Instead, all we have is a bundle of perceptions, held together by memory. This is Hume's attempt to show what exactly it is we refer to when we talk about the self. Hume rejects that we have any real idea of the self because he assumes that the self must be something unchanging and constant. He finds no im-

28. Lisa Battaglia Owen, "Toward A Buddhist Feminism: Mahayana Sutras, Feminist Theory, and the Transformation of Sex," *Asian Journal of Women Studies*, 3(4), December 1997.

pression of such a thing, so there can't be an idea of it. This, at least, seems right. There doesn't seem to be any unchanging underlying substance that we can point to and assert that 'that thing' is the self that binds all perceptions together. The Buddha proposes a metaphysical view of the self that is similar to Hume's notion. The similarity lies in Hume's claim that the self is a bundle. But in Buddhism, the self is not merely a bundle of perceptions. Remember the five skandhas include the body, perceptions, feelings, innate tendencies, and consciousness. Each of these components is constantly changing. That is, *change* is their essential feature. What the Buddha denies is the claim that there is a soul or self that underlies the thing that we point to when we point at each other. Buddha is denying the existence of Atman, the unchanging eternal soul or Self of Hinduism. It's not a denial of the self per se, but merely a denial of a constant underlying existence. There's *something*, just no unchanging and essential something."[29]

"What are some of the other teachings of Buddha? You mentioned the Four Noble Truths and the Eightfold Path."

"The Four Noble Truths: First, all life entails suffering, called *dukkha*. As we saw, the appropriate response to suffering is compassion, gentleness, respect, kindness, and understanding. Second, the cause of suffering is desire. The appropriate response to desire is detachment. Third, if one removes desire, one removes suffering. The *sangha* provides a refuge from the world of desire. Of course it's not to everybody's liking. Most Buddhists are householders who support the sangha instead, which helps them gain good karma. Originally, the sangha only included monks, but after some convincing (actually, eighteen years' worth, if I remember correctly), the Buddha allowed nuns too. The Buddha was a *reluctant* feminist." Jessica chuckled. "Indeed, on three different occasions the Buddha refused to allow his aunt and foster mother Prajapati Gautami and her women to join the monastic community. Even after the Buddha permitted women to become nuns, he insisted that a monk always take precedence over a nun in matters of respect and deference, and a nun must never teach a monk. So despite ultimately allowing women to become nuns, the Buddha preserved male dominance within the order.... Finally, the fourth noble truth: the way to remove desire (Buddha's prescription for eliminating all suffering) is to follow the Eightfold Path: right speech, right action and right livelihood; right effort, right mindfulness and right concentration; and right view and right intention. They are often divided into Morality, Meditation, and Prajna. When we observe the Eightfold Path, we follow in the footsteps of Buddha in eliminating desire, attachment, and ignorance, and we ultimately achieve enlightenment and parinirvana."

"Can you say more about the Eightfold Path? Does Buddha give more specific instructions?"

"Sure. Let's start with right speech. Many of us underestimate the power of the spoken word, and we often regret the words that we say. Many of us have been deeply hurt by harsh criticism or the spreading of gossip. But we also know how good it feels when somebody extends kind words or offers a compliment. Words can encourage us, unite us, and heal division. But they can also destroy relationships and start wars. If we resolve to never speak unkindly, we move closer to compassionate living."

"I like that." Aapo smiled.

"Right action asks us to consider others and the world we live in. It includes taking whatever steps possible to safeguard the world for future generations, includ-

29. Their discussion is based on Alan Tomhave, "Cartesian Intuitions, Humean Puzzles, and the Buddhist Conception of the Self," *Philosophy East and West*, October 2010.

ing nonhuman life, of course. Right action also encompasses the five precepts which Buddha gave: do not kill, steal, lie, avoid sexual misconduct, and do not take drugs or other intoxicants. Right livelihood follows from right action. If your work lacks respect for life, it will become an obstacle to spiritual progress. Buddhism promotes equality of all living beings and respect for all life. Buddha thus discourages particular types of work, including those that deal in harmful intoxicants and weapons, and those that harm human and nonhuman life. A Buddhist would never own a liquor store or a gun shop, for example. He'd never be a butcher, and he'd certainly never engage in slave or animal trade."[30]

Aapo squeezed his face as he felt a slight headache coming on.

Jessica didn't notice his discomfort. She continued, "Buddha also taught the doctrine of *Dependent Origination*. Most of us see the world as a composite of different, separate, individual things, existing independently of one another. But this is an illusion. Buddha taught that reality is deeply interrelated and interdependent, and nothing exists apart from anything else. All things depend on other things for their coming-into-be, their origination. This is especially true of the psychological and bodily states that condition a person's bondage to suffering and rebirth. Buddhists use the image of a 'wheel of becoming' with twelve links. The wheel shows the cycle of interdependent stages reflecting the movement from a past life through the present one and into the future. But it doesn't stop there, since the future life will lead to old age, death, and rebirth. The wheel will keep turning around and around, until the person seeks enlightenment."

"I like that Buddha welcomed nuns too—although reluctantly. Since the sanghas admit nuns, it seems that Buddhism, unlike Hinduism, allows women to achieve liberation from samsara."

"Exactly right, Aapo, at least in the Mahayana tradition. Through compassionate living, mastering meditation, and achieving wisdom, both men and women can realize nirvana and parinirvana."

"Do Buddhists have sacred texts?"

"They do. The Buddhist canon consists of the many *sutras*: the words and teachings of Gautama Buddha. A Buddhist priest once joked with me that Buddhism is neck-deep in sutras. My favorite is *The Lotus Sutra*, a beloved text of the *Mahayana* school. There are three main Buddhist schools: The Mahayana or Great Vehicle, the *Theravada* or Elder Traditionalists (which is much more conservative and claims to represent the original and authentic teachings of Buddha) and the *Vajrayana*—the dominant form of Buddhism in Tibet. (I'm sure you're familiar with the Dalai Lama, the spiritual leader of the *Gelugpa* or Yellow Hat Buddhists of Tibet.) While most agree that the Vajrayana or Tantric School is just another form of Mahayana Buddhism, Vajrayana Buddhists claim that their tradition can be directly traced back to Gautama Buddha. I have a copy of *The Lotus Sutra* in my backpack. I'd love to share it with you sometime. In that text, Siddhartha Gautama, called The World Honored One, is teaching the Dharma to the many multitudes of creatures here on our Buddha world (Earth) in a most spectacular display. It's a fascinating and outrageously fun book, which introduces wonderful new teachings."

"I'd like that." Aapo smiled.

"There are also a number of non-canonical texts."

Is Buddhism as pluralistic and diverse as Hinduism?"

"It is, but not in having 330 million gods. Buddha is not worshipped as a god,

30. See https://www.buddha101.com/p_path.htm.

but revered as a fully enlightened human being. I mean of course the historical Buddha, the living Siddhartha Gautama. *The Lotus Sutra* seems to tell a different story. The World Honored One has an assortment of supernatural powers, as you'll see. All sorts of magical things happen in that book, including people being transported by giant lotus flowers that move like flying saucers. Gautama Buddha had very little to say about gods and even discouraged people from devoting themselves to them. While he acknowledged their existence, he taught that they're of no help in our quest for spiritual enlightenment. While gods might help us from time to time, liberation from samsara can only be achieved through our own efforts. So instead of devoting ourselves to gods, we should devote ourselves to putting the Dharma into practice. *The Lotus Sutra* is chockfull of supernatural beings (the Buddhas and *bodhisattvas*) who are objects of devotion—but whether they're gods really depends on how you define the term. Whenever we get a chance to look at *The Lotus Sutra*, you'll get what I mean."

"It's a deal. So how is Buddhism pluralistic?"

"Mahayana Buddhism teaches that since people are so different, many different approaches, called skillful or expedient means, are needed to get everyone on the so-called One Buddha-Vehicle Path to Buddhahood. The Lotus Sutra promises that all living creatures will eventually become a Buddha. Buddhist teachers and philosophers offer many different interpretations of Buddha's teachings, and this is very much in line with the Buddha's wishes. He insisted that no one person or institution should fix a single canon or orthodoxy in doctrinal interpretation. As a result, by six hundred years after Siddhartha's death, several different canons of collected teachings were created, and the sanghas aligned under the two main schools: Mahayana and Theravada. The Vajrayana School began much later, in the sixth or seventh century CE. Despite this great diversity, what gives the religion unity is reverence for the so-called *Three Gems*: Buddha, Dharma, and Sangha."

11 am, Philip S.W. Goldson International Airport, just outside of Belize City
After a three-hour layover in Houston and an overnight flight, Finn Lauder and the real Jessica Kraus arrived at the Philip S.W. Goldson International Airport, just outside of Belize City. Before they'd caught their flight, Jessica had convinced Finn to take her shopping on Rodeo Drive, but only after she agreed to an emergency session with his stylist who bleached her hair platinum blonde. They both loved her new look. Four hours before their flight, they stopped off at Bar Nineteen 12 at the Beverly Hills Hotel and had a few cocktails and fancy appetizers on their terrace. They now stood at baggage claim awaiting Jessica's brand new, cherry red leather luggage, stuffed full of Dolce and Gabbana dresses and a Louis Vuitton two-piece swimsuit.

"So where do we go from here? How're we supposed to find them?" Finn asked somewhat anxiously.

"I don't know. Mr. Chan's gorilla manservant wasn't exactly forthcoming with a lot of details. But I called my Uncle Nick and he told me they'd be somewhere outside the Chiquibul Forest Reserve. I'm sure they can't be *that* hard to find."

"Where's that? Can we take a taxi? Is there a hotel nearby? I need a shower." He ran his fingers through his hair.

"Like I said, I don't exactly know. But this place can't be *that* primitive."

A guy wearing dreadlocks and sporting a yellow slouchy beanie hat, a guy who was way too dark for Jessica Kraus' taste, stood next to them. She forced a smile to hide her discomfort. The guy had been listening to their conversation with a certain amusement. He smiled at Jessica and then said, "You want to go to Chiquibul Forest Reserve? It's about a five-hour drive, and some of the roads are extremely rough in places. No taxi will get you there. You'll need to hire someone with a four-wheel drive. I'll happily take you—for a price. But Chiquibul Forest Reserve is a huge place: 147,000 acres with a perimeter of 119 kilometers. Where exactly do you want to go?"

Jessica Kraus was trying to convert kilometers to miles. She remembered running a 5k once, which was a little over 3 miles. *If 5k equals 3 miles, then 119—let's just make it 120, it's easier to do the math—divided by 5 equals 24. And 24 times 3 equals—let's see...*" Jessica began writing numbers in the air. "*4 times 3 equals 12, that's 2 carry the 1...72 miles!* (Actually the answer was 74.56, but close enough. Jessica Kraus was never particularly good at arithmetic and always took the most discombobulated route in arriving at an answer.) Just then she had the most remarkable insight:

"We're *never* going to find them!"

But Finn wasn't paying any attention. He had been watching the carousel. One, after another, after *a-fucking-nother* bag dropped onto the conveyor belt. When he had begun cursing at the thought of having to talk to one of those *Stupid Lost Baggage People*, he spotted it. "There's your luggage."

But Jessica Kraus wasn't paying any attention. She was looking up at the departure board: *A Tropic Air flight to Cancún leaves in four and a half hours.*

"Let's go to Cancún!" she exclaimed.

Finn shook his head, dumbfounded. "What? What are you *crazy*?"

"Come on…. *P-l-e-a-s-e*?" She stretched out the word and gave her most adorable look. "I mean look at us. We don't have much of a plan. What were we thinking? Your fiancée will be there for almost six weeks anyway. We can try to find them later, after we think things through some more—on the beach." This was probably the smartest thing that Jessica Kraus had said in her thirty years of existence.

Finn eyed the departure board and then eyed Jessica. She was almost a ten with her new hair color. *She would be a ten if I took her to Dr. Rak for a new set of tits.* He grinned widely. "Sure—OK, let's go up to the ticket counter. We'll see if they still have seats."

Jessica bobbed up and down like an excited little girl and then gave Finn a big squeeze. "Thank you!"

"Anything for you, Jess." He took her hand as they walked up to the ticket counter.

Meantime, back at the limestone steps

"You mentioned the wheel of becoming," Aapo began. "It just occurred to me. I think I've seen it depicted in Buddhist art. It was beautifully and colorfully detailed, and a little frightening, from what I remember. A monster-type figure was clutching the wheel with his four limbs."

"You're right. The monster figure is most commonly Yama, the god of death of Hinduism who was later absorbed into Buddhist mythology. Each of Yama's limbs symbolizes suffering in samsara: birth, old age, disease, and death. The wheel is fascinating. It really helps answer the question 'Who am I?' The answer requires understanding the various components of the wheel. I've already mentioned the twelve links. Typically, the cycle of twelve interdependent stages constitutes the outer rim of the wheel. Inside there are six spokes which divide the center into six wedges depicting the six possible realms into which beings can be reborn in samsara. First is the realm of gods or *devas*, which are not like the gods of Hinduism, but are long-lived spiritually advanced beings. These devas are not as enlightened as Buddhas and will eventually be recycled back into samsara. Then there's the realm of *asuras*, the so-called angry gods. They are fueled by hatred and jealousy and often fight with each other and the devas. There is also the realm of hell, the realm of hungry ghosts, the animal realm, and of course the human realm. One can only escape samsara by way of the human realm, and so one is considered blessed to be born a human. That's why Buddhism teaches that a human life should not be wasted and that we should live with purpose, seek enlightenment, and exercise compassion and kindness."

"There are also animals at the center of the wheel, if I remember correctly. What are they?"

"You're right, Aapo. At the center or hub of the wheel we typically find pictures of a pig, a bird, and a snake. These three animals turn the wheel of samsara and represent the *Three Poisons* or Unwholesome Roots, which are considered to be the source of all evil: ignorance, hatred, and greed. Ignorance, represented by the pig, is the chief root and the primary cause of all evil and suffering. The cure for ignorance is wisdom. Hatred is represented by the snake. Hatred arises from ignorance, because we fail to understand the interconnectedness of all things and instead experience ourselves as separate from everything else. As a result, we desire things and want to take them for ourselves, or we detest them and want to avoid or even destroy them. We're likely to become angry with anyone who gets in the way of what we desire, and we become envious of others who have what we want. The cure for hatred is loving kindness. Greed or attachment is represented by the bird and refers to our desire for things that we mistakenly think will make us happier. But such things rarely satisfy us for long and put us at odds with others whom we then manipulate or exploit to get what we want. Greed often results in our harming nonhuman nature too, by destroying their environment or robbing them of their freedom, because we value our own lives above their own. The cure for greed is generosity: generously giving of ourselves, generously relinquishing any sort of claim on what we might desire."

"My grampa used to tell a wonderful story about greed, a classic folktale from West Africa. It's about Anansi the spider and explains why he has no hair. Want to hear it?"

"Absolutely. Would your grandfather sing 'Palmer William' as a fattening song for this story?"

"You bet…. He'd start with all that crickin' and crackin' and make such goofy faces. Lottie and I would just laugh and laugh."

"Crick crack, twelve o'clock, monkey sit down pon a rock." Jessica grinned as she thought about the camp dance party the night before.

"Sometimes he would say 'fish sit on a rock' instead." Aapo chuckled. "Gramma would come in and say 'You pickaninnies want some pie?' She made the best cashew pie. I don't think that word was offensive then. Or at least Gramma didn't know any better."

"So what is the Anansi story?" Jessica was so thoroughly enjoying herself that she had all but forgotten that she had chores awaiting her back at the camp.

"There are a lot of Anansi stories, but the one about the beans is my favorite, probably because Gramma would always cook such wonderful beans. It goes like this: Once upon a time, when time was time, Anansi went to visit his Gramma's house. She was throwing him a party. Anansi wore his finest clothes and a nice tall hat just for the occasion. When he walked into Gramma's house, all of the guests smiled at him.

Anansi strutted around showing off his fancy clothes. They were very impressed by how he dressed. He was very proud. He was also very hungry. He walked up to the table. Gramma had prepared so much wonderful food for Anansi: guinea fowl eggs and fufu, sweet potatoes and fish stew, palm wine, and cassava cake with spiced butter. Anansi ate and ate until he couldn't eat anymore. But then he noticed something: Gramma had forgotten to make the beans! How could Gramma forget to make his favorite beans? He frowned, but then he caught a whiff of Gramma's beans coming from the kitchen. He snuck into the kitchen and, sure enough, he found a pot of beans on the stovetop. Gramma had followed Anansi and told him, 'The beans aren't ready yet, Anansi. Don't eat them.' Then Gramma left the kitchen. Anansi just kept looking at the pot of beans. Finally, he could no longer resist them. He found a little pouch on the counter, then took off the lid and filled the pouch with spoonful after spoonful of Gramma's wonderful beans. When the bag was full, Anansi placed it on his head and covered it up with his hat so that nobody would see what he did. Then he walked back out to the party and announced 'I have to leave now.' But Gramma told Anansi, 'This party is in your honor. You can't leave.' By now Anansi's head began to sweat because the beans were so hot. Anansi announced again, with even more urgency, 'I have to leave now.' At this point the beans began scalding his head. Sweat poured down his face. Anansi was in serious pain. He lifted his hat a little in order to cool off his head, and when he did the beans spilled out of the pouch, down his head, and onto his fancy clothes. Everybody was shocked, especially Gramma, when they noticed that Anansi's head was now bald. The scalding beans had burned off all his hair! And that's how Anansi the spider became bald."[31] Aapo smiled widely.

"Bald from his greedy desire for Grandma's scrumptious beans!" Jessica laughed.

"Isn't this a great story? It was my favorite. Grampa would often tell it because he knew how much I loved Gramma's beans. I would often sneak into the kitchen for a spoonful—or five." Aapo chuckled and then asked, "What about your grandparents, Jessica? You suggested they weren't the best of people."

"I'd rather not talk about them. Too distressing. Actually my grandma wasn't that bad, except that she didn't protect me from Grandpa. But Grandpa was hurting her too. Anyway, let's not talk about it."

"How'd you end up with them in the first place? Did something happen with your parents? —Oops, sorry. I didn't mean to press."

Jessica's eyes teared up. Aapo reached out and held her hand.

Eighteen years earlier, Tempe, Arizona

Twelve-year-old Jessica Kraut was lounging by the backyard pool. Her parents, both administrators at Maricopa County Community College District, were inside the house with her little brother, James. Jessica was thinking about Kenny Madrid for the hundredth time that day. He used to be so mean. Just a couple months ago he stuffed orange peels in her mouth and tied her to a tree for the *ki-otes* to get her. But at Emma's birthday party last week he kissed her on a dare. Now Jessica couldn't get him out of her mind. Just then Jessica's mother opened the patio door. Her little brother was by her side. "Jess, I'm off to get a pedicure. I need you to watch James while I'm gone. Daddy is too busy." Two-year-old James ran up to Jessica with a bright orange bouncy ball, smiling all the way.

'Sure, OK.' Jessica didn't mind watching her little brother. Sometimes he was an-

31. See http://www.uexpress.com/tell-me-a-story/2010/4/25/anansi-and-the-pot-of-beans.

noying, but mostly he was just ridiculously cute and funny. Jessica got up from her chair. James kicked the ball to her, giggling. Jessica kicked it back. They took turns kicking the ball back and forth when Jessica suddenly noticed that Kenny Madrid was standing at the fence with his bike.

"Sit down in the grass, James. Don't go anywhere, OK? I'll be right back." Jessica walked up to the fence, face beaming. Before she reached it, she turned back around and said, "Stay right there."

James sat in the grass with his big orange bouncy ball and watched his sister. After about three minutes he decided to stand up and play kick the ball by himself.

Kenny smiled at Jessica. "Want to ride bikes?"

"OK…." She smiled back. But then she frowned. "I can't. I have to watch my stupid little brother." She rolled her eyes. Then she turned and looked at James, who was standing in the grass with his ball. She smiled at James and then turned her attention back to Kenny.

James set the ball on the grass and kicked as hard as he could. It landed in the water. He walked up to the edge of the pool, knelt down, and stretched out his hand to grab the ball. It was just out of his reach. He leaned further—and fell in.

Several minutes passed before Jessica heard her father screaming. She turned around and saw him pulling a lifeless James out of the water. It would be years before Jessica could step foot near a pool again.

As Jessica was telling Aapo the story, her voice cracked. "After that, my parents would fight all the time. They wouldn't stop screaming at each other. One day my father told me to pack my suitcase, that I would be staying at my grandparents' for the weekend. *But he never came back to get me.* I haven't heard from him in eighteen years."

Aapo looked at Jessica tenderly. So much pain he wished he could just kiss away. He gave her a hug and as he released his embrace he let his lips gently touch her own. Then it struck him *What am I doing*? He was afraid to look at her, but he did anyway.

"Sorry," Aapo said. He looked over at the jaguar carving. It was baring its teeth at him. Or at least Aapo thought it should be. Just then they heard footprints—distinctly *human* footprints—well at least to Aapo's trained ear. He reached for his gun.

"There you two are." This time it was Chicken Eyes, who smiled.

"Does *everybody* know about this place?" Aapo asked, a bit irritated.

"This is just like the time I walked outside to feed the rabbits and there was an avocado just sitting there *in the grass.*" Chicken Eyes' smile grew bigger.

"What?" Aapo shook his head.

Chicken Eyes thought that what he had said was so obvious that it didn't need repeating, but he repeated it anyway: "An avocado. Sitting in the grass. *In the Bronx.*"

"Oh, well that explains it." Aapo rolled his eyes. "So how long have *you* known about this place?"

Chicken Eyes did not answer. Instead he said, "This spot is so peaceful." Then he addressed Jessica, "There's a big tarpon waiting for you back at the camp. I covered it with canvas to keep our friend, the kite, away." He laughed. But then he noticed Jessica's face. It was covered in tears. "Are you OK?" He sat on the other side of her and rested his hand on her knee.

Jessica wiped her face with the back of her hand. "I'm fine."

"Don't worry about dinner. We'll help you," Chicken Eyes said, trying to cheer her up. "Hey, how about a story? Want to hear about Sisimito?"

"Sisimito?"

"He's like Big Foot," Chicken Eyes explained. "Sisimito lives in a cave. At dusk, he ventures out, kidnaps women, and forces them to have his children. Women are warned never to stay out late when they wash their clothes because...."

Aapo gave Chicken Eyes a stern look.

"Oh, sorry." Chicken Eyes grimaced.

"How about Xtabai?" Aapo offered. "She's a beautiful seductress who preys on Belizean *men*."

"What does she look like?" Jessica was trying to cheer up.

"Maybe that's who she saw at the stream," Chicken Eyes said with a smile.

"Maybe so," Aapo answered.

"So what does she look like?" Jessica repeated.

"She has long, flowing, raven black hair, and a sweet, melodic voice. She lures the unsuspecting man into a passionate embrace with her sweet love songs and then transforms into a thorny ceiba tree, piercing every part of his body."

Jessica cringed. "Does she hang out by the water?"

"Often," Chicken Eyes said.

"Well then maybe so...." Jessica said. Her face brightened up a bit.

Chicken Eyes stood up and extended his hand to Jessica as if asking her for a dance. "Let's get back. The tarpon awaits us."

"I can hardly wait," she said with the hint of a smirk.

Aapo stood up. "Never mind me. I'll be hobbling along behind you." He watched them disappear. Then he walked up to the jaguar carving and placed his hand on its head. "Jaguar God of the Underworld, if only you would invoke your black magic for my own selfish ends...." He gave a heavy sigh and then headed back to the camp.

Meanwhile, were Finn Lauder not about ready to step onto a single engine turbo-prop bound for Cancún with the real Jessica Kraus alias *the Jessica he always wanted Jessica to be*, he would have been at home just in time to catch the following update on the local news: Jessica Kraut, the woman police suspect somehow stole the prized scarlet macaw from the Los Angeles Zoo, had last been spotted (according to Belizean authorities and the LAPD, who were now combining their efforts) being carried out of a white Isuzu Trooper and into a villa in San Ignacio owned by a Mr. Edin Chan. Authorities now suspected that she might have been drugged and was being held against her will, although they couldn't find any sober witnesses to corroborate the account. Police raided the villa only to find it empty but recently inhabited. Neighbors who were interviewed by police called Mr. Chan a prominent community member and "charming" but "mysterious."

Spider monkey (top); Slaty-breasted tinamou (bottom)

Ferruginous pygmy owl

Peccary

SIX

Finn Lauder looked at his companion. He couldn't get over how much she resembled his fiancée, Jessica. He thought about his meeting with Maggie's shrink just a few days before.

Dr. Giles Nutt looked down at his open appointment book atop his crescent-shaped desk, handmade from a mix of exotic woods. A new patient, Finn Lauder—his last appointment of the day. Dr. Nutt opened the little drawer and reached for his pill box. He popped two Valium into his mouth and gulped them down with a swig of Evian before buzzing his receptionist, Lola. After a couple of minutes, his door opened, and there stood a man, complete with wavy dark hair, chiseled chin, and high cheekbones, looking every bit the model he never was, wearing a grey knit button-down shirt ($695), navy virgin wool twill trousers ($874), and suede and leather low-top sneakers ($924), all by Brunello Cucinelli. The man gave a nervous smile. Dr. Nutt got up from his desk, walked up to the man, and shook his hand, while saying, "Welcome. You must be Finn Lauder. Please, have a seat." Dr. Nutt motioned Finn to the ecru leather sofa, and then took a seat in the matching chair opposite him.

Finn sized up Maggie's shrink: a middle-aged man, each strand of silver hair gelled perfectly in place, with sapphire blue eyes sitting behind black square frame glasses. He was wearing a baby blue cashmere sweater. Finn was certain that Maggie was fucking him. He wrinkled his nose. The room reeked of the competing smells of his Stephano Ricci men's fragrance ($699), and Dr. Nutt's Lalique's Encre Noire a L'Extreme Eau de Parfum Pour Homme, as well as this morning's oversized bouquet of white gardenias—a gift from Lola who had spent the past two years trying to woo her employer with thoughtful little presents. Alas, this was all in vain, since women weren't exactly Giles Nutt's type—but he didn't have the heart to tell her. Finn's eyes slowed passed over a framed print of the three panels of Hieronymus Bosch's *The Garden of Earthly Delights,* ca. 1500, which hung on the wall behind the shrink's head. Finn was transfixed by the fantastical animals, the nude figures, and the bright pink and blue formations. But then his eyes froze on the right panel depicting a dark otherworldly hellscape, and he shook his head. Finally, he said, "Interesting choice."

Dr. Nutt had been studying him. "Bosch is one of my favorites…. So you mentioned this encounter with the frog. Let's start with some free association."

"OK." Finn sounded more nervous than he thought he was.

"I'll start," Dr. Nutt began. "Frog."

"Frog legs." Finn had never played this sort of game before and felt uneasy. It was bad enough that he admitted on the phone that he had a hallucination. What else might his responses disclose about his mental state?

"Frog legs," Dr. Nutt echoed.

"France."

"France," Dr. Nutt echoed again.

"The Louvre."

"The Louvre."

"Jessica… This is how my fiancée, Jessica, wants to spend our honeymoon. At a fucking museum! God, that goddamn little frog hallucination is about Jessica!"

Dr. Nutt smiled at Finn's insight. "Good, good. Go with that. Tell me more."

"I've got to go through with this. I don't want to sound like some greedy little bastard, but I really want that Donnelly account," Finn said, sounding like some greedy little bastard.

"Let's stay with your fiancée, Jessica. Do you love her?"

"Seriously?" Finn caught himself rolling his eyes. "Who falls in love anymore?"

"People do all the time...."

"I don't know. Maybe…. Probably not." Finn gave a heavy sigh. "But the Donnelly account."

"So it sounds like any woman would do, so long as it gives you the Donnelly account."

"Well, Doc, I do have high standards, but yes: *any woman would do.*" He frowned.

Meanwhile, the real Jessica Kraus was thinking about this …

The last clients of the day had just left. Jessica Kraus, dressed in a gray and black Boho peasant dress with plunging neckline, black leather kitten-heel mules, and dark hair flowing past her shoulders, walked to the door of her Uncle Nick's gallery and locked it.

Just then, Nick Kraus emerged from his office. He had short gray hair, a circle beard, and hazel eyes. He was dressed in a black Armani button-down shirt with rolled up sleeves and tan twill pants. He walked up to his niece and said, "I see you just sold *Three Orioles with Hanging Nest from the North Wall*…. Well, done." He smiled warmly.

"Yes, they loved that piece." Jessica smiled back.

"So are you ready for your big adventure with Mr. Chan?" Nick walked over to a small wooden table lined with colorful wine glasses and poured them each a glass of Sauvignon Blanc, which sat chilling in a bucket of ice.

Jessica thought about the eviction notice that almost certainly awaited her when she returned to her apartment that evening. She was nose-deep in credit card debt, but was too embarrassed to tell her Uncle Nick. She thought that maybe she could sleep on the couch in his office until she could come up with a more long-term solution. But where would she shower? And so she answered, "Of course, I'm always up for new experiences."

"You'll be pampered when he takes you to Buenos Aires. He'll give you fancy dresses and expensive jewelry to wear—Whatever you'd like. You'll look like a princess." Nick smiled, and then he added, "He'll introduce you to some of the wealthier clients who will take you out for lavish dinners. Only the best."

"Can't wait!"

"What happens *after* the dinners is up to you, of course, but you're a grown woman. I'm sure you can handle it." Nick paused before stating, "Chan expects this from you." He had convinced himself that his niece was a grown woman, and in any case Chan would certainly never put her in any real danger. He continued, "So are you OK with that? Your flight leaves tomorrow."

"Are you kidding? Of course! Believe me, Uncle Nick, I've gone to bed with my share of men in exchange for fancy dinners…. This is called '*dating.*'"

Nick chuckled. "Of course it is…. Good girl." He clicked his glass against hers. "I knew I could count on you. Chan trusts me. He's like a brother to me. I told him you'd be cool with it."

He was right: Nick Kraus and Edin Chan *were* like brothers. Nick was like the brother who always needed to be bailed out. He had a gambling problem and Chan was in the regular habit of paying off his debt. Chan had a soft spot for Nick, and he absolutely loved his ceramic pieces, with which Nick would invariably surprise him every time they would meet. Nick's usual response to Chan's generosity: "I owe you one." And so when the woman who was charged to oversee the camp in Chan's latest job canceled at the very last minute (and for good reason: she had taken a tumble off her bike and was badly bruised), Chan asked Nick if he knew anyone he trusted who'd be willing to step in. Nick didn't have to think about this for very long. His niece was a perfect fit for the job.

Late morning the next day, April 12

Jessica Kraut was busily sweeping one of the tent floors when she was interrupted by the jingling of keys behind her. She turned around and saw Chicken Eyes standing at the entrance.

"I'm off to the village to pick up a few supplies. Want anything?"

"How're you going to get there? Didn't Mr. Chan take the SUV?"

"He did. He was off to meet his contacts across the Guatemala border, who would then take him by private plane to brokers in Buenos Aires…. No worries, though. We've got a few Jeeps hidden about 150 meters away. Need anything?"

Jessica thought about the crescent moon pendant that Aapo had given her the day before. "This might sound like a weird request, but if you happen upon a chain, maybe something made of silver or leather, can you pick it up for me? Something for a pendant."

"Sure, OK. Some of the ladies sell their handcrafted jewelry at the market. I might be able to find something like that—That *is* a weird request." Chicken Eyes twisted up his face. "I thought maybe you were craving some tasty treat. Like a chocolate pastry?"

"Just the chain." Jessica smiled, but then she felt more than a little anxious. "But what about tonight's dinner?"

"I told Aapo that *he* was responsible for that. I put a fishing pole in one hand and a bottle of rum in the other and ordered him to go sit by the stream." Chicken Eyes chuckled. "Worst case, I trust you'll be creative with your cooking and fancy up those sweet potatoes…. By the way, I doubt I'll be hungry when I return. Today is 'Feast Day' for the village leader, Sachihiro. He's said to be 200 years old."

Jessica chuckled, but then she noticed that Chicken Eyes was completely straight-faced.

Noticing her puzzled look, he clarified, "Of course, he's 200 years old according to the Tzolk'in or nahual calendar, which only has 260 days, not 365."

"Sure, but that would still make him …"

"One hundred and forty-two years old." Chicken Eyes grinned. "The villagers believe that Sachihiro is immortal. They venerate him like a god. They also say that he is a nahual—a shapeshifter. Oftentimes, when Sachihiro takes a walk deep into the forest, some of the villagers will spot an ancient jaguar just outside the village. A jaguar so old he's lost all his teeth. His fur even has bald patches, and he has a scar across his face—just like Sachihiro. They only see the jaguar after Sachihiro has disappeared on his walk. As jaguar, Sachihiro rules wisely and justly. A jaguar is known for his keen eyesight, especially at night, which means Sachihiro can look into the darkest places of the human heart and help guide his people into the light."

"You mean the very same villagers who *have your backs*, who keep their eyes and ears open for anything *suspicious?*" Jessica asked (*accused really, as she reflected upon Aapo's words the other day*), but Chicken Eyes was oblivious to her snark.

"The very same." Chicken Eyes smiled.

Jessica gave a frosty look, which he did notice. Once again, Chicken Eyes was left wondering whether he should try to 'explore feelings.' However, after some reflection, he only offered, *"I'll try to get that chain."*

For a few moments, Jessica thought about accompanying Chicken Eyes to the village. Once there, she could excuse herself to search for a chain, only to contact the village police who'd then come in and shut down Mr. Chan's operation. But then she thought about all the chores she still had to do, about making sure the guys had a meal when they returned. So she waved Chicken Eyes off and attended to her sweeping. Maya however, who had been keeping Jessica company, took the opportunity to exit the tent as Chicken Eyes was leaving.

Maya flew deep within the Chiquibul Forest Reserve to a little-excavated part of the Caracol Ruins, landing atop the remnants of a limestone wall. As she did so, she transformed into a beautiful dark haired woman—the same woman whom Jessica was so mesmerized by just a few days before.

The plot had been in the works for some time now, though nobody really knew how long or who initiated it. Was it King K'uk Mo's idea to include Jessica Kraut? Was it Sachihiro's? And what a brilliant idea to involve Sachihiro's granddaughter, Maya (whom the villagers call 'Yatzil' –*Loved One*). Yatzil's nahual is the scarlet macaw. How ingenious to have her get a job at the Los Angeles Zoo, passing herself off as a zoo veterinarian specializing in avian medicine. After all, Yatzil knew how to treat animals better than anyone. Her grandfather had made certain of it by ensuring she learn from the best: at the feet of the ancient monkey king from the time she was a little girl. All Yatzil had to do, once she secured the job at the zoo, was get into the rainforest exhibit and then transform herself into a macaw. They'd wonder where their new vet disappeared to, but that could be handled by a letter saying she had an unforeseen emergency and had to quit without notice. There would also be the worry of where a new $25,000 scarlet macaw came from, but that was solved by Yatzil trading places with a resident scarlet macaw, whom she then arranged to be transported back to the Belizean rainforest. What a beautiful plan. The keel-billed toucans and macaws said it was Yatzil's idea (and they would know about such things). The baboons and spider monkeys attributed the idea to King K'uk Mo. After all, only a *monkey* king could come up with such an intricate, well-orchestrated scheme. Of course neither Yatzil nor the king were speaking about the matter, leaving everyone to their own speculations.

The king's council sat high in their places and watched from above. King K'uk Mo emerged from his chamber. Yatzil smiled as he approached. The ancient one extended his hand and welcomed her in her native Q'eqchi:

King K'uk Mo: "Yatzil. Ma sa' laach'ool. Chan ru wankat?"

Yatzil: "Ma sa' laach'ool. Sa' linch'ool b'antiox."

King K'uk Mo: "Sa' b'antiox."

After this brief exchange of pleasantries, the king sat next to her on what remained of the wall and smiled widely.

Historians and biographers, who might write about these events, would have to answer questions such as why, given that Yatzil and her grandfather Sachihiro knew about Chan's operation, they didn't just go directly to the local authorities and report the whole thing in the first place. The fact is—they did. But Edin Chan (and indeed even his father before him) had paid them off to look the other way. It would require an extremely elaborate plan which at first appeared only to involve capturing a US citizen facing felony charges for stealing a zoo animal—but who would end up having intimate connections with Mr. Chan. Once LAPD got involved in the case, they watched every move the Belizean authorities would make—which meant Belizean police would have to follow the facts wherever they would lead. They found themselves no longer able to protect Mr. Chan once it became clear that he was somehow involved. All the more so when they were led to believe that he might have kidnapped the woman—a nefarious act even for Chan! King K'uk Mo saw that Jessica Kraut only needed a nudge to help her see a way to escape from her entanglement with Finn, and hence she was the perfect candidate to play the lead role in their scheme. And of course he'd be helping her step back into the light.

King K'uk Mo and Yatzil discussed the final steps of their plan, and then the ancient one bid Yatzil—now Maya—goodbye, as she flew back to enjoy her grandfather's Feast Day.

Mid-afternoon, back at the camp

Aapo returned empty-handed and a bit tipsy. He found Jessica sitting beneath the rainbow eucalyptus tree, whose painted bark was slowly pouring over her, coloring her body in pale blues, purples, oranges, and pinks. She hoped that, chameleon-like, she would disappear into the bark. A green chameleon, who inspired her thinking in this manner, perched above her on a limb. His left eye swiveled to spy a keel-billed toucan teetering on a large, climbing, woody vine. His right eye swiveled to an opened page of *The Lotus Sutra*, held between Jessica's two hands. Jessica looked up as Aapo approached and smiled broadly.

"Where's the catch?"

"Still swimming about in the stream…" Aapo crinkled up his face.

"Guess we'll have to order take-out." Jessica laughed. "I'll go start a big pot of rice and beans." She stood up and handed him her book.

Aapo smiled when he read the title. "*The Lotus Sutra*…."

"Why don't you start reading the first chapter while I start dinner. It's a delightfully magical storybook, and one of the most widely read and revered of Buddhist scriptures, at least of the Mahayana School. It was written between the first century BCE and the second century CE. *The Lotus Sutra* instructs that it is the final, highest teaching, superseding all previous teachings. It utilizes a unique literary device: This is a text that constantly refers to itself." Jessica grinned. "You'll see…."

"Why *Lotus*?"

"Because in India, the lotus flower is considered to be the most beautiful and sacred flower in the world. While it grows from the mud at the bottom of a pond, its petals remain unstained. The way I conceive it, below the water's surface represents suffering in samsara, and the flower itself liberation."

Aapo followed her to the table, sat down, and began to read.

The Lotus Sutra

Jessica had started the rice and beans and was now sitting as patiently as she could while Aapo pored over the first five or so pages of one of her favorite books. Finally, Aapo let out a grunt and then took a swig of rum.

"What a weird book." He shook his head. "Honestly, I've no idea what's going on, except that some innumerable gazillion billion creatures, human, nonhuman, dragons, chimeras, centaurs, griffins, pythons—why pythons?—are surrounding the World Honored One (Buddha) who is deep in meditation, as brightly colored flowers rain down from the sky. He seems to have some extraordinary magical powers, emitting a beam of light from the tuft of white hair between his eyebrows and illuminating all the living beings of the eighteen thousand worlds (whatever that means) including the Buddhas who currently exist in those worlds. Huh? Obviously his audience is about to witness some extraordinary event...."

"It's weird, but fun, don't you think?"

"Sure—if only I could understand it."

Jessica chuckled. "I guess it does require some translating. You're right, many of the main characters in the text are human—monks and nuns, bodhisattvas, including *Maitreya*, the future Buddha of *our* Buddha world, Earth. And others are nonhuman, including the mythical creatures you just mentioned. The central character is, of course, the Buddha, and while he does have supernatural powers, the text constantly reminds us of the historical Siddhartha Gautama. The significance of the eighteen thousand worlds is that the beam of light makes possible for the audience to witness the innumerable skillful means being utilized across all Buddha worlds to get all living creatures on the One-Buddha Vehicle Path."

"Who are the bodhisattvas?"

"Bodhisattvas are future Buddhas who, because of their tremendous compassion for all living beings, choose to remain in the world, delaying parinirvana, in order to help *all* creatures (human and nonhuman) get on the One-Buddha Vehicle path toward Buddhahood. Everyone will eventually become a Buddha. This is the promise of *The Lotus Sutra*. The bodhisattvas accomplish their task by teaching the Dharma."

"So what's the big event?"

"Buddha, the World Honored One, will teach *The Lotus Flower of the Wonderful Dharma*—none other than *The Lotus Sutra*."

"As you said, a text referring to itself!" Aapo beamed.

"As I said...." She smiled. "It's most obvious in the chapter entitled 'Devadatta.' The World Honored One says that, 'In the future, if there are any good sons or good daughters who, hearing this Devadatta chapter of the Wonderful Dharma Flower Sutra, faithfully respect it with pure hearts and are free from doubt...will be born into the presence of the Buddhas of the ten directions.'"

Aapo studied Jessica, wondering whether he should say anything about how his lips had accidentally landed on her own. He decided against it. Perhaps she had forgotten already. Perhaps she didn't think anything of it. What was he doing anyway? She likely realized that he was just trying to comfort her. Wasn't that all that it was? It was the wrong thing to do and the wrong time to do it. He felt himself grow smaller.

Jessica beamed in the manner of someone completely enthralled by the conversation. She loved how Aapo seemed so interested in her favorite subject. She thought for a few moments about how she would begin before extending her hand. "Might I have that back for a minute?" she asked, referring of course to *The Lotus Sutra*.

By now they had gathered something of an audience: the teetering toucan, the green chameleon (whose name was, you'd hardly believe, Abraham Lincoln), even the monkey and his wife, who proudly wore her lavender jade pendant which hung from a garland of twisted vine. Jessica noted their presence and smiled.

"One of the main teachings of *The Lotus Sutra* is skillful means,[32] doing whatever it takes to get a person on the One-Buddha Vehicle Path, including lying—though the World Honored One does not call it a lie since the goal was achieved." She opened the book to Chapter 3. "In Chapter 3, the World Honored One teaches the famous parable of the burning house. It goes like this: There was, in a certain kingdom, a great elder, whose house was large and spacious but had only one gateway. Its rooms were old and decaying, its walls crumbling, its pillars rotting at the base, and so on. All at once, all over the house, fire suddenly broke out. The elder's many children were busy playing in the house, oblivious to the fact that it was now engulfed in flames. The elder became alarmed and thought: 'My children are in the burning house, enjoying themselves, engrossed in play, with no awareness, alarm, or fear. While pain and suffering threaten, they have no thought of trying to escape.' He called out to his children: 'Get out quickly, all of you!' The children, absorbed in their play, paid no attention to him. And so the elder thought: 'If my children do not get out at once, they will certainly be burned alive. I must find some skillful means to get my children to escape from this imminent disaster.' Knowing what his children liked, the elder said to them: 'A variety of playthings, extraordinarily rare—goat carriages, deer carriages, and ox carriages— stand outside the gate for you to play with. You must get out of this burning house quickly, and I will give you whichever ones you want.' When the children heard their father describe all the rare and wonderful playthings, they eagerly rushed outside the burning house. Once outside, the children said to their father: 'Those playthings you promised, please give them to us now.' Their father gave each of his children a carriage. It was not what they expected, but they were delighted nonetheless. The carriages were exquisitely decorated with jewels, and bells, and garlands of flowers, with beautiful rose-colored pillows inside, and they were pulled by powerful, handsome white oxen, fast as the wind. And each child had many servants to attend to them. The children in the burning house represent all of us who are suffering in samsara and are distracted by worldly attachments. The elder, of course, represents the Buddha, and the fancy carriages represent parinirvana on the One-Buddha Vehicle Path. The three promised carriages represent three different approaches on that path: the shravaka way of the traditional monks and nuns in the monasteries, the pratyekabuddha way of the forest-dwelling monks who pursue enlightenment in isolation from others, and the bodhisattva way. *The Lotus Sutra* promotes the bodhisattva way, the most difficult path to Buddhahood. Indeed we discover that the bodhisattva way is the only path to Buddhahood. The other two ways are used as skillful means to help the practitioners ultimately find their way onto the bodhisattva path, which otherwise seems too daunting."

Thoroughly enjoying the lessons of the story, Aapo all but forgot his earlier angst. "What makes the bodhisattva way so difficult? I'd think that the forest-dwelling way would be the most difficult. This reminds me of the forest-dweller stage of Hinduism's four stages of life."

"It should…." Jessica smiled and then said, "The bodhisattva way is the most difficult because it demands that we treat *all living beings* (human, nonhuman, friends, enemies) with gentleness, compassion, kindness, respect, and understanding. Sounds easy in theory, but it proves to be incredibly difficult, as any person can attest. Indeed, the Buddha teaches that, of all the sutras, *The Lotus Sutra* is the most difficult to believe and difficult to understand. He promises that anyone who hears this Dharma

32. All references to *The Lotus Sutra* are to the translation by Gene Reeves.

and receives it with joy (that is, who embraces the message and exercises great compassion for all living beings) will attain supreme awakening. Imagine what the world would be like were everyone to practice the bodhisattva way."

Aapo looked at her affectionately and then said, "Want to take a walk?"

"Sure, I'd love that. Dinner's all but ready and just waiting for the guys to get back. Where to?"

Aapo grabbed her hand and pointed, "This way. It's a bit of a steep climb, about 50 meters, but on a clear day like today you can see all the way to the Guatemalan border town Melchor de Menchos, as well as the Xunantunich ruins."

"But your foot…."

"Is better. Come on, let's go."

Jessica grinned widely.

Meanwhile, at the Four Seasons Hotel in the exclusive La Recoleta district, Buenos Aires

Edin Chan had just finished his algae body wrap and therapeutic head massage. The spa therapist was beginning a full-body application of sweet almond massage oil when an attendant walked up to Chan with a telephone.

"Teléfono para usted, Señor Chan." The attendant handed Chan a towel.

Chan wiped off his hands before grabbing the phone. "Gracias…." And then speaking into the phone, he said, "Esto es Señor Chan."

It was none other than Chan's gorilla manservant (as the real Jessica Kraus so colorfully described him) on the other end. By now the two hotel staff had stepped away and were busying themselves in some corner, pretending not to pay any attention. Of course it didn't help that Mr. Chan was speaking a mix of Spanish and English. (They knew just enough of the latter to flatter their English-speaking clients into giving bigger tips.) But Mr. Chan's voice was loud with rage, which all but undid his 7732 pesos' worth of relaxing spa treatment. Here's what they made out:

"¿Qué estás tratando de decirme? [Followed by English words they didn't understand.] No puedes ser serio. [More English words they couldn't understand.] ¿Estas bromeando? Debes estar bromeando! ¿Ahora qué hacer? ^%&#! [This is universally understood.] ^%&#! [Chan repeated with even more frenzy.] ¿Ahora qué? Now what?" He slammed down the phone, got up from the table, slipped on a robe, and stormed out of the room.

Jessica and Aapo take a walk to a summit, 0.8 kilometers away

Jessica held onto Aapo's hand as he pushed their way through hundreds of thumb-sized, cream colored orchids tinged with bronze which dangled from the tree limbs like vines. They reminded Jessica of the beaded room dividers of her Auntie Jack's apartment. As they continued along, they heard the chirps, grunts, whistles, and snorts of nearby coatis foraging for food. Aapo was carrying a small canvas bag of craboo, which he had harvested just that morning. He was eating the little yellow cherry-looking fruit by the handful. Jessica refused when he offered her a few. They smelled faintly like vomit, or maybe a dog food factory, or a …

Just then, a wobbly, raccoon-monkey-dog-looking fur ball began enthusiastically tugging on Aapo's pant leg, causing them both to laugh.

"I wish I had my camera. How utterly adorable! She's the cutest little thing I've ever seen," Jessica chirped.

Aapo tossed the baby coati a few pieces of fruit which she eagerly gobbled up. The mother, who anxiously stood but a few feet away, couldn't bear her worry any longer, walked up, and carried her baby off with her mouth. The whole scene lasted a mere twenty seconds.

They passed a tree with cascading yellow flowers which looked like a fancy ball-room dress. Jessica lifted some up with her palm. "Aapo ..." She hesitated.

"Yeah?" Aapo smiled.

"What use are fancy dresses out here? Mr. Chan had me bring some."

"I don't know.... I've never really thought to ask. I guess because Mr. Chan likes to treat the women who oversee the camp to a few days' escape to be dazzled by the grandeur of Buenos Aires."

"I guess that makes sense. But I don't want to go to Buenos Aires...."

"You'll have to take that up with Mr. Chan."

As they continued along, they heard wails so distressing that Jessica winced. Aapo ran to the noise, Jessica following close behind. There before them was a young howler monkey, caught in a snare trap. The blood-soaked rope was pulled tightly across the top of his blood-soaked foot. Aapo rushed up to him.

"He's young, maybe three years old. He shouldn't have struggled so much." Pause, then, "Why did he struggle?" Another pause. "Snare traps tighten the more they are pulled on, like a Chinese finger trap. He shouldn't be bleeding this much—unless the rope lacerated an artery."[33]

Aapo pulled out his knife, cut through the rope, and cradled the monkey in his arms. The monkey looked up at him with frightened eyes. Jessica watched, frozen in horror. Aapo applied pressure to stop the bleeding, but nothing worked.

"We have to save him. Hold him while I take off my shirt. I need to make a tour-niquet."

Jessica stood motionless, arms down by her side, as Aapo tried to hand her the monkey.

"Take him, Jessica. Take him, dammit!"

Jessica kept staring at Aapo blank-faced.

"Please Jessica, I need your help." Desperation strained his voice.

Jessica opened her mouth—and then turned and ran away.

"Please come back, Jessica. I need your help. I need your help. Don't run away. Come back!" Aapo continued to cradle the monkey as he watched Jessica disappear into the darkness.

Jessica could hear Aapo calling out to her, and she stopped after about 10 meters. She stood there alone, as if the whole rainforest had abandoned her. She closed her eyes.

I can't do this.

Aapo yelled out again, even more desperately.

After a few minutes, Jessica opened her eyes and ran back.

By now, Aapo had taken off his shirt and made a tourniquet, but the bleeding wouldn't stop. He was covered in blood.

"Shoot him! Please shoot him to put him out of his pain. Please...." Jessica begged, tears spilling from her eyes.

"No. I can save him. I can save him, Jessica." Aapo looked shaken.

A couple of minutes passed, and mercifully the little monkey died.

33. Thanks so much to Dr. Randall Sunshine for educating me about this.

Aapo collapsed to the ground and burst into tears.

Aapo dug a shallow grave, buried the little howler monkey, and then sat down beside Jessica on a flat rock. They sat there in silence, the rest of the forest seemingly oblivious to what had just transpired. After about an hour, Aapo looked at Jessica and said, "We must shut down the camp right away."

Jessica wiped the wet of her tears. "Yes, but Mr. Chan…."

"… is away. Now's the perfect time to do it. We must do this right away!" Little did they know about King K'uk Mo and Yatzil's masterful plan.

Jessica reached over and gave Aapo a big hug. "Thank you," she whispered.

Aapo looked at her with great urgency and said, "We'll have to get some of the guys on our side. *Or maybe I could just tell them…. I could* just tell them that Mr. Chan has *ordered* this. I'll figure out how to deal with Mr. Chan when he returns." His head was swirling. "There's too much to think about right now, Jessica. Tell me more about the bodhisattva way. I too want to become a bodhisattva."

Jessica was feeling a mix of joy and sadness. "OK…." She wasn't sure she could carry on as if nothing had happened, but she tried anyway. "Chapter 20, my favorite chapter, is called 'Never Disrespectful Bodhisattva.' It tells about a bodhisattva-monk named Never Disrespectful who would bow before everyone he met and praise them, saying 'I deeply respect you. I would never be disrespectful or arrogant towards you. Why? Because all of you will become Buddhas.'" Jessica looked at Aapo and asked, "Should I continue?"

Aapo wiped a tear and nodded.

Jessica continued, "OK…. Never Disrespectful would never read or recite the sutras. He was a lousy monk. He simply went around bowing to people and repeating these words. Regardless of whom he came across, he would always say: 'I would never dare disrespect you, because surely you will all become Buddhas.' Never Disrespectful became despised as an ignorant monk who gave empty promises. He was constantly cursed, but he would never become angry. He just kept saying: 'I will never disrespect you. You will all become Buddhas.' People became so enraged that they threw sticks, tiles, and stones at him. But he would persist in saying, 'You will all become Buddhas.' When this monk was nearing death, he heard from the sky two hundred million billion verses of the Dharma Flower Sutra. He received and embraced them all. As a result, he acquired purity of vision and great divine faculties, and his life was extended for 'two million billion myriads of years.' He possessed powers of joyful and eloquent speech, and powers of goodness and tranquility. When people would hear him preach, they all believed and followed him. Guess who this bodhisattva monk was. None other than Siddhartha Gautama—the Buddha."

"What a great story. Does *The Lotus Sutra* really teach that *everyone* will become a Buddha? Even the most wicked? Can I become a Buddha too?"

"Yes, anyone can become a Buddha. Chapter 12 promises that even Devadatta, Siddhartha's infamous cousin and brother-in-law who tried to kill him multiple times (including by a drunken elephant), will become a Buddha. The Devadatta story is immediately followed by the delightful story of a little eight-year-old girl, a dragon princess who is so compassionate, respectful, gentle, and kind that she instantly transforms into a male-bodied Buddha in front of a mocking, disbelieving audience."

"Why male-bodied?"

"Because all Buddhas share the same thirty-two characteristics. Many are quite funny, especially when taken all together: webbed fingers and toes, hands reaching below the knees, forty teeth, long eyelashes like those of a royal bull, a long and flexible tongue that when extended can touch the hairline, well-grown body hairs which curl distinctly to the right, saliva that imparts delicious taste to anything that is eaten. An additional characteristic is the tuft of soft white hair between the eyebrows. Yet another is having a penis 'concealed in a sheath.' Hence the impossibility of a female-bodied Buddha. Some say that the dragon girl's transformation into a Buddha in a society that discriminated against women is a ringing declaration of women's rights. Others note that dragon girl, being the daughter of the dragon king, must have had a dragon—that is, *animal*—body, which further proclaims animal rights. Actually, dragon girl isn't a dragon at all, but a member of the Naga race—beings who are half-serpent, half-human and enjoy the status of the devas. Most artistic depictions of dragon girl give her a female *human* body."

"But the thirty-two characteristics of the Buddha don't explain *why* the Buddha must be male-bodied, just that it is," Aapo insisted.

"You're right," Jessica began. "It has to do with female bodies being associated with polluting fluids such as blood. As with so many other religions, women's bodies are considered defiling, and hence not suitable for someone so perfect and enlightened as a Buddha. Indeed, the monk Shariputra, a disciple of Gautama Buddha, says as much: 'The body of a woman is filthy and impure, not a vessel for the Dharma.' Thus enlightened females must become male-bodied Buddhas, although there are many female bodhisattvas who figure prominently in Buddhist culture. Interestingly, the popular male bodhisattva of compassion, Avalokiteshvara, appears as the female-bodied bodhisattva Guanyin or Kanon in China and Japan. That being said, there are some Mahayana sutras in which an enlightened female refuses to change into the male sex. For example, in the Vimalakirti Sutra, Shariputra asks a goddess why, if she is so wise, she cannot transform from her female state. What prevents her from doing so? In response, the goddess uses her magical powers to cause Shariputra to appear in her form and herself to appear in his form. Then the goddess, in Shariputra's form, said to Shariputra (now in the goddess' form), 'What prevents *you* from transforming yourself out of *your* female state?' The goddess continues, 'All women appear in the form of a woman in just the same way as Shariputra appears in the form of a woman. They are not women in reality. They just *appear* in the form of women. In the same way, the Buddha said, in all things there is neither male nor female.' Then the goddess released her magic and each returned to their ordinary form. The goddess *refused* to transform her sex, noting that sex is an illusion, empty of any inherent characteristics, which is consistent with Buddha's teaching that all things are devoid of essence."

"I love how *The Lotus Sutra* plays with numbers. Just how long are two million billion myriads of years exactly? How long is a myriad anyway? —Any other new teachings?"

"Yes, that there is only one long-lived Buddha, but many embodiments. We see this in Chapter 16 when the World Honored One announces that 'there have been innumerable, unlimited hundreds of thousands of billions of myriads of eons since I became a Buddha.' He also explains that 'I have constantly been in this world— preaching, teaching, and transforming. And in other places, in hundreds of thousands of billions of myriads of countless other lands, I have led and enriched living beings.' The outrageously long life of the Buddha can be explained in part by the fact that the Buddha and his Dharma are alive in all of his bodhisattvas. We learn in

Chapter 15 that the World Honored One has 'innumerable tens of millions of billions of bodhisattvas' all golden-hued and possessing the thirty-two characteristics of the Buddha. Some say that, rather than merely long-lived, the Buddha is eternal. Others say that he is none other than the Dharmakaya, who manifests physical and celestial buddhas across the buddha worlds in the ten directions. Whenever the Dharmakaya senses that the living creatures of a particular world need to hear the Dharma, it sends a Buddha. Our Buddha world, Earth, is awaiting Maitreya, the next Buddha, who features prominently in *The Lotus Sutra.*"

After a few minutes of silence, Jessica reached out and touched Aapo's hand. "That little monkey...."

Aapo nodded. "I know...."

Meanwhile at Sachihiro's "Feast Day," eighteen kilometers away

The entire village was present, except for Ikal and his very pregnant wife, Akna. That morning they had taken the one and only car in the village to Belmopan. The village's midwife and granny healer had exhausted their methods with his wife's particularly complicated pregnancy, and so Ikal drove the almost 120 kilometers to the hospital. He would check Akna into the hospital and then return to the village, since the villagers never wanted to be long without a car in case of an unexpected emergency, as had happened with Ikal and his beloved wife.

Sachihiro's Feast Day began with music, dancing, prayers, and speeches all around. Then came the food, Sachihiro's favorite: cak'ik (spicy turkey soup), tamalitos, fresh fruits, and stacks of steaming corn tortillas. He sat in the center, Yatzil by his side, surrounded by young girls carrying baskets of brightly colored flowers (lilies, orchids, and daffodils) which they playfully tossed upon Sachihiro's head, causing him to laugh. Chicken Eyes was there, of course. The villagers knew him as Mr. Chan's trusted and beloved employee. And he fit in. After all, they were no strangers to the fantastical: Nahuales, Xtabai, Sisi....

Just then clanking and clunking interrupted their festivities. The men of the village got up and ran toward the noise—Chicken Eyes too (indeed, everyone except Sachihiro, who was slow to move about, being 200 years old after all). When they finally arrived at the road just outside the village, there stood the village car with a banged-up fender and a dazed Ikal behind the wheel. "What happened?" they all asked in their native Q'eqchi. Chicken Eyes knew Q'eqchi and he too expressed his concern. Ikal just sat there, dumbstruck. After some time, one of the men opened the car door and helped Ikal out. He was shaking.

"What happened?" they all repeated. Finally, Ikal whispered, so slowly they could feel every syllable, "Sisimito...."

Sisimito: The Belizeans' version of Big Foot.

Chicken Eyes immediately glanced down at the fender. There was still fresh blood and a tangle of mysterious hair. But Chicken Eyes recognized it. Ikal seemed all right. Just a bit shaken. But what about Big Foot?

After some moments, Chicken Eyes asked, "Sisimito.... Was he badly injured? Where is he?"

Ikal finally mumbled, "He.... He ran away."

The men began walking Ikal back to the village, promising him that a bowl of cak'ik and some fresh tortillas would quiet his spirit. Ikal was more interested in the rum. But Chicken Eyes stayed behind. He studied the fender. Given the size of the dent, he imagined that Big Foot had not been terribly injured.

And he was right. Sisimito (whose reputation with the ladies was entirely un-founded), known as Alix to the many residents of the rainforest, made his way to none other than King K'uk Mo, who had prepared a magical, plant-based concoction which would help heal his cuts and bruises. Alix was currently sharing swigs of rum from a hollowed out coconut shell with the ancient one. Alix was doing so well, in fact, that the two of them were belly-laughing about *who-knows-what*.

Meanwhile, Chicken Eyes grabbed his knife and carefully removed the hair from the fender. He placed it in his pouch. Then he rubbed the knife against the fresh blood and wiped it on a piece of paper which he had ripped from his notebook. He folded the paper and placed it in his pouch. Then he sat down by the right front wheel and crafted a letter:

> *Dear Mr. Chan, Aapo, my beloved brothers, and dearest Jessica,*
> *I have been vindicated. I have evidence of the most extraordinary sort and have gone to Belmopan to convince the researchers at the University of Belize to test the samples.*
> *Very truly yours,*
> *Dr. Nathaniel Jackson III*

Although the letter was hastily written, it was legible enough. Now how to sneak back into the camp and put the letter in a conspicuous place? Chicken Eyes hated weepy goodbyes. He decided to return to Sachihiro's Feast Day, which would go well into the night. He'd drive back after everyone had gone to bed. What use was he at this point, anyway? Aapo could help Jessica for the remainder of the job. And so that's how it all went….

Later that night, back at the camp

Everyone had retreated to their tents for the night. Earlier, Jessica had fancied up the rice and beans with sweet potatoes, getting her inspiration from Chicken Eyes who had already snuck back into the camp, leaving his note on the table underneath a half-empty rum bottle. He placed Jessica's chain there too. While most everyone slept, Aapo sat in his tent and thought about none other than the Obeah love spell.[34] He had never tried it. He always feared its power and consequences. He knew that the love spell didn't work by manipulation or tricks. The Obeah love spell won't harm the person or go against the person's will. Instead, it would strengthen and bring about the realization of already existing feelings of love and affection. It just "helps" true love. Did Jessica love him? If she didn't, the spell wouldn't work anyway.

But if she did….

But Aapo had a problem. He lacked many of the items needed for the spell. His gramma had taught him how to perform it. She claimed that his grampa had used it on her to get her to marry him. He would need a photo of Jessica (or an item she had touched), a photo of himself, a piece of parchment paper, a piece of black yarn, a pink candle, and a toothpick. It was easy to find items that Jessica had touched, and there had to be toothpicks somewhere around, but he couldn't very well perform the spell with just these two items. He wondered if he could improvise a bit: something *he* had touched rather than his photo, string instead of yarn, a white lantern candle, a piece

34. See https://www.magic-love-spells.com/obeah-true-love-spell/.

of notebook paper…. He laughed out loud at the nonsense of it and crawled into bed.

Meantime, Jessica sat on her cot. She had been thinking about Aapo, and Mr. Chan, and all that had transpired that day. Her lantern illuminated her opened notebook as she began to write:

Amanda Macaw didn't know a thing about love. So why was she writing a love story, for crying out loud?!

Jessica closed her notebook and frowned.

White-crowned manakin

Agouti

Red-eyed tree frog

Gray-headed kite

SEVEN

Jessica thought long and hard about getting up. This wasn't a good morning. But she needed to make the coffee. Chicken Eyes was certainly back from the village by now. Perhaps *he* had started the coffee. In any case, he shouldn't be doing the work that *she* was getting paid for. But she was exhausted. It wasn't the sounds of the night denizens of the forest that had kept her awake. By now she was used to the howler monkeys, jaguarundis, ocelots, and the occasional tree-shaking roar of the jaguar. By now she was used to the crickets chirping, toads croaking, owls hooting, and the barking of the "honey bears" or kinkajous. By now she was used to the glow of the fireflies dancing about her tent and the many phosphorescent bugs illuminating her tent floor. Indeed, these lights and sounds were comforting. No, she had had a nightmare of her little brother, pale and lifeless, being pulled from the water. Jessica had become quite good at keeping such thoughts at bay, but sometimes they would haunt her sleep. She lay on her cot and thought about the time she had visited her mother, right after her father's stroke just a couple of years ago. She hadn't seen her mother in almost fifteen years.

Jessica had flown to Phoenix Sky Harbor Airport, the closest one to Tempe. Her Auntie Jack had told her about her father's condition. He was now out of ICU, seemingly out of grave danger, and resting in a hospital room. Jessica had asked her father through Jacqueline whether she could see him. He refused. But her mother agreed to meet her at a restaurant near the airport. Jessica chose Indian, which was a mistake. Her mother complained the whole time about how much she hated curry—and how the place smelled so bad.

As Jessica sat across the table, her mother looked *old*. Much older than her 51 years. Her hair had grayed. Her face was haggard from too much sun and alcohol. Auntie Jack had told Jessica that her mother had become a drunk, that she had lost her job because of that some years ago. Now Jessica worried that her father wouldn't be able to work again.

Jessica's mother was already on her second glass of wine, and they'd only sat down about twenty minutes before. She tore a piece of naan and put it in her mouth—the only thing she said she'd eat from the whole buffet. Jessica's plate was towering with vegetable samosa, paneer pakora, aloo mattar, and chicken curry. She had been chatting it up with the owner. Jessica presumed he was Hindu, given all of the marvelous artistic depictions of Krishna which adorned the place. She asked if he was and whether she could bother him with a few questions. He was flattered. They talked about Krishna's teachings in the *Bhagavad Gita*, about whether karma yoga led to moksha or heaven. Jessica's mother just shook her head.

"Jacqueline tells me you got your Ph.D. and are now teaching in Charlotte. Eastern religions?" Jessica's mother said in the manner of one making polite conversation. She looked about the room and then said, "Is that why you chose this place?"

"I chose this place because I like Indian food…. Sorry, I hadn't remembered that you didn't."

Jessica's mother tried to smile.

"How is dad?" Jessica's voice strained a bit. "Is he going to make it?"

Jessica's mother shrugged and then finally muttered, "Yes, he's going to make it."

She took her last gulp of wine and then waved her hand to get the server's attention to bring her another.

Jessica looked at her mother with pained eyes. "Maybe you shouldn't drink so much…."

"I know my limit."

"Even still…." Jessica turned away, hoping to spot the owner who could engage her in more conversation.

"Why are you here, Jessica? You know your father won't see you, especially in this condition. This has all been very difficult for him—*for us.*"

Jessica's voice cracked even more and she felt herself holding back tears. "What are you going to do, if dad can't work again? Do you have a plan?"

"We'll manage." Her mother took another bite of naan. Jessica pushed her food about her plate with her fork.

She finally got the confidence to say, "Would you and dad be willing to move in with me? Charlotte is a really nice place. Charlotte is called the New South. It's got lots of…."

But Jessica's mother cut her off. "You know we can't do that." After a few minutes and just as her third glass of wine arrived, she said, "Can we go now? I'm not very hungry. I have an upset stomach."

"But you just ordered another glass of wine." Jessica sounded more pleading than she wanted to. She needed her mother. She needed her parents. Was there anything she could do to make things different?

Jessica's mother stood up. "I've really got to go, Jessica. I'm glad we made time to meet. It's been entirely too long. Have a safe trip."

Jessica watched her mother grab a handful of pastel candies from a ceramic bowl as she walked through the door, then reached across the table for the abandoned glass of wine and downed it in one gulp.

An hour later at the camp

Aapo sat at the table, Chicken Eyes' letter in hand. He hadn't seen Jessica yet this morning. He had gone to her tent, which was empty. He imagined that she was bathing in the pool upstream (she was). Maya had joined her. Aapo had started the coffee, even started a pot of beans and made the batter for johnnycakes. Anything to distract him from thinking about Chicken Eyes' cryptic letter. He wasn't sure what to make of it. What evidence? Was he ever coming back? Vindicated? Just as Aapo was about to busy himself with another chore, he saw Jessica approaching.

"Good morning," Jessica said and smiled.

"Maanin. Da how yu di du?"

"What a beautiful morning." Jessica was trying to make the best out of the day, despite the way it had begun. But then she noticed Aapo's long face. "What's wrong?"

He was still holding the letter. "Chicken Eyes" were the only words that came out of his mouth.

Jessica flew into a panic. "Is he all right?" She felt her words catch in her throat. Aapo handed her the letter. After reading it, she said, "What does this mean? Should we go to Belmopan?" Just then, she noticed a leather chain on the table. She tried to smile. "He got me the chain," she said, just above a whisper. She picked it up and placed it in her pocket. Aapo just sat there speechless.

"Thanks for getting breakfast started." She looked at the cake batter. "I best start on these. The guys should be waking up anytime."

Finally, Aapo said, "He'll be OK," mostly to reassure himself.

Soon the guys woke up and of course everybody was talking about Chicken Eyes' perplexing letter. By the end of breakfast, they had all agreed that Chicken Eyes knew what he was doing. That he must be on to *something of the most extraordinary sort* to abandon them like this. Eventually he would return and let them know. There was nothing to worry about.

Aapo declared: "*I mean Cheese 'n Rice!* [This was the Kriol way of avoiding taking the Savior's name in vain.] *Not much can happen at the University of Belize—of all places. And he's a grown man. Let's stop treating him like a little boy.*"

Satisfied with Aapo's proclamation, the guys headed out for the day. Jessica, on the other hand, was far less convinced.

Chicken Eyes' letter had sufficiently distracted Aapo from his plan to shut down Mr. Chan's operation. After seeing the guys off, it promptly came back to mind. He looked over at Jessica who was busy clearing off the dishes.

"Tonight…. Tonight I'm going to tell them that Mr. Chan said to release the animals, stop the job, and go home," Aapo said with tremendous authority.

Jessica stopped what she was doing, looked at him, and said, "Won't they ask the obvious?"

"What do you mean?"

"How was Mr. Chan able to contact you? None of our cell phones works out here."

He thought on her words for a few moments. "You're right…." He frowned. "So what should we do?"

"I don't know. Maybe we can talk with them about the divine within all living creatures, about compassion, kindness, and respect. All the things I taught you from Hinduism and Buddhism. Maybe they'll come around."

"I guess that might work, but what if they don't? Then what? Then what do we do?"

"Do we have another car? Maybe we could drive to Belmopan and tell somebody. We could check in on Chicken Eyes too."

"We do, but that won't work, Jessica. Mr. Chan is very well connected. There's a reason his family has been in this business for sixty some odd years."

"What then?"

"I just don't know." Aapo sighed heavily. "I guess our best chance is for you to teach the guys some of the lessons you taught me. But that could take days, if they're even up to hearing about it. As you know, after a hard day's work, they usually like to forget about it all. They'd rather drink, play music…."

Jessica interrupted him. "You're right." She looked over at the rainbow eucalyptus tree. All its color had puddled to the ground.

Early afternoon, Department of Science, University of Belize, Belmopan

Dr. Nathaniel Jackson III, formerly and affectionately known as Chicken Eyes, sat at the conference table, surrounded by the Dean of Science and Technology, and faculty from Biology, Chemistry, and Physics.

"Thank you for seeing me with such short notice." Nathaniel smiled appreciatively.

The dean smiled back. "We're glad to have you, Dr. Jackson. You say you're in possession of groundbreaking evidence? How can we help you?"

Nathaniel placed his pouch on the table. "I am. Yesterday, in Red Creek Village—you know the place?"

"I do," she began, "Q'eqchi, right? About 200 inhabitants…."

"Yes…. As I was saying, yesterday one of the villagers—he was actually returning from Belmopan—hit Sisimito."

"Sisimito?" the biologist asked with a curled lip.

"Yes, Sisimito."

"But this is just legend…."

"Many think so, but they're mistaken. When I was at Columbia, I encountered one too. Big Foot. I have evidence here…."

"Is that what's in your pouch? The evidence?" the dean asked.

"Yes ma'am. Hair and blood samples. Like I said, one of the villagers hit him. The villager's wife is staying at Western Regional Hospital, by the way. She's due to have a baby any day now."

"Let's see what you've got," said the physicist.

Nathaniel opened the pouch and placed the items on the table. "I've become something of an expert on Big Foot." He smiled widely, his confidence growing with every word. "I've written several papers on it, all unpublished so far. I think we've got a gold mine here."

"Could it have been something else? Something else that this villager hit?" asked the chemist, skeptically.

"Nothing that resembles Sisimito. We've only got the big cats in Belize, as you well know. There's nothing resembling Sisimito."

"Did the villager hit a person? Maybe he hit a person…. That's a more reasonable hypothesis, with all due respect, Dr. Jackson, for you and your work," said the biologist.

"Let's examine the evidence," said the physicist.

Nathaniel smiled. "Thank you for your confidence, sir."

"We can go to my lab," suggested the biologist.

"I'll leave the four of you to do just that," said the dean as she got up from the conference table. "I'll be in my office awaiting any preliminary conclusions."

It turned out, as one might have suspected, that the four scientists couldn't make any inferences with the university's limited lab equipment, but the hair looked unusual enough that they decided to prepare the two samples for DNA testing at a pre-eminent wildlife forensic DNA laboratory in the US. They also invited the Biodiversity Center of Belize to join the investigation. It took the biologist and chemist some while to get onboard (the physicist already had a soft spot for Nathaniel, being in the same discipline and all) but once the lab results came back, no one could contain their excitement.

The hair sample was a bust. DNA is isolated from the root of the hair shaft, and the sample proved inconclusive. But the blood sample disclosed a male of unknown species. The University was so delighted that they hired Nathaniel Jackson III to become the head researcher of what was turning into an international research team. All of a sudden, Nathaniel's papers would be published and cited the world over. Ikal would become a celebrity too, making regular national television appearances. And tourists would begin flocking to Red Creek Village by the hundreds. Soon the village would open a Sisimito and Big Foot Museum. The revenue would enable the village to build a new school and medical center which also served the surrounding villages. They were even able to purchase their own school bus and medical van! Both the school and medical center would be named after none other than their beloved Sachihiro.

Meanwhile, back at the camp...

Aapo found Jessica at the stream, rinsing and hanging the soiled laundry on nearby tree limbs. He had a fishing pole in hand.

"Want to join me? I need my lucky charm." He smiled widely.

"Walk the bodhisattva way," she whispered, and then in a louder voice she proposed, "How about we hunt wild mushrooms instead. I could add them to a big pot of rice and beans. —I don't know why this came to mind just now. Maybe make some corn tortillas. Are you good at spotting edible mushrooms?"

Aapo's face lit up. "I haven't done that since I was a boy. Gramma used to take me into the forest to hunt wild mushrooms. She'd tell me stories about the Hashishi Pampi, little miniature people or fairies who live in the forest. They're usually found playing in the ashes wherever milpas are burned or forest fires often occur. They're also called 'Duenditos' since they're smaller than the Duendes—have I told you about Tata Duende?"

"I don't think so."

"I'll have to do that some time. Anyway, the Hashishi Pampi are very playful, but they can also be quite mischievous…. Belize has a lot of edible mushrooms, and they're easy to find on old rotting wood. They even grow on coconut husks. I've seen them grow in garbage dumps too—no kidding. My friends and I would go to the dumps to find discarded toys. What a great idea, Jessica."

She smiled. "Super! Let's grab a bucket and get to work. What kinds of mushroom grow here anyway?"

"All kinds. Oyster mushrooms, Pig's Ear mushrooms, Turkey Tail, Hairy Turkey Tail (these last two are medicinal), even Paddy Straw mushrooms. They're a staple in the Far East, but they also grow wild in Belize."

After about an hour of foraging about the forest, their bucket was full of dozens of delectable mushrooms. Jessica especially admired the purple color of the underside of the Pig's Ears. They were lucky to find such a big cluster of them, surprisingly untouched by the many creatures of the forest. They made their way to the limestone steps and sat down. They looked over at the jaguar stone carving and marveled again at what an incredible find. But then it suddenly struck Aapo where they were and what had happened the last time they found themselves at this place. He was glad that Jaguar God had not disclosed his secret desire. He instinctively began rubbing the front of his neck, which brought about a certain calm.

"I remember the first time you took me to this place. The night we arrived. You teased me about the Lords of Xibalba." Jessica chuckled. "Seems like forever ago."

"Not even a week…." Aapo rubbed his neck some more. Jessica noticed.

"Are you OK?"

"Sure. Why do you ask?"

"You seem nervous or something. Don't worry, I'll finish dinner long before the guys get back. I just want to sit here for a little while." She gave a sweet sigh.

"Thanks for suggesting that we hunt mushrooms. I'd forgotten how fun it was." Aapo smiled.

"I thought about what it really means to walk the bodhisattva way. Or to recognize the divine within all creatures. You know, I used to be a vegetarian. During grad school. I used to be a lot of things. I really strayed from that path. In any case, I didn't hear the guys complain about not having meat yesterday."

"You weren't around when they teased me incessantly." Aapo laughed.

"Well maybe so…. Did you know that Jains believe that even plants have souls?"

"Really?"

"We haven't talked about Jainism and Sikhism. Both of these religions come from Hinduism too. We haven't got a lot of time, but would you like to hear a little about them?"

"I'd love you." Aapo blushed when he realized his quite obviously Freudian slip. Jessica only grinned.

Introduction to Jainism and Sikhism

"Jainism is a minor religion," Jessica began. "It only has about five to eight million followers. Like Buddhism, it came out of the shramana movement. Do you remember what that is?"[35]

"Weren't they ascetic seekers who rejected most of the Vedic teachings, especially the spiritual and social hierarchy established by the Brahmins?"

Jessica smiled. "Right. Shramanas rejected the hierarchical caste system and the spiritual elitism and elaborate liturgical practices of the priestly caste. Jainism founded its religion on the existence of twenty-four sages called *Tirthankaras*, all of whom have lived in this current world cycle. The most recent sage, *Mahavira*, was a contemporary of Siddhartha Gautama (the Buddha), though there's no indication that they'd met. Mahavira lived in the same region of northern India, and like Buddha he came from the Kshatriya caste. Like both Hinduism and Buddhism, Jains believe in eternally recurring cycles of creation and destruction. The Tirthankaras appear during predictable times in the cycle. Mahavira is the last sage in our current morally and spiritually depraved time period. In the next cycle, another twenty-four sages will appear, and then yet another twenty-four sages, and so on through all eternity."

"So what do Jains believe, besides that plants have souls? Do they share any similarities with Hinduism, as Buddhism does? Karma? Samsara?"

Aapo suddenly smiled when he noticed a speckled racer, about three feet long and black with its characteristic yellow and blue spotting, dart toward an unsuspecting red-eyed tree frog. He nudged Jessica to watch. She cringed and then squeezed her eyes shut as the snake crushed the struggling little frog, bit it several times, and then swallowed it whole. His little red-eyed friends sat atop the fan-shaped leaflets of a maidenhead fern, one of the species used by the ancient Maya to decorate ceremonial altars. They averted their eyes and then paid their respects before they resumed catching botflies.

Jessica dared to open one eye. "Is it over?"

"It's over." Aapo couldn't help but chuckle at Jessica's delicate demeanor. She opened her other eye as the snake slithered away.

She grimaced. "Poor little frog." After a few moments she said, "So back to the lesson. Yes, Jains believe in both karma and samsara. They even worship Hindu gods. However, like Buddhists, they understand gods to be nothing more than powerful beings still stuck in samsara and destined to eventual rebirth. And like Buddhists, they don't believe that gods can help us in our quest for spiritual enlightenment."

35. This discussion is based on Chapter 4, "Jainism" in Brodd, Chapter 4, "Jaina Traditions" in Oxtoby, et al., and Chapter 3 "Hinduism, Jainism, and Sikhism" in Esposito.

"What about the Tirthankaras? Are they considered to be gods?" Aapo asked.

Wait— (Sorry). That little red-eyed tree frog. This truly was a dreadful event. All his friends called him 'Busta Rhymes.' He had the most beautiful voice in the forest. Sorry, I'll resume the story.

"No, the Tirthankaras are humans, not gods, nor avatars of gods. However, they're venerated and their lives emulated as the highest expression of the Jainist ideal. The twenty-four sages are revered for having achieved moksha (Jains share this term with Hinduism). The Tirthankaras taught that the only way to escape samsara is through non-action and doing no harm to any living thing, called *ahimsa*. A person can avoid harming other living things only through complete inaction. Any violence we commit increases negative karma, even when the harm is unintentional. But *any* sort of action, even actions which produces *good* karma, keeps us in samsara."

"That seems extreme."

"It is. Their beliefs are founded on their understanding of reality. They divide the world into two categories of existence: *jiva* (soul) and *ajiva*. Jiva is eternal and conscious. Ajiva is substance without consciousness. Ajiva is divided into four types: motion, rest, atoms, and space. Jiva and ajiva comprise all that exists in the universe. Jiva interacts with ajiva. Indeed, both are thoroughly enmeshed. All living things are a combination of jiva and ajiva. Further, all jivas/souls are considered equal regardless of the body they inhabit: whether plant, insect, animal, human, or god. Jains categorize living things according to the number of senses they engage. Plants and microbes only engage the sense of touch. They are often called 'one-souled' for that reason. Humans, gods, and most animals engage all five senses and are thus 'five-souled.' Worms are thought to be two-souled, insects that crawl on legs, three-souled, and flying insects four-souled."

"Seems like the only way you can achieve moksha is by fasting to death, since being a vegetarian even causes harm to one-souled beings."

"Believe it or not, Jains advocate this practice," Jessica explained. Aapo shook his head incredulously. She continued, "While not a universal practice, it's not uncommon even amongst householders—those who support the Jainist monks and nuns in the sanghas. The key, if you're going to stick around on this Earth, is to do as little harm as possible in your practices. Monks and nuns aren't even allowed to prepare their own food, since harvesting plants, even boiling water, causes harm to living beings. Indeed, monks and nuns are altogether dependent on householders for their food, but they're only allowed to take a small portion, and they can only eat 'leftovers' —food that hasn't been especially prepared for them. They're only allowed to drink as much water as is absolutely necessary so as to minimize the harm to the living organisms in the water. Finally, all food and water must be cooked, boiled, or peeled to ensure that it is completely without life. Householders obviously accept that they will do a certain amount of harm to living things, but in supporting the sanghas they also know that they are earning good karma for their next life in samsara."

"You know I've been wondering about this since you first introduced Eastern religions: how is it that karma sticks to the soul or consciousness? Just what is karma, really? You've noted that karma refers to good and bad actions which inform how we will be reborn in samsara, but karma is also the stuff that sticks to us in light of those good and bad actions."

"Actually Jains have a good answer to this question. They believe that karma is a physical substance that's found everywhere in the universe. Karma particles are attracted to the jiva (soul) by the actions of that jiva. It's helpful to think of karma as floating dust which sticks to the soul (or consciousness, if you're a Buddhist), or as atomic particles which attach to the soul, as a result of our actions, words, or thoughts.[36] When karma particles stick to a soul, they affect the life of that soul. The good or bad karma that sticks also colors that soul: in gold, lotus-pink, and white (good karma), and black, blue, and gray (bad karma)."

"But how can physical substance stick to a nonphysical substance like the soul or consciousness? Jains believe that jiva interacts with ajiva, that they're thoroughly enmeshed, but do they say *how* they are?"

"Not that I'm aware. But you know, certain Western philosophies and religions face this same sort of problem. Consider the view called substance dualism, which was championed by the seventeenth century philosopher Descartes. How does non-material substance like mind or soul interact with material substance like the brain? Descartes suggested the pineal gland as the point of contact between the two, but that's only because it didn't seem to have any other function. But locating *where* the contact might happen doesn't get us any closer to understanding *how* it might happen. We'll have to chalk this up to one of the many mysteries of the universe." Jessica smiled.

"Do Jains believe in anything like samadhi or prajna?"

"Yes. It's called *kevala* or 'omniscience.' Kevala is knowledge of everything, including one's inner self, one's past lives, other living beings' past lives, all the world and all the things in it. Kevala is a quality of all souls, but it's hidden by the karma (both good and bad) that sticks to the soul."

"I want to experience kevala. Of course I don't want to do what it takes to get there." Aapo grinned. "You mentioned monks and nuns. So women are able to achieve moksha too?"

"That depends on which sect one belongs to. A couple of hundred years or so after Mahavira's death, there was a sectarian split due to differing interpretations of ascetic practices and women's spiritual capacity, among other things. The so-called 'Sky Clad,' who moved south, required male monastic nakedness. Those who remained in the north called themselves 'White Clad' because of the white robes they wore. They believe that women can attain moksha too. They even believe that the nineteenth Tirthankara was a woman." Jessica smiled.

"So what do *you* think about Jainism, Jessica? Seems too extreme for my taste."

"I love the idea that all living things are ensouled. I believe this too."

Just then something quite fantastical occurred: King K'uk Mo insisted that his council keep an eye on Jessica and the camp. More often than not they'd stay quite hidden. But that afternoon they decided to have a little fun. First came a shower of brightly colored flowers raining from the treetops: perfumed plumeria in whites, yellows, oranges, reds, and pinks—Mother Nature's aphrodisiac. The fragrance was almost dizzying. Jessica and Aapo looked up, spotted the culprits, and laughed. Ankle-deep in plumeria, Aapo continued:

"So tell me about Sikhism. Aren't Sikhs the ones who wear the turbans and breeches?"[37]

Jessica bent over and picked up a hot pink flower with a pale orange center,

---

36. See http://www.bbc.co.uk/religion/religions/jainism/beliefs/karma.shtml.

37. This discussion is based on Chapter 5, "Sikhism" in *Invitation to Asian Religions*, Jeffrey Brodd, et al., Chapter 3 "Sikh Traditions" in *World Religions: Eastern Traditions* (Fourth Edition), ed. Willard Oxtoby, et al., and Chapter 3 "Hinduism, Jainism, and Sikhism" in *Religions of Asia Today* (Third Edition), ed. John Esposito, et al.

brought it to her nose, closed her eyes and inhaled deeply. After a few moments, she opened her eyes and said, "They are. Sikhism was founded during the era of Muslim rule by a bhakti guru named *Nanak*. He was probably a bhakta of Vishnu and born into the Kshatriya caste. Other scholars say that he was a Vaishya, that his parents were merchants. In about 1498, when Nanak was thirty years old, he underwent a life-changing spiritual experience that would lead to the founding of the religion. Nanak went down to the river to bathe but never resurfaced from the water. Everybody assumed he'd drowned, though his body couldn't be found. Three days later, Nanak emerged from the river, returned to his village and proclaimed his spiritual message which he professed to have received directly from God (he was taken to God's court, as he'd explain): 'There is neither Hindu nor Muslim, so whose path shall I follow? I shall follow God's path. God is neither Hindu nor Muslim, and the path which I follow is God's.' This led to twenty years of traveling far and wide and in all directions to learn the variety of religious customs. While abroad, Nanak also proclaimed his own teachings, often to hostile audiences. He was famous for bucking 'proper' religious protocol. He believed that this was his divine commission."

After Jessica was done speaking she smiled at Aapo and said sweetly, "That was romantic," referring of course to the shower of plumeria, which caused Aapo to blush. (Aapo would be doing a lot of blushing that day.)

"Bucking protocol as one's divine commission—this sounds like Jesus, or Socrates," Aapo said, trying to recover some of his composure.

"How do you know about Socrates?" Jessica gave a playful smirk.

"Like I've told you, Mr. Chan ensured that I had a good education."

Jessica smiled at that.

Twenty years previously, Green Hills Memorial Park, 4 miles from Mr. Chan's estate in Rolling Hills

Mr. Chan and Aapo stood up from the marble bench which sat next to Lottie's freshly turned grave. The air smelled of lilacs and freshly mown grass. The Palos Verdes Peninsula and the Pacific Ocean could be seen off in the distance. A kaleidoscope of Palos Verdes Blue butterflies (the world's rarest butterfly with wings dipped in silvery blue and found only on the Palos Verdes Peninsula) fluttered about. How they got there only the gods know. The private ceremony had ended about ten minutes before. The sun shone brightly. Mr. Chan gave Aapo's shoulder an affectionate squeeze.

"Are you ready to go now, son?"

"Sure, I guess so."

"So are you excited about your first semester at college? It starts in just a couple of weeks." Mr. Chan now had his arm around Aapo's shoulder.

"I don't know, Mr. Chan. I'm not going to fit in at UCLA for all kinds of reasons, including the fact that I'll be the oldest freshman in its entire history." Aapo frowned.

Mr. Chan chuckled. "Well, you got a late start, that's all. You were quite a bit behind in your education when I first met you. In any case, you're only twenty-two. You're not *that* old."

"Almost twenty-three." Aapo cracked a smile.

Mr. Chan continued, "You know how much I value education. People respect you, you get what you want. My father insisted that I get an education for that very reason. He never did. After he left the village—well, you know. Have you decided what you want to study?"

"I love history, literature, studying other cultures. Something like that."

"So follow your heart. You'll always have a job with me. Study what you're passionate about."

"I'm not sure what I want to do after I finish school," Aapo began, hesitantly. "I'm not sure I ever want to go back to Belize."

Mr. Chan looked at him sternly. "Remember what I taught you? A lesson my own father taught me: A son *always* obeys his father. This is a matter of respect. —And you'll be paid well. You'll never have to worry about money."

"You're right," Aapo surrendered. "Let's get home, Mr. Chan. It's been a hard day."

Edin Chan tried to smile as they began their short walk to his grey metallic Aston Martin. "Indeed it has…."

Jessica bent down, grabbed a red plumeria with a bright yellow center, and extended it to Aapo with a smile. "Guru Nanak gathered a large following, and at about the age of fifty, he established the first Sikh community in what is now Pakistan. There have been ten gurus. The tenth guru, Gobind Singh—he was born in 1666 and died in 1708, and was considered the greatest guru after Nanak—declared before he died at the hands of a Mughal assassin that their religious text, the *Adi Granth*, would thereafter be considered their guru. Indeed, their scripture is now called *Guru Granth Sahib*. The text is a collection of hymns and sermons composed by Guru Nanak and others."

All of a sudden a big ball of black yarn dropped from the treetop, landing at Aapo's feet. He picked it up, studied it, then placed it on his lap. Jessica gave a puzzled look and gazed upward. The monkeys made funny faces. Next dropped a little pink candle, followed by a roll of parchment paper. Suddenly, Aapo felt his heart flutter. Nobody knew about the Obeah love spell—*nobody!* This had to be some outrageous coincidence. Something that'd make a great story over a few beers at some pub back home. Then Aapo looked over at the Jaguar God. It had one of those faces of someone who knew more than he was letting on. Aapo gathered up the candle and the paper and set them on his lap with the ball of yarn.

Jessica looked at the items and then at Aapo who had an almost guilty expression on his face. "What's all this?" she asked, more than a bit perplexed.

Before Aapo could answer, the monkeys laughed uproariously. And then the head councilmember roared, causing Jessica to cover her ears. The troop quickly scattered.

"You said monkeys like to collect weird things…" was all that Jessica could offer.

Aapo pretended as if what had just occurred was more commonplace than he could let on. "So what are their teachings?"

Jessica played along and proceeded with her lesson. "There is only one God, but it is entirely beyond human understanding, beyond any human categories. Nanak referred to God as 'Om-kara,' which means 'Divine One.' He also used the name 'Nirankar' which means 'Without Form.' God resides within each of us. Indeed, God dwells within all creation. Here Nanak used the name 'Sat Guru,' meaning 'True Teacher.' Sat Guru bestows grace upon us when we approach him through loving devotion which then liberates us from samsara. The most prescribed way to engage in loving devotion, according to *Guru Granth Sahib*, is by meditating on the divine nature of God (called *nam*). Another name Nanak used for Sat Guru, by the way, was 'Akal Purakh.'"

"So liberation from samsara is their goal too."

"Right. Liberation from samsara is called *mukti*. Mukti leads to being in the presence of God—a state of eternal bliss. The most appealing thing about Sikhism is how progressive it's been since its very founding: Sikhism promotes equality and community service. Nanak affirmed the social equality of all people, regardless of caste, race, and creed—even gender. The Sikh organization, called the *Khalsa*, which was founded to defend their faith after the fifth guru was tortured and martyred by order of the Mughal emperor, is open to women. Sikh women aren't required to conform to the gender practices of Hinduism or Islam. There's no priesthood or ordained ministry, men and women pray together, and anyone can teach or read from the scripture. Sikhs also provide a community kitchen which welcomes anyone, regardless of caste, gender, race, or station in life, to enjoy a common meal. These teachings were revolutionary at the time—they still are, even today."

"Wow, that's amazingly progressive. So tell me more about the Khalsa." Aapo glanced at the items on his lap and his heart fluttered once more. He pounded his chest to scare the flutters away, looked at Jessica, and smiled.

Jessica smiled back. "There was relative peace between the Sikhs and Mughals through the sixteenth century. But within a year of the Mughal Emperor Akbar's death in 1605, the new emperor, Jahangir, ordered the fifth guru Arjan's execution. Guru Arjan's execution was for *political* not religious reasons. Emperor Jahangir had exercised the same religious tolerance as his father, Akbar. Guru Arjan's martyrdom pushed the Sikh community into separatism and militancy. The Sikh community, called the *Panth*, took up arms to defend itself against Mughal hostility. The tenth guru Singh required that his male followers dress a certain way to make them instantly recognizable. This is called the "Five K's", since each of the requirements begins with the letter K in their language, Punjabi: uncut hair covered with a turban, a small comb worn in the hair, a steel wristlet, a sword, and breeches. While the wearing of the sword once suggested their readiness to fight, now it's merely symbolic and often concealed under their clothing so as not to appear threatening to others."

Suddenly Aapo noticed the hour. "We should be getting back now. Not much time to make our concoction." He placed the three items on top of the bucket of mushrooms, stood up from the limestone steps, and extended his hand to Jessica. They made their way back to the camp.

This really shouldn't bother me so much, being such a commonplace event. My therapist even says that I should let this go. But Busta Rhymes could truly bust out the most beautiful songs.

Late night, Cancún

Finn Lauder and the real Jessica Kraus walked into the Mandala, one of Cancún's hippest, most upscale lounges with its Indian-inspired décor in rich vibrant colors and lush fabrics. Jessica wore a sleeveless Dolce and Gabbana dress in loud pink with yellow pineapple print ($1945) and matching pink iguana leather mules embellished with sparkling gemstones (a veritable bargain at $1175). Finn wore a short sleeve black D&G cotton shirt with white palm print and Italian collar (his favorite). Only $745.

Everybody's eyes were on them (some were even pointing) as they were escorted to their private table in the VIP section. Jessica imagined that this was because they were such an attractive couple, and she said as much. This *might* have been the reason, had what transpired not actually transpired just a few hours before. Everybody was staring (indeed, many were sniggering) at their matching tattoos: His and Hers. Jessica's was completely visible in her sleeveless dress. Finn's short sleeves covered the top half of his, but the word was clear enough. Ordinarily His and Hers tattoos wouldn't cause such a ruckus, but theirs were different. When the happy couple walked into the tattoo parlor, they were already liquored up on champagne mojitos from the Congo Bar. It was Jessica who decided to get matching tattoos. Finn thought that this was just another one of her silly ideas, but the champagne got the best of him, and with a little arm twisting he found himself going along. The tattoo artist, noting their intoxicated state, decided to have a little fun at their expense. And so he tattooed "Hers" on Jessica's arm and "His" on Finn's. So far they hadn't noticed this permanent "mistake" (that would come later and would result in the near-strangulation of the tattoo artist, which would land them in jail for several hours until Finn bribed the police to let them go). But the club goers had certainly noticed and found this more than a little amusing.

Once seated at their table, Finn said in the most serious tone of the evening, "This has been fun, Jess, but we really should be thinking about flying back to Belize."

"Let's give up on that plan," Jessica replied with her most adorable smile.

"Huh? What do you mean?"

Here's what Jessica meant: She had already given up on the idea of finding Jessica Kraut, already given up on getting her promised one million dollars. After all, Finn Lauder III offered a far sweeter deal. Of course, she couldn't say *that*, so instead she said: "Let's get married."

"What? Are you nuts?" Finn shook his head.

"Let's get married. Think about it. You wouldn't even really have to change the invitations. Wouldn't you rather marry a Kraus? I mean what kind of name is *Kraut* anyway? You'd be marrying some poor mensch's side dish. Who'd go out of their way to eat *fermented cabbage*?"

"Personally, it gives me gas." Finn grimaced.

"Exactly. And we've been having so much fun. Don't tell me you'd have more fun with fermented cabbage."

"It *has* been fun." He grinned.

"So you'll marry me then? Think about it. Imagine the embarrassment if there's no wedding. Imagine all that money down the drain. All those disappointed guests."

"You're right…."

"So does that mean 'yes'?" Jessica reached out and touched his hand.

"You're asking me at my weakest moment, Jess. Think about how much we've had to drink."

"Well, we could wait until we get back to the hotel room…." She gave a playful smirk.

"I guess that would be a *considerably weaker* moment." He gave a seductive smile.

Jessica leaned over and gave Finn a big kiss. "So it's a 'yes'!"

"*Yes*. Yes, I'll marry you Jessica Kraus!" It didn't take long before Finn was convinced. After all, his new Jessica would become anything he wanted her to be.

"Hurray! Let's order a bottle of their best champagne. I can't wait to shop for a ring tomorrow. How many carats? Five? Can I get five carats?"

"Anything for you, Jess."

EIGHT

Jessica Kraut had just finished the dishes and was sitting with Maya enjoying a big cup of coffee sweetened with coconut sugar. Aapo approached her with a big grin.

"Are you up for an adventure today?"

"Adventure?"

"I thought maybe we could take a couple inner tubes and headlamps and hike to this river I discovered last year. It flows through a cave. You wouldn't believe what's inside! It's my favorite place."

"Better than the limestone steps and our new stone jaguar friend?" She smiled.

"Better than the limestones steps and our new stone jaguar friend," he repeated. "I call it *Ah-Puch Cavern*, after the ruler of Xibalba." His excitement shone on his face.

"Xibalba *again*?" Jessica shook her head in mock-exasperation.

"Don't worry, Jessica. If you get scared, just scream! Shriek! Moan! If you're convincing enough, Ah-Puch will leave you alone, believing that his lesser demons have already gotten hold of you."[38] Aapo laughed.

Jessica cracked a smile, and then said, "So what about dinner?"

"Rice and beans." Aapo smirked. "In any case, we should be back in a few hours."

"Won't the guys eventually revolt? I mean this will be our third day in a row serving rice and beans."

"Belly full, body glad," Aapo quipped.

Jessica chuckled at that. "Yeah and I guess they really don't have a choice but to eat what's put in front of them. Is your foot still getting better?"

"It's only about a twenty-minute hike, and yes, it doesn't hurt nearly as much."

Jessica finished her last sip of coffee and stood up. "OK, then—let's do it!" she chirped.

Aapo found himself pathetically grateful.

"So what's in the cave anyway?" she asked.

"You'll see…." He smiled widely.

Aapo and Jessica grabbed their gear and headed deeper into the forest. The ground squished and crunched from moss and fallen leaves. Soon the air reeked of rotting meat. Jessica crinkled her nose at the offense.

"What's that godawful smell?"

"Not sure…. It might be a fresh kill. Though I don't see any vultures around. Our King Vulture, by the way, is such a beautiful bird." Pause, then, "I know what you're going to say: 'How can a *vulture*, of all things, be *beautiful*?' Maya believe that the King Vulture carries messages between humans and the gods."

As they pushed through a snarl of vines, they came upon the answer to Jessica's question:

To the left stood a large climbing vine showcasing an ENORMOUS purplish-brown heart-shaped flower with a dark center. Suddenly they found themselves surrounded by a kaleidoscope of iridescent butterflies.

"It's a pelican flower, one of the world's largest flowers. It smells like that to attract flies and other pollinators," Aapo said squinty-eyed. A streak of sunlight glared in his

38. See http://www.allabouthistory.org/mayan-death-god-faq.htm.

face. "When the butterflies consume its nectar, they're no longer so tasty to would-be predators."

"What on earth would possibly eat a butterfly?" Jessica asked, not really caring for an answer. She peered into the center and noted a shiny blue butterfly inside. "Thanks for suggesting this adventure. What fun!" She beamed.

As they continued along, Aapo noticed long claw markings on the trunk of a cedar tree. He walked up to it and moved his fingers down the grooves.

"These are older. Definitely not fresh. Maybe five to seven days old."

Jessica walked up to his side. "What are they? Claw marks?" A tinge of fear ran through her.

"Tiger." Aapo looked down and noticed they were standing on a reddish-orange leafcutter ant nest, stretching some fifteen meters long. "We're standing on a leafcutter's nest. Kriol call them 'wee wee ants.' Look carefully around. These nests are perfect for showing tiger tracks." They walked about, eyes fixed on the ground.

"I'm getting scared," Jessica squeaked.

"Don't be. Remember what I said? Tigers rarely attack people." Aapo was about three meters away when he called out, "Come over here!"

"What? Did you find something?" She walked over to him and looked down. Next to Aapo's worn leather work boot was a huge pugmark. She squatted down and put her hand in it. She looked up at Aapo and asked, "Is this old too?"

"Almost certainly—yes."

Satisfied with Aapo's answer, Jessica picked up her inner tube. "Let's keep going."

It wasn't long before they heard a booming roar, which caused Jessica to all but jump out of her boots. "Jaguar!" She ran up to Aapo. He couldn't help but chuckle. Jessica had heard the howler monkeys roar a hundred times over, but the jaguar signs had made her more than a bit edgy.

Aapo reached out and touched her shoulder. "Baboons, Jessica."

She tried to laugh. "Of course…. You have a gun, though, right? You brought your gun?"

He patted the large thigh pocket of his cargo pants. "Right here."

After a few minutes, he said, "You remind me of the Victorian hunters' view of the African jungle. You're the nervous white man—er, *lady*. You know, Mary Midgley…?"

"Sure, but how do *you* know about Mary Midgley?" Jessica asked, cutting him off. But before Aapo could answer her, she answered, "Mr. Chan…."

"Right…." He smiled. "Anyway, Mary Midgley said that the nervous white man was the most dangerous thing in the jungle, because he assumed every creature he met would attack him, and so he shot on sight. Why would the nervous white man, who would shoot at anything big enough to aim at, think that the beasts of the jungle were more savage than he? *Why do whites still think so?*"[39]

"You're right. Sorry." Jessica frowned.

"Did you know that the baboons use their roar to compete for territory? Instead of fighting each other, when two troops meet to compete for a territory, both sides sit down and howl their loudest. The side that makes the most noise wins. Entirely bloodless—and I dare say *fun*."

As they continued on their adventure, Jessica had an overpowering feeling that something bad was going to happen—she could feel it. They had walked another twenty meters or so when Jessica noticed eyes peering at her from the dark underbrush. Great big dark eyes. She dropped her inner tube and ran to Aapo, grabbing

39. See The Essential Mary Midgley, "Animals and the Problem of Evil."

him so tightly he thought his *own* eyes would pop out.

"Eyes—there are big eyes in the bushes."

"You want me to save you from Big. Eyes. In. The. Bushes?" ... words for dramatic effect, and then cracked a smile. "Beware t... They'll *stare* you to death!" Aapo laughed hard at his joke.

"Stop teasing." She furrowed her brow.

"Let's sit over here," Aapo said, as he plopped down on a big flat rock. Jessica opened up her backpack, grabbed her thermos, and took a big gulp of water.

He extended his flask. "You might need something a bit stronger. Nervous white lady...." He smirked.

Just then, a red brocket deer jumped out from the underbrush.

Aapo burst out laughing. "You really need to learn to go with the flow, Jessica."

She smiled. "You're right. Sorry.... 'Go with the flow'—that is Taoist teaching. I haven't yet told you about Confucianism and Taoism. Want to hear about them?"

"Sure, but we've only got about 500 meters to walk before we reach the place where the river swoops into the cave."

"Won't it be more difficult to talk while we're floating along? In any case, you've billed this cave as all kinds of amazing, and I don't want to be distracted from the enjoyment of it."

"Fair enough." Aapo took a swig of rum from his flask.

"Tell you what, how about if I just tell you about the ancient Chinese religion from which Confucianism and Taoism emerged? Then on the way *back* I can tell you about Confucianism and Taoism," Jessica proposed.

"Deal." He reached out and touched her hand. For a few minutes, Aapo and Jessica just sat there. Aapo, for his part, couldn't figure out what was going on. Usually Jessica was so talkative.

Jessica looked at Aapo. A wave of calm washed over her. All at once, the birds chirped chirpier—and she noted a myriad of little insects swarming in the yellow light which filtered down from the treetops. All the trilling and buzzing made her intensely aware of the ground beneath her feet, of the agouti rummaging through the leaves and finally nabbing the small orange fruit of a nearby breadnut tree. She caressed the cold stone on which they sat, covered by moss and jungle. These sights and sounds, so foreign to her when she first arrived at this place (it seemed like forever ago), were now like welcome hosts. What words could possibly capture this moment? She finally found them, getting some inspiration from Goethe: *The world came to life in my soul.* A smile spread across her face. She closed her eyes and breathed deeply.

Aapo had been studying her. On cue, he shut his eyes and joined her meditation.

After some time, Jessica opened her eyes and began to speak, which jolted Aapo out of his contemplation.

Ancient Chinese Religion

"Both Confucianism and Taoism arose from an ancient Chinese religion which began around 1600 BCE," Jessica began.[40] "They can be understood as two divergent extensions of this ancient religion. The *I Ching*, or *Book of Changes*, compiled by the end of the second millennium BCE, depicts the earliest expression of ancient Chinese

40. This discussion is based on Chapter 6, "Confucianism and Daoism," in Brodd. See also Chapter 5, "East Asian Religions: Confucianism, Daoism, Shinto, Buddhism," in Esposito, and Chapter 6, "Chinese and Korean Traditions," in Oxtoby.

beliefs."

What were some of the beliefs of this ancient religion? Did they have a creation ↕h? As you know, I love creation myths." Aapo smiled.

"The ancient Chinese believed that from an original state of undifferentiated chaos, two opposite, and yet complementary, energies or life force (*qi*) emerged: *yin* and *yang*. Yin and yang interact dynamically and harmoniously, generating the myriad elements of creation. Many dualities found in nature—light/dark, hot/cold, dry/wet, masculine/feminine—are manifestations of these energies."

"The yin yang symbol looks like an interracial sperm couple having a naked party." Aapo gave a goofy face.

Jessica chuckled. "Humans are a combination of material body and immaterial soul. The immaterial soul is divided into *hun* (the yang component—light, pure, and upward-rising) and *po* (the yin component—heavy, opaque, and downward-sinking). At death, hun departs from the body and rises skyward, and po settles down into the earth alongside the interred body. After death, if the energy remains to keep hun and po together, the spirit of the deceased lingers. Otherwise, hun and po eventually dissipate and reconfigure to form future beings."

"The Chinese honor their ancestors, right?"

"They do. Ancestors play an active role in the lives of their descendants. They're often consulted on matters both great and small. The spirit of the person who dies in old age and has been properly cared for by descendants becomes *shen*—a benevolent spirit that protects and benefits the living. But the spirit of the person who dies tragically or prematurely, or who's not properly cared for by descendants, becomes *gui*—a vengeful and malevolent ghost. Shen and gui also refer to benevolent gods and demons, respectively. During the Shang dynasty, the earliest known historic period in China, dating from 1600 to 1046 BCE, the spirits of ancestors carried messages to the Lord on High, *Shangdi*, the most powerful god in the Shang pantheon of spirits and who also happened to be the ancient ancestor of the Shang imperial house."

"That's rather convenient." Aapo smirked. "So what made up the Shang pantheon of spirits?"

"At the top was Shangdi, followed by Nature (the spirits that animate natural phenomena like rivers and mountains). Then came the Celestial Spirits, such as the sun and moon. Next were the Former Lords of the Shang, and finally the Direct Ancestors. Shangdi controlled the cosmos and monitored the behavior of the royal descendants, distributing rewards and punishments. The Shang ruler assumed the role of shaman, communicating with Shangdi and the other ancestral spirits. The Shang ruler needed to maintain good relations with Shangdi and the spirits, since they were his source of imperial power. This power was called *de* or 'virtue.' It was only through the correct performance of sacrificial rituals to Shangdi and the ancestors that the Shang ruler could claim legitimate authority. In 1046 BCE (although historians disagree about the date, some dating it as early as 1122) a rebellion overthrew the Shang dynasty and founded the Zhou dynasty (1046–256 BCE). The defeat of the Shang family was interpreted as the will of Shangdi (now named *Tian* and often translated as 'The Sky,' 'The Force Above,' or merely 'Heaven'). Like Shangdi, Tian only supported virtuous kings. Virtue gave them their legitimacy to rule. This was called the 'Mandate of Tian' or the 'Mandate of Heaven.' Should the ruler lack virtue, Tian could withdraw the mandate and transfer it to another person or family. Good (that is, *virtuous*) governance was thus a duty to Heaven. Tian's working in nature and the human world was called its *Tao*, or 'Way.' By following the Tao, both the natural and human worlds would reach their greatest fulfillment. In the human world, this meant virtuous behavior. The ruler's duty was to implement the Tao and serve as a virtuous role model for his subjects. As the chosen representative of Tian in the human world, the Zhou ruler was called *Tianzi* or 'Son of Tian.' As such, he was both a political and religious leader. As king and priest, he was required to observe a set of rituals called *li* as the way to implement the Tao. Tao (the Way) became the ideal course of human conduct, through practicing li. Only the correct and sincere performance of li would convince Tian of the king's virtue. The king thus served as a role model for his subjects through the proper performance of li. *Confucius* lived during the end of the Zhou Dynasty."

"Remember, Jessica, that in the interest of time—we want to at least *try* to get back to make some sort of dinner for the guys, right?—you said we'd talk about Confucianism and Taoism on the way *back* from the cave … although this is fascinating stuff." Aapo smiled.

"Right, but I'd like to give some background about Confucius (also known as Master K'ung),[41] since he lived during the Zhou dynasty and was informed by their religious beliefs and practices. That is, if you don't mind." Jessica gave a flirtatious smile.

"Go on…. You have the floor—the *forest floor.*" Aapo chuckled.

"Thanks." Jessica grinned. "The Zhou system resembled feudal Europe. Although the fiefdoms were governed independently, the feudal lords owed their allegiance to the Zhou king, paying tribute to the royal court and serving the king during times of war. By the time of Confucius' birth (551 BCE), however, the Zhou kings had been reduced to mere figureheads. The feudal lords had altogether usurped the kings' power and the fiefdoms were largely run as independent states. Eventually, even the feudal lords' power was usurped by more powerful clans. This was true of Confucius' state, Lu (in modern Shandong province), which was ruled by the powerful 'Three Families': Ji, Meng, and Shu. Confucius came from a humble economic background and held only minor government posts throughout his life, despite his aspirations. He saw himself as an emissary of Tian. Confucius believed that his contemporaries had lost the Tao or Way, and it was up to him to get them back on the virtuous path. Only then could there be a return to a harmonious and stable society. He looked at the early Zhou period as a golden age (a time when the Way prevailed) and he longed for a return to that time. While Confucius achieved only marginal influence during his lifetime, he did gather a fairly large following of disciples, some of whom were able to secure high government posts. His vision was later taken up by prominent Confucian teachers Mencius (Mengzi) and Xunzi, both of the Warring States Period which followed the Zhou. Not getting respect in his own state of Lu, Confucius would often take his message to neighboring states—unsuccessfully. He died in 479 BCE, almost assuredly believing that his entire life had been politically and practically worthless.[42] It wasn't until the later Han dynasty (206 BCE–220 CE) that Confucius was officially recognized by Chinese rulers as China's first great teacher. Confucius, like Buddha, Socrates, and Jesus, never wrote anything down. But during the Han period, the *Analects*, a book which purported to be a record of his teachings, became required reading for every educated Chinese. Unfortunately, after the collapse of the Han Dynasty, Confucianism was gradually eclipsed by Buddhism, which became the region's dominant philosophy. It wasn't until the Song Dynasty, which began in 960 CE, and

41. See "Introduction," Confucius: The Essential Analects, translated by Edward Slingerland.
42. See "Introduction," *The Analects of Confucius: A Philosophical Translation*, translated by Roger T. Ames and Henry Rosemont Jr.

the later Ming Dynasty (1368–1644), that China saw a revival of Confucianism, and the rise of the Neo-Confucian philosophers."

"*Neo*-Confucian?"

"It's an umbrella term for the various schools of Confucianism which arose during the Song and Ming Dynasties. They were considered conscious reactions against the dominance of Buddhism and the 'anti-social' influence of Taoism. Their goal was to bring China back to the original teachings of Confucius. They also saw Mencius as the true follower of Confucius. Mencius, unlike Xunzi, believed that human nature is essentially good and people should be led by virtuous example rather than by authoritarian rule.[43] In Book 2 of the *Analects*, Confucius makes clear this teaching: When the ruler leads by virtuous example, the people will submit." Jessica smiled and then said, "I'm done now."

"I love history. I can't wait to hear the rest." Aapo stood up and extended his hand to Jessica who happily took it, and they were on their way.

After about ten minutes of relatively uneventful hiking (Jessica did have an "Oh look!" moment when she spotted a blue-ping-pong-paddle-tailed motmot bird in a cacao tree) they arrived at the mouth of the cave. As they were getting ready to put their inner tubes into the cool water, Aapo noted a tiger print the size of his open hand in the mud of the riverbank. Jessica tried not to freak out. She'd done enough of that already on this adventure. She tried to reason instead: "Is it fresh? I mean, this is mud. How can you tell whether it's a fresh print or an older one when it's in mud? There's really no way to tell, right?"

"Mud banks hold the shape of pugmarks well…. You're right, it becomes more difficult to determine the age of the print. It'd be easier were we to find some scat. That'd give us a good idea of how recent he's been around. It's definitely tiger though."

"Do they live in caves? Does this jaguar live in *this cave*?" It was clear that Jessica's freaking out got the better of her reasoning.

"Occasionally a tiger will wander into a cave while stalking a gibnut or agouti, but they don't live in caves. Tigers often sleep in trees, near water. Sometimes they'll bed down in a soft pile of leaves. They'd not likely live in a cave—certainly not this one. Did you know that tigers love the water? They catch fish and turtles."

As Aapo was speaking, he spotted a cracked turtle shell about two meters away. "There's what's left of his breakfast." He smiled.

Aapo walked over, picked up the shell, and studied it. "Tortuga Blanca—the river turtle. They're critically endangered, hunted for their meat, eggs, and shells. The tiger isn't helping them stick around in this world."

"Maybe so. Of course if only the jaguars hunted them, they wouldn't be endangered in the first place." Suddenly it struck her, "Hey, does this mean the jaguar was here just this morning?"

"Looks like it…. There's the turtle's foot over there." He pointed to a webbed foot about a meter away. "It looks fresh. No signs of decay. But don't worry, Jessica. As I told you, tigers don't generally attack people. Now, turn on your headlamp, we'll be entering into the underworld. We'll be entering Xi-bal-ba."

Jessica couldn't help but laugh.

As they plopped their inner tubes into the river, they startled a gibnut lapping up

43. See "Introduction," Confucius: The Analects, translated by Raymond Dawson and "Appendix 4," *Confucius: The Essential Analects*, translated by Edward Slingerland.

the water. It was dark with several horizontal lines of white blotches, heavy in appearance, with a pig-like snout. He dove into the river and disappeared.

"What was that? He looked so weird."

"Gibnut—Royal Rat."

"Why is it called a Royal Rat?"

"Queen Elizabeth was famously served one for dinner during one of her visits to this country. That's how it got its nickname."

"Will he drown?"

"Not at all. They're great swimmers. They love the water. They can even stay submerged for up to fifteen minutes. We frightened him. He'll reemerge once we've moved on."

As they began floating along, sinister limestone stalactites loomed from above, while stalagmites jutted up from the water.

"Maya used the caves to perform sacrificial rituals. They would carry flaming torches, burning incense, and ceramic pots holding various kinds of gifts as they led people to their deaths (usually by blunt force to the head) as offerings to their gods."

As Aapo was speaking, they floated past a giant stalagmite by the cave wall. It was some fifteen feet tall and resembled what Jessica could only describe as a serpent-bird.

"I call it Q'uq'umatz (Quetzal Serpent), after the Q'eqchi feathered serpent god of the *Popol Vuh*. He's one of the creation gods. Q'uq'umatz moves in the water and is associated with the underworld. Isn't it incredible that there'd be a stalagmite which so closely resembles Q'uq'umatz?"

"I'm not scared, if that's what you're trying to do." Jessica was trying desperately to convince herself.

"No, no. Not at all. But don't you find it remarkable? The water's not that deep right here. Get out of your inner tube…."

"But the water's cold."

"Get out of your inner tube and follow me over here, to this pool away from the current."

Jessica followed Aapo's directions and waded waist-deep, inner tube in tow, to a placid pool by the cave wall, turning fifty shades of … BLUE (this is not *that* kind of story) as she did so. Catfish and little translucent crayfish, who were not accustomed to such a disturbance, grumbled as they swam away. A one-foot wide (no kidding) whip spider scaled the slippery shiny wall. Thankfully, for Jessica's sake (and for the reader's sake, too), it was eleven feet above her, and she didn't think to look up.

"Look over in this corner," Aapo said. Carved jade in the shapes of various animals lay along the cave's ledge atop broken ceramic vessels, dinnerware, and pots (many in indigo blue). Jessica picked up a jaguar-shaped mask and studied it.

"How old is this stuff?"

"Twelve, thirteen hundred years probably, from the Classic period. Did you know that Maya would smash the ceramic pots during these ceremonies to release the energy or 'life force' within?"

"Life force. That sounds like qi. The animated force in all living things…."

After a time, they walked back to the current, plopped into their inner tubes, and were on their way. Soon they floated past an underground waterfall which screamed at them in a mouth-gaping way. It had announced itself some time earlier, but Jessica hadn't expected it would try to provoke her into a cussing fight. They rounded a bend which opened up to a chamber the size of a cathedral. The yellow sunlight filtered through openings from above.

Until now, Jessica had been thoroughly enjoying Aapo's favorite place.

Until now.

At the back of the cathedral stood a large limestone altar. Encircling it lay piles of human bones, sparkling and puffy in appearance. Hundreds of pieces of broken pottery surrounded them. One skull, slightly elongated which gave it an alien-look, stared Jessica right down to the rubber of her inner tube. And then came the colony of bats, whizzing by her, screeching like little flying mice, one brushing her shoulder. Jessica let out a scream which could have rattled the bones back to life.

"Get me out of here!"

"Don't worry, Jessica. The bats only feed on insects and fruit. We're not in a Dracula movie."

Aapo's calm only infuriated her more. "Get me out of here!"

"There's only one way out. The current only flows one way. We've only got another 100 meters or so. The exit is at the other end of this corridor." He pointed off to the right.

"I hate you for this!" Jessica cried through her screams. "Why did you do this to me? How could you possibly have thought I'd like this?"

Aapo couldn't get a word in. Finally, "I'm sorry" was all that he managed to say.

After a few moments of awkward silence, and as they exited the main cathedral leaving death behind, Aapo thought they needed a distraction: "Tell me about Confucianism and Taoism."

"WHAT?"

"Remember how we started this adventure? Go with the flow. You're safe, I promise. I wouldn't let anything hurt you…. I want to hear about Confucianism and Taoism."

Jessica looked at Aapo as if he were some kind of alien with seven eyes.

He smiled. "So what do you say? I know a bit about Confucius. Don't his sayings appear in all those little fortune cookies in Chinese restaurants across America?" He couldn't help but laugh.

Jessica cracked a smile through her tears. "Maybe so…."

"So what do you say?"

Jessica wiped the smear off her face. "OK."

Introduction to Confucianism

"As I mentioned, Confucius inherited a tradition of ancient Chinese religious views. The *Analects* is the single-most important work that comprises his main teachings. Confucianism's texts include the *Analects* in addition to the so-called *Five Classics* (*Record of Rites, Book of Odes, Book of History, I Ching,* and *Spring and Autumn Annals*). Tian ('Heaven') is central to Confucius' teachings. Tian 'calls' people to return to the Tao or Way. Confucius understood the Tao to be the ideal course of human conduct, which included li (proper ritual behavior) and *ren.* Ren is extraordinarily difficult to translate. It's commonly translated as 'humaneness,' 'humanity,' 'benevolence,' and 'goodness.' I think the best attempts at explaining ren try to capture the entire person: a person's cultivated cognitive, aesthetic, moral, and religious sensibilities as they are expressed in his ritualized roles and relationships. Ren also includes a person's bodily posture, comportment, and communication. Any definition that fails to capture all these various elements impoverishes ren.[44]

"So what are these ritualized roles and relationships?"

"Each person has overlapping roles in society. The cultivation of 'correctness' in human relationships is crucial to a harmonious, secure, and stable society, and to humans flourishing. These relationships are civil, familial, and filial. Confucius identified what he called the *Five Hierarchical Relationships*: ruler and minister (that is, state official), father and son, husband and wife, elder and younger (including siblings), and friends. Each relationship is guided by ren, and the way to ren is through li. We see this clearly when Confucius' beloved disciple Yan Hui asked him about ren and Confucius replied, 'Do not look at what is contrary to li, do not listen to what is contrary to li, do not speak what is contrary to li, and make no movement which is contrary to li.' Confucius says in Book 12 of the *Analects* that if someone returned to li, even for a single day, then all under Heaven would ascribe ren to him. Li encompasses the entirety of proper human conduct. Filial virtue, the proper respect paid to one's father, is called *xiao*. Filial virtue also includes the living's relationship to their ancestors. Confucius used the word *Junzi* to describe the gentleman of noble moral character, committed to cultivating ren, li, and de (virtue). Historically, the Junzi was 'son of a lord,' and referred to a Zhou member of the aristocracy. But Confucius said that *anyone* can be a Junzi. The Junzi became a kind of *moral* aristocrat, an exemplar of ren. In Book 4, Confucius explains that the Junzi never shuns ren, not even for the time it takes to finish a meal. In fact, ren is so important for the Junzi that he doesn't overly cherish his own life at the expense of ren. In Book 15, Confucius says that the Junzi will sometimes even sacrifice his own life to achieve ren. The Junzi cultivates mastery of one's heart-mind, called *xin*. There are four components of xin: compassion (which leads to benevolence), shame (which leads to li), respect (which leads to duty), and right and wrong (which leads to wisdom). You know, there was only *one person* whom Confucius seemed to suggest was a true Junzi. (He didn't even consider himself to be a Junzi.) This was his beloved disciple Yan Hui, who died tragically at an early age. Yan Hui was also homeless (for a time, anyway), living in an alleyway and surviving on a bowlful of rice and a ladleful of water a day—proof indeed that anyone (well, any male) can become a Junzi. And yet Yan Hui clearly never thought of himself as such. We get a sense of this in Book 9, where Yan Hui says that the more he looks up to the Tao, 'the higher it is; the more I penetrate it, the harder it becomes; I see it ahead of me, and suddenly it is behind…. But even though I long to pursue it, I have no way of doing so at all.' Of course he's expressing the extreme difficulty of following the Tao."

As Jessica finished speaking, they popped out of the other side of the cave and into the speckled sunshine.

Hiking back to the camp

"You made it out alive," Aapo teased.

"Barely…. I'll say this: your adventure definitely aged me." Jessica smiled. She looked around. Everything looked different, of course, since they had been spit out on the other side, but after about ten minutes' walk, they made their way back to the cave entrance.

"Are you sure we can find our way back to the camp?" Jessica dreaded the thought

44. "Introduction," *The Analects of Confucius: A Philosophical Translation*, translated by Roger T. Ames and Henry Rosemont Jr.

of any more surprises.

"I know this forest. Trust me." Aapo smiled warmly.

"We should've been like Hansel and Gretel and left a trail of breadcrumbs to mark the way." She chuckled.

"Like the fairytale, my dear, the birds would have long gobbled them up."

"True. Well then we should have tied string around tree limbs along our way. We could have put that black yarn the monkeys gave us to some good use." She smiled widely thinking about how magical that was.

Aapo felt a strange tinge of guilt, although it really wasn't warranted. He gave a nervous laugh. "So what time is it anyway?"

Jessica checked her watch. "2:15… Actually 2:12, but who cares about three little minutes?"

"I do. I care about them very much. I think about them night and day. They are so neglected."

She laughed.

"We'll have plenty of time to make a wonderful dinner AND there's still time for you to tell me about Taoism. Assuming we don't have any surprise encounters, like shaking hands with an elephant or something, we should be back in about twenty minutes."

"Did *you* ever shake hands with an elephant?"

"No, but I've always wanted to."

Introduction to Taoism

"The earliest Taoists were *Laozi* (Master Lao) and *Zhuangzi* (Master Zhuang). Laozi is the reputed author of the *Tao Te Ching*, the oldest existing book of Taoism."[45]

"I've read *The Tao of Pooh* and *The Te of Piglet*. I love Winnie the Pooh. 'People say nothing is impossible, but I do nothing every day!'" Aapo laughed.

"Remember when Pooh asks Christopher Robin 'How do you do nothing?' and he responds, 'It's when people call out at you, just as you're going out to do it, and you say 'Oh nothing,' and then you go and do that,'" Jessica joined in. "Anyway, the *Tao Te Ching* is actually multi-authored, but attributed to Laozi. Laozi was a contemporary of Confucius. Laozi met Confucius and even gives an account of what he had learned from him on the subject of li (rites). Laozi was critical of Confucius' emphasis on li, attacking it as 'social decorum.'[46] Both Laozi and his successor Zhuangzi (who lived during the Warring States period) were self-consciously non-Confucian in that they expressed markedly different understandings of the Tao, de, and ideal human conduct. They both believed that Confucians harmed society by imposing rules and artificial practices that interfered with people's natural inclinations. Taoists argue that a harmonious society is only possible after humanity has harmonized itself with Nature and the Tao. Taoists redefined Tao as the primordial entity that exists in an undifferentiated state prior to the coming into being of the 'myriad things' including Nature itself, and from which the yin yang forces emerge. This is similar to the original state of undifferentiated chaos found in the Ancient Chinese creation myth. The Tao, as the ground of all being, displaced Tian. Taoism also vehemently attacks Confucian-

45. Their discussion is based on Chen, *The Tao Te Ching*; Chapter 5, "East Asian Religions: Confucianism, Daoism, Shinto, Buddhism," in Esposito; and Chapter 6, "Chinese and Korean Traditions," in Oxtoby.

46. See "Date and Authorship of the *Tao Te Ching*," Chen, *The Tao Te Ching*.

ism for taking humans to be superior to other creatures. The *Analects* do not even mention nonhuman creatures. Well, I guess they do in the following way: in Book 2, a young disciple asks Confucius about xiao (filial piety). Confucius replies that in the present day (a time when almost no one was following the Tao) it means 'providing sustenance.' But, he says, even dogs and horses receive that. The *Tao Te Ching* demands that people stop lifting themselves above the rest of nature, which results in alienation from the natural world. We must reject our urge to transcend nature. We must renounce our so-called right to dominate nature. Nature is humanity's true home and teacher. We really see this is in Taoist art. If a human subject is included in a particular work, such as a painting, he does not figure prominently. That subject is merely a small part of a larger, more magnificent nature scene. Nature is the most direct and faithful revelation of the Tao. Our knowledge of the Tao comes through our observation of nature—that is, of nature uncorrupted and undistorted by human action which tends to run counter to the Tao."[47]

"So Taoists redefine de too. It's hard to keep track of all these terms in Eastern religions. It's like learning a foreign language." Aapo chuckled.

"You're right—and try to spell them all! In Taoism, 'de' no longer means (Confucian) 'virtue.' De is the concrete expression or manifestation of the Tao in all things, pervading every aspect of existence. De is also the power attained when one harmonizes oneself with the Tao. The person in harmony with the Tao no longer perceives Nature as threatening, as something to be feared. That person possesses the power of the Tao, and becomes immune to Nature's most frightening 'dangers.' This power is wisdom. The person who possesses this wisdom is the sage. Taoists teach that the Tao cannot be adequately described in words. The opening lines of the *Tao Te Ching* state: 'Tao that can be spoken of, is not the Everlasting Tao. Name that can be named, is not the Everlasting name.' Even though it cannot be adequately captured in words, the Tao is compared to a mysterious female, water, an infant, and an uncarved block. Confucianism is grounded in rules, order, rituals, and correctness in our various roles and relationships. Taoism, on the other hand, maintains that the Tao can only maintain its pristine form when humans leave it alone. Leave the Tao alone to be Tao. This teaching is best exemplified by *wu-wei*, actionless action or the path of non-interference—harmonizing with the Tao. 'Do nothing, and nothing will be left undone.' Nature is run perfectly by the Tao, and so people are not needed to improve it. The ideal Taoist society, the only truly harmonious society, is a simple, primitive state, governed by Nature and the Tao."

"Go with the flow...." Aapo smiled.

"Going with the flow is the Taoist sage 'doing nothing.' This is the only way to peace, justice, and happiness: knowing that all creatures (human and nonhuman) have the same origin, live in the same environment, and share the same destiny. Although the *Tao Te Ching* is the earliest Taoist text, I really love the stories of the *Zhuangzi*. Zhuangzi was such an interesting figure. He was a contemporary of the Confucian sage Mencius (Mengzi). Zhuangzi was known for the way he dressed: his clothes shoddy and patched, his shoes held together by string. He really exemplified the person free from worldly attachments and living according to the Tao. Like Laozi, Zhuangzi taught that the Tao that can be known and spoken of is not the Tao. He also taught the all-pervasive, omnipresent Tao. In Chapter 22, when Zhuangzi was asked 'Where is the Tao that you speak of?' he replies, 'There is nowhere it is not.' Indeed,

47. See "The *Tao Te Ching* as a Religious Treatise," Chen, *The Tao Te Ching*.

when pressed to explain what he meant, Zhuangzi responds: in ants, crickets, grasses, weeds and, lower still, in tiles and shards—even in (these are his words) piss and shit."[48]

"He sounds like a colorful guy." Aapo chuckled. "What are some of your favorite stories of the *Zhuangzi*?"

"They include the Butterfly Dream, Peng and Dove, and Cook Cuts Up Ox. Several of Zhuangzi's stories (especially Peng and Dove found in the first chapter) demonstrate the relativity of perspective in tension with the vastness of the Tao, and in particular the perspective of the Small as contrasted with the Vast. The perspective, and thus understanding, of the Small is confined and defined by its limitations. While the Vast loses sight of the distinctions noticed by the Small, the Vast still encompasses the Small in virtue of being Vast. The Peng is a magnificent creature. The *Zhuangzi* states that 'When Peng journeys to the Southern Oblivion, the waters ripple for three thousand li' (a Chinese unit of distance equal to half a kilometer, and not to be confused with Confucian li—ritual). Spiraling aloft, he ascends ninety thousand li and continues his journey without rest for half a year.' When Peng looks down, he sees only the blue of the sky and nothing more. That's how vast his perspective. The dove and the cicada laugh at Peng. But as Zhuangzi notes, 'What do these little creatures know? A small consciousness cannot keep up with a vast consciousness…. The morning mushroom knows nothing of the noontide; the winter cicada knows nothing of spring and autumn.'"

"What a great story." Aapo touched Jessica's shoulder affectionately and smiled.

They finally made it back to the camp—not three, but almost six hours later. Luckily, they still had enough time to make a big pot of rice and beans, this time sweetened with coconut water, and a hearty stack of corn tortillas. Jessica even thought to make a pot of stewed fruit, spiced with cloves, cinnamon, and nutmeg—and of course rum!

An hour before sunrise, April 15, at the camp

The culmination of King K'uk Mo's elaborate plan involving Yatzil and her grandfather, Sachihiro, required four six-foot long, fifty-pound Columbian mammoth tusks, soft clay, crustacean shells (shrimp and lobster), herring sperm DNA (don't ask how the ancient one acquired this—he'll never tell), jet oil (which involved Maya/Yatzil and the Philip S.W. Goldson airport), and matches. As well: one eight-foot long, thirty-pound boa constrictor, four jaguars in procession (and a fifth—none other than Sachihiro-jaguar—to carry the king), plus two baboons from King K'uk Mo's council. One can hardly imagine how such disparate things were needed to pull off such a magnificent feat. This requires a bit of explaining.

It's a little known fact that while international trade in elephant ivory has been banned since 1990, it's *legal* to sell mammoth ivory. Indeed, smugglers often sell elephant ivory claiming that it's mammoth ivory. All the more so that they look the same to the untrained eye (to the trained eye, mammoth tusks are more curved than elephant tusks). Most mammoth ivory comes from the woolly mammoths whose remains stayed buried under layers of ice in Siberia and elsewhere. That is, until recently, when warming temperatures melted the ice and uncovered their ivory tusks. But King K'uk Mo did not have Siberian woolly mammoth tusks. His were from the *Columbian* mammoth which, despite its name, actually lived all up and down North

48. All textual references and commentary are from *Zhuangzi: The Essential Writings with Selections from Traditional Commentaries*, translated by Brook Ziporyn.

and Central America—from the northern US to Costa Rica. King K'uk Mo was gifted these tusks by another ancient monkey king, Xelajú, some 74 kilometers away in Tikal Guatemala.

But what use are Columbian mammoth tusks and how did they figure so centrally into the ancient one's plans?

King K'uk Mo came up with the idea after he got word that Uhuru Kenyatta, the president of Kenya, was set in only two weeks' time to burn 105 tons of elephant ivory in order to send a strong anti-poaching message to the world. In Kenyatta's words, "Ivory is worthless, unless it's on our elephants." King K'uk Mo knew that the tusks would take an incredibly long time to burn down to ashes—indeed, so long that somebody would most certainly spot the massive billow of black smoke long before the fire threatened any damage.

The four jaguars, each having the strength enough to haul a large kill up a tree, carried the tusks to the center of the camp a safe distance away from the tents where everyone was sleeping. But just to ensure that the camp (as well the rest of the rainforest) would be out of danger, King K'uk Mo concocted a natural fire retardant composed of soft clay, crustacean shells, and herring sperm DNA. (Don't believe me? Just Google it.) Once the procession arrived at the camp, the ancient one hopped off Sachihiro-jaguar and rubbed a thick layer of the retardant carefully along the belly of the boa constrictor, which made her laugh. The mongrels never made a sound, for they too were apprised of the scheme.

Then the two baboons from King K'uk Mo's council carefully arranged the four tusks in the manner of an eight-pointed cross—a Maya symbol representing the sacred ceiba tree. The monkeys were able to lift them with ease because (as they love to boast) they are four times stronger than human creatures. After the tusks had been arranged, King K'uk Mo stood over them, and with hands reaching skyward offered a prayer to the heavens. Then the boa constrictor (whose name was Aretha, after her favorite singer) slithered around the cross to set the protective barrier. Next came the dousing of jet fuel, as mammoth tusks won't burn unless they are subjected to incredibly high temperatures. Not a single creature in the rainforest wanted to start the fire, leaving it to Yatzil. After King K'uk Mo's procession had cleared the camp, Yatzil lit a match, dropped it, transformed into Maya, and flew away.

NINE

Jessica had smelled it first: a heavy acrid odor, not but five minutes after the fire had started. She ran out of her tent, saw the big billow of black smoke, and screamed to wake up the guys. At once they all rushed out of their tents, some stumbling over themselves as they tried to pull up their breeches. Fearing that someone would most certainly notice the smoke once day broke and then they'd be found out (given the incriminating evidence about the camp), they ran like blazes toward the direction of their hidden vehicles, leaving only Jessica and Aapo to put out the fire. Aapo had already run to the supply tent to grab the fire extinguisher. It wasn't long before the flames were out, but the smoke kept billowing.

As Aapo stood over the smoke trying to determine the source of the fire, Jessica handed him a towel to cover his nose and mouth. She grabbed another for herself. Suddenly Aapo's eyes went wide in disbelief.

"What on earth? Looks like *elephant tusks!*"

Jessica approached. "*Impossible!*"

"Just look!" He shook his head. "This makes no sense. The closest thing we've ever had to an elephant around here would be the Columbian mammoth, but that was during the *Ice Age*! Who would've done this? And for what possible reason? Where'd they come from?"

Just then, Jessica remembered King K'uk Mo's words in the telling of his story—the one about the baboon, the crocodile, and the jaguar that he told her on her first full day at the camp: *The story involves a baboon, a crocodile and a jaguar, though the characters don't really matter in the telling of the story. Instead of a jaguar, it could have been an ocelot—or even a WOOLLY MAMMOTH!*

Jessica smiled at her epiphany.

"This is part of a plan—perhaps a divine plan." She squeezed Aapo's arm affectionately. "King K'uk Mo told me a story…." She wondered just how much she should tell him (as if he'd believe it anyway). She finally just said, "In any case, we needn't fear."

Aapo looked at Jessica as if she spoke in some garbled tongue. "Who's King K'uk Mo?"

"The ancient king of this forest." But Jessica's explanation only further confounded him.

"Huh?"

She smiled at his confusion. "Trust me…."

Jessica had never fully convinced herself that her encounter with King K'uk Mo had actually happened. Then again, so many weird things had transpired since she arrived. But *burning mammoth tusks*? Without doubt she would see the ancient one again. She looked up and away from the smoke and saw the colors of sunrise painted across the tree tops.

"Someone will be coming soon. Someone will notice the smoke (how can they not?) and Mr. Chan's operation will be permanently shut down. You'll see—Want some coffee? I'll go make some coffee," Jessica said.

For his part, Aapo couldn't figure out how Jessica—the woman who freaked out over bugs and bats and the littlest things—could be so *composed*. He shook his head. *I don't know ANYTHING about women.* But the fire was out, the smoke would eventually dissipate, and she was right: someone would notice, probably as far away as

Belmopan. And so he said, "Sure, I'd love some coffee."

To see the two of them sitting beside a smoldering pile of mammoth tusks and behaving so untroubled, as if this were just another typical morning at the camp, was nothing short of ... (no word will do, really).

The villagers were the first to see—and smell—the smoke, and they quickly rushed to tell Sachihiro. The village leader, knowing full well what would transpire, assured them that everything was under control, and in any case, what could they do? No need to worry, he told them, Belmopan emergency personnel were on their way as he spoke.

And he was right. After about an hour, a helicopter flew overhead, as Jessica and Aapo enjoyed their morning coffee. Well, perhaps "enjoyed" is too strong a word, since even Jessica had felt a tinge of unease, thinking she just might be wrong. The chopper pilot looked down at Jessica and Aapo, who waved from below. He radioed authorities that the fire was out, but something needed to be done to contain the smoke. Emergency vehicles were soon underway. But nobody knew what they were driving to, what they would discover, when they arrived. A couple officers from the LAPD assigned to the missing macaw case accompanied them, after hearing someone say that the smoke was in the direction of Mr. Chan's camp.

Once the copter had disappeared out of sight, Jessica said, "Let me tell you about Shinto."

"Now?" Aapo was genuinely baffled. He looked over at the smoldering mammoth tusks, and then at Jessica who was so uncharacteristically self-possessed.

"Sure, why not? What else can we do while we wait?"

"OK...." After all, Jessica was right. What else *could* they do?

And so she began....

Introduction to Shinto

"Shinto is the oldest religion in Japan. The word 'Shinto' comes from the Japanese pronunciation of the Chinese word 'shen'...."[49]

"I remember that word. Shen are benevolent spirits that protect and benefit the living—or benevolent gods." Aapo grinned. Sure he could play along, if Jessica insisted that they treat this morning like any other.

"Right. Here 'shen' refers to benevolent gods. 'To' or 'do' is the Japanese way of pronouncing the Chinese word 'Tao' or 'Way.' So 'Shinto' means 'The Way of the gods.'"

"Cool." Aapo poured himself another cup of coffee and then pointed at her cup. "Would you like some more?"

"Sure." Jessica gave a pleasant smile. "The term 'Shinto' did not appear until the Japanese began to use it to distinguish their religion from Buddhism, which was first introduced to the region in 538 CE. It was known as 'Butsudō,' by the way, meaning 'The Way of Buddha.'"

"Isn't Shinto the religion of the *kami*?" Although Aapo engaged Jessica, he was ever mindful of the noxious smoldering tusks, making sure he didn't spot a glowing ember that threatened to rekindle the blaze.

"Wow, you continue to impress," Jessica said a little too excitedly. "Yes, it is. In

49. Their discussion is based on Chapter 5, "East Asian Religions: Confucianism, Daoism, Shinto, Buddhism," in Esposito, and Chapter 7, "Shinto," in Brodd. See also Chapter 7, "Japanese Traditions," in Oxtoby.

fact, Shinto is known more colloquially as 'Kami-no-michi' or 'The Way of the Kami.' So what do you know about the kami?"

"Kami are the gods and the spirits of the whole of nature—the birds, beasts, forests, seas, and the mountains. They are also the spirits of the ancestors. Kami is most evident in nature. Since the whole of nature is regarded as kami, nature is considered an expression of divine presence."

"Right." Jessica smiled widely. "As scholars have pointed out, 'Kami' actually refers to anything that is out of the ordinary, awe-inspiring, mysterious, powerful, and beyond our control or comprehension. Of course this includes everything you just mentioned. Most kami are the source of blessing and protection, and so people worship them hoping to receive divine favors or gifts, or to offer thanksgiving. Other kami are malevolent and ill-tempered, and people worship them to avert misfortune or disaster."

"Who was the founder of Shinto? So far you've told me about Siddhartha Gautama, Confucius, Laozi and Zhuangzi. Oh, and Mahavira of Jainism and Guru Nanak of Sikhism. Does Shinto have a founder, or is it more like Hinduism?"

"No, it doesn't. At least no known founder. Nor does it have any official sacred texts like the sutras or the Vedas. The religion is based on highly revered texts from the eighth and ninth centuries, especially the *Kojiki*, or 'Records of Ancient Matters,' which consists of a collection of myths. One of the most important is the creation myth."

"How does this one go?"

"It begins with several generations of invisible deities, all of whom have titles ending with the word 'kami'...." She chuckled.

"Not a surprise...." He laughed along.

"They all have titles ending with the word 'kami,'" she repeated, "until there appears the primordial pair: *Izanagi* and his wife, *Izanami*. The divine couple brings the world out of its original chaos. Standing on a heavenly floating bridge, they lower a jeweled spear and stir the ocean below. When they lift up the spear, the brine dripping down from its tip form the many islands of Japan. The *Kojiki* creation story reflects the Japanese belief that their island nation was created by kami as a paradise on Earth."

"Japan as a divine creation. I love the imagery."

"There's a beautiful artistic depiction of this event at the Boston Museum of Fine Arts: a hanging scroll of ink and color on silk, by the artist Kobayashi Eitaku, from the mid-1880s. Anyway, the divine couple descends from the heavens and takes up residence on the islands, and through their sexual union they produce all the various natural deities, plants, animals, and people. Izanami is burned to death while giving birth to her last child, the fire god, Kagutsuchi."

"I guess that would do it." Aapo smirked. "What happens next?"

"Izanagi follows his wife to Yomi—the underworld. There he sees her decomposing body. Horrified and repulsed, he flees to the world of the living and washes off in a stream. As he washes out his eyes, the sun goddess Amaterasu and the lunar god Tsukuyomi are born. As he washes off his nose, the powerful and ill-tempered storm god, Susa-no-o, is born. So the procreative power of the primordial pair...."

"Say that ten times fast...." Aapo gave a goofy face.

Jessica laughed. "As I was saying, the procreative power of the primordial pair continues after Izanami's death, when Izanagi gives birth to more deities through ritual washing."

"As you seem to suggest, this story also emphasizes the importance of ritual purification," Aapo began. "Izanagi followed his wife to the underworld because of his profound love for her. But even so passionate a love that would send a man to the land of the dead was overpowered by the horrific sight of his wife's decomposing body—so much so that he abandoned her and hurries back to the world of the living where he washes himself clean."

"I really like what you said." Jessica smiled. "This story teaches that death, disease, and other pollutants make a person who comes in contact with them spiritually unclean. Such people must be ritually purified before they can approach the kami. Back to the sun goddess, Amaterasu—she is also the ancestress of the Japanese royal family. Indeed, up through the tenth century, it was not uncommon for the imperial ruler to be a woman. The emperor was considered to be a descendent of Amaterasu, and thereby deserving of veneration and worship. This sentiment was expressed by both nationalists and royalists from the fourteenth century onward, but it found its most extravagant expression during the Shinto revivalist movement of the eighteenth and nineteenth centuries. It wasn't until Japan's defeat in 1945 at the end of World War II that the cult of the emperor was officially abolished."

"I wonder: Does the red disc against the white background of Japan's national flag represent the sun goddess Amaterasu? I bet it does, especially since the emperor was said to be her descendent."

"I hadn't really thought of that—without doubt." Jessica smiled.

"Does Shinto have any teachings about how to live well, such as the importance of compassion and respect that we see in Hinduism and Buddhism? Any notion of good and evil, or sin? Anything like that?"

"Well, Shinto has nothing resembling God-given moral instruction or laws, and there's certainly no cosmic battle between good and evil forces. Instead of sin, what's most offensive to the gods is pollution and defilement, and of course there is great emphasis on fertility, as suggested in the story of Izanagi and Izanami. These values are reflected in Shinto purification and fertility rituals. Such rituals prepare the practitioner to directly experience the presence of the divine kami."

As Jessica was speaking, Aapo felt an intense sense of urgency. At first he mistook the sensation for too much caffeine, and especially on an empty stomach (his belly was, after all, grumbling—should he pick a couple of sapodilla, dangling from that tree?). But then it struck him that soon Belmopan emergency responders would arrive (the sight of the helicopter all but assured that), and this might be the last day he would ever spend with Jessica—and so the last opportunity he had to tell her how he truly felt. He looked at her tenderly and began, "Jessica, I…"

But Jessica cut him off: "Aapo, I'm not who you—" Just as she was about to finish her sentence with the words "think I am," Mr. Chan appeared, seemingly out of nowhere.

"Mr. Chan," Jessica said, more than a bit startled. Aapo was surprised to see him, too.

"You're back early," Aapo said and smiled.

Mr. Chan approached. He looked at them with flat, cold eyes. "What's going on here? Where is everyone? Where're our vehicles? Who started this fire?" His voice grew loud with rage.

"Everything's under control," Aapo said, trying to reassure himself more than anything.

"Is that right?" Mr. Chan said with a sneer, and then to Jessica he demanded,

"You're coming with me."

Jessica looked at Mr. Chan and then at Aapo. Aapo had seen that terror on her face before: when they came upon the piles of human bones in the cave—never mind the bats that brushed up against her.

"Where are you going?" Aapo asked anxiously.

Mr. Chan did not answer. Instead, he pulled out his gun and pointed it at Jessica. "Jessica is not who you think she is," he said through gritted teeth. He grabbed her arm and started leading her away.

Jessica went pale. She looked at Aapo, whose face was strained.

All at once, Aapo lunged at Mr. Chan. In the ensuing scuffle, Chan whacked Aapo across the face with his gun, shattering his cheekbone and sending him flying to the ground. Aapo struggled to get up, struggled with everything within him, but he had reinjured his foot in the fall, and so lay there helplessly. "Jessica!" he cried out in utter desperation. "Please don't hurt her!" he begged in a choked voice.

As Mr. Chan led Jessica away at gunpoint, she spotted King K'uk Mo sitting on a low branch of the ceiba tree which stood by Chan's tent. The ancient one smiled at her, put his hands together, and gave a short bow.

And then he ROARED.

At once, twelve howler monkeys jumped down from the trees and moved toward them.

Mr. Chan, knowing that he didn't stand a chance against them, dropped his gun and ran deep into the forest. The baboons chased after him, barking and grunting along the way. Jessica rushed over to Aapo and sat by his side. She leaned in and kissed him ever so tenderly on the bloom of his cheek.

Meantime, Chan kept on running. The howler monkeys could have overtaken him, could have ripped him into twelve equal pieces. Instead, they chased Chan right to one of his own traps. As Chan was scooped up, his straw fedora fell to the forest floor. The twelve monkeys looked up at Chan from below. There he was, tangled up in netting and dangling precariously from a heavy limb.

A tiger slowly walked along the bough from which Mr. Chan dangled, licking her chops. Chan froze in terror as she crouched over him and began pawing at her breakfast:

Edin Chan Tartare.

TEN

As Jessica and Aapo huddled together a safe distance away from the most mal-odorously smoldering mammoth tusks, Belmopan's emergency response team ar-rived: two police cars, a small fire truck, and an ambulance. One can only imagine how they crowded into such a small place as the camp. Everyone left their vehicles at once and approached. What followed was a dizzying exchange of words:

"Jessica Kraut?"

"That's her."

"He needs a hospital."

"Are you all right, Miss Kraut?"

"You have the wrong person. She's Jessica *Kraus*."

"That's the guy who was spotted with Edin Chan."

"Ask her if she's being held against her will."

"His name is Aapo Abram."

"Are you OK, Miss Kraut?"

"*I'm* OK, but *he* needs a hospital. Please get him to the hospital!"

"Be sure the flames are out and let's do something about that godawful smoke."

"I don't need a hospital. I'm OK, really."

"What's going on here?"

"Jessica Kraut, where's the macaw?"

"What?"

"OK, the smoke should be gone in no time. It's all under control."

"Turn over the macaw or face felony charges."

"Arrest her."

By now, the paramedics were attending to Aapo. He refused to get into the ambu-lance, but promised that he would go to the hospital on his own, once he was assured that Jessica would be all right. Meantime, the Belmopan police officers, accompanied by one of the officers from the LAPD, began scouring the camp, turning up piece after piece of incriminating evidence. It was clear that the Belmopan police could no longer protect Chan.

"Did you find the bird?"

"No, but we found these …"

"So no bird?"

Getting no response, the other LAPD officer said, "Jessica Kraut, you are under arrest for the theft of a scarlet macaw from the Los Angeles Zoo." He cuffed Jessica's hands behind her back.

"What's going on?" Jessica asked. "I was never at the Los Angeles Zoo. Not since I was a girl, anyway."

"Jessica wouldn't do that. That's not the Jessica I know. This must be a mistake," Aapo protested. "Let her go."

"You'd best keep quiet, Mr. Abram. You've got troubles of your own…. Where's Chan?"

As the other LAPD officer began escorting Jessica to the police car, Maya flew down and landed on the ground before them. As she did, she transformed into a beautiful dark haired woman, the same woman Jessica had seen bathing at the stream just days before.

"Nahual!" the Belmopan police cried out in fear. The officers from the LAPD had already run to the police car, locking themselves safely inside.

"Nahual!" they repeated.

Jessica stood there open-mouthed.

Aapo also said nothing.

Yatzil looked at Jessica and smiled sweetly. She extended her hand in greeting. "Jessica, my name is Yatzil, though you know me as the feathered one whom you call 'Maya.'"

"I don't understand." Jessica shook her head. "What's going on?"

Yatzil addressed the Belmopan police, "I'm the scarlet macaw whom you're looking for."

"What's going on?" asked the officers.

"Jessica committed no crime. Release her," Yatzil insisted.

One of the officers removed the cuffs. Jessica went over to Aapo.

"Arrest him," the other officer said, pointing at Aapo.

"What for?" Aapo asked.

"You work for Edin Chan?"

"I did."

"Where is he?"

"He ran off," Jessica jumped in. "Aapo's done nothing wrong. He's been nothing but gentle and loving. Go chase after Chan."

"She's right," Yatzil began. "Aapo is innocent. It's Mr. Chan you want, though I dare say, I fear *somebody* has already gotten to him…."

"What's going on here?" the other officer said with a wrinkled nose.

"You'll find the animals about two kilometers that way. You'll soon meet up with a road," Aapo explained. "Follow that."

"So is there a crime here?" The other officer wrinkled his nose again.

"There's no crime here," Yatzil assured them. Once they were convinced, Yatzil watched them drive away, and then she looked at Aapo. "You'd best get to a hospital." She gave a gentle smile.

"Thank you," Jessica said to Yatzil as she clutched Aapo's hand.

"You're welcome…. It's about time I get back to the village and attend to my grandfather." Yatzil's eyes twinkled as she transformed into Maya and then flew off.

After some silence, Aapo looked at Jessica and asked, "So what're you going to do now?"

Jessica shook her head. "I don't know. I've got nothing to go back to…. What about you?"

"I've saved up some money. I was thinking I'd go to Belmopan, maybe buy a small farm. Find Chicken Eyes…. I guess he's the only family I've got."

"That sounds like a wonderful plan. You'll be so happy there."

"Why don't you come with me, Jessica? You said you've got nothing to go back to. I can't offer you a lot, but I can give you my heart."

Jessica felt a wild happiness she had never known before.

NOW she could write that love story.

One year later, April 15, 2017, a little farm three kilometers outside of Belmopan

The day couldn't have been more glorious. They had gathered in an open field— *their* field—surrounded by mango, coconut, and cashew trees. Sachihiro had offici- ated. Presently, they all sat on the front porch of their freshly painted yellow wooden house: Sachihiro, of course, Yatzil and King K'uk Mo, Nathaniel "Chicken Eyes" Jackson III and his new girlfriend, Mina.

Just then the door opened. Jessica's mother stepped out carrying a three-layer, white frosted cake adorned with freshly picked lavender-colored hibiscus—Jessica's favorite. Jessica's father followed with a bottle of champagne.

The happy couple would soon be on their way. Nathaniel had already put their suitcase in the car. He opened the passenger door. "You lovebirds ready?"

Jessica looked at her mother somewhat anxiously. "You'll take care of the chickens and cows?"

Jessica's mother smiled reassuringly. "We'll take care of the chickens and cows."

"Don't worry about us," Jessica's father piped in. "Nathaniel will help us finish the remodel of our 'mother in law' house while you're gone." He squeezed his wife affectionately and smiled. "Now get out of here...."

"I love you, Daddy."

"Back at ya, kiddo."

ELEVEN

For those of you who like to peek at your presents before your birthday: you're the same people who read the last pages of novels before reading the rest of the story.

DON'T.

Go back to the beginning, and I'll see you make it back here.

If you're one of those who delights in magic, our story ends with Chapter 10. But for the rest of you who are moved by the power of love which transcends all possible worlds, read on, for there is more to reveal.

Alternative Ending 1

Jessica was jolted awake as the wheels touched the ground. The captain just announced that they had arrived in LA, where the weather was a comfortable 72 degrees. Jessica grabbed her carry-on from the overhead compartment and made her way off the plane. She decided to get a coffee before heading to ground transportation just outside the baggage claim. What was she doing here anyway? Did she really want to know the truth? All men cheat. Isn't that what Auntie Jack said? Why should Finn be any different?

She walked into the Coffee Bean and Tea Leaf and stood in line. A fat black man with sad brown eyes accidentally bumped into her. Jessica's heart leapfrogged over her right lung. She smiled broadly. "It's you…."

"Have we met?" the man asked.

"Oh, sorry. No, I don't think so. You remind me of somebody though."

"Can I buy you a coffee? That's the least I can do for smacking into you. Does your flight leave soon?"

"I just landed from Charlotte. How about you?"

"Me too. Belize City. So what would you like?"

"Latte. Decaf. I've already liquored up on caffeine this morning."

The man chuckled. "So what brings you to LA?" he asked as they sat down at a little table.

"A … *friend*. He's not really expecting me. Not any time soon, anyway." Just then, Jessica noticed the necklace the man was wearing: a crescent moon made of purple jade hanging from a leather chain.

"Your pendant…." She smiled sweetly.

"You like it? I got it from some ladies in a Q'eqchi village. They sell them at an open air market." He grasped the pendant in his hand as he spoke.

"It's beautiful."

The man removed the necklace and extended it to her. "Here. Why don't you have it? I've got plenty more. I make a point of buying them every time I go back. It helps support their families."

"Are you sure?"

"Of course. Please take it."

"Thank you." Jessica blushed. "Well I really should be going. Thank you for the coffee." But then she wondered: Why the rush?

"Do you have a pen?" the man asked as Jessica stood up. She fumbled through her backpack and extended one to him. He wrote down his name and phone number.

"If you find time while you're here in LA, I'd love to meet up again."

Jessica looked down at the paper and smiled. "My name's Jessica."

"I hope to see you again, dear Jessica."

Alternative Ending 2

Jessica was jolted awake as the wheels touched the ground. The captain announced that they had just arrived in LA, where the weather was a comfortable 72 degrees. Jessica grabbed her carry-on from the overhead compartment and made her way off the plane. She decided to get a coffee before heading to ground transportation just outside the baggage claim. What was she doing here anyway? Did she really want to know the truth? All men cheat. Isn't that what Auntie Jack said? Why should Finn be any different?

Jessica walked into the Coffee Bean and Tea Leaf and got a decaf latte (*I've already liquored up on caffeine this morning*) and a one-touch milk frother with automatic shut off (only $40). *How did I ever live without one?* She put the frother in her backpack, forgetting to zip the pack back up, and made her way to the baggage claim.

When Jessica arrived, she sipped at her latte and pulled out her phone to check the time: 2:54 pm.

Just then, a scarlet macaw flew through an open door at LAX, landing smack dab in the middle of Jessica's opened backpack....

DISCUSSION AND REVIEW QUESTIONS

Chapter 1

1. Explain the Maya creation story, the Popol Vuh.

Chapter 2

1. Discuss the significance in Hinduism of the Purusha creation myth "The Hymn of Man."

2. Discuss the effects of British colonialism on the Indian subcontinent and British Honduras.

3. Discuss the similarities and differences between Krishna and Jesus.

Chapter 3

1. Compare Western and Indigenous approaches to nature and the natural world.

2. Recount the Hindu epic *Ramayana* and the significance of the relationship between Rama and the monkey god Hanuman.

3. What are the philosophical lessons about Atman (the Self) found in the Katha and Brihadaranyaka Upanishads?

Chapter 4

1. Discuss the evolution of religions leading up to the Axial Age.

2. What is the significance of religions during the Axial Age?

3. Explain what is meant by Earth losing its reality during the Axial Age and cite specific examples which demonstrate this phenomenon.

4. Discuss the core teachings of the Advaita Vedanta school of Hinduism. Explain how it is monistic.

5. What makes Hinduism one of the most diverse and pluralistic religions in the world?

6. Explain how a Hindu is liberated from samsara. Be sure to discuss the preferable and pleasurable paths.

7. Explain the importance of karma yoga, introduced in the *Bhagavad Gita*.

8.   Explain how Atman informs Hindu ethics. How do dharma and caste relate to Hindu ethics?

9.   Discuss the differences between Eastern/Indigenous and Western religions in their approach to the human and natural worlds.

Chapter 5

1.   Do Hindus believe in freewill? Provide examples to support your answer.

2.   Explain the true nature of reality for Hindus and for Buddhists.

3.   Discuss Buddha's core teachings, including the Four Noble Truths and Eight-fold Path.

4.   Discuss the similarities between Buddha's and eighteenth-century philosopher David Hume's conceptions of the self.

5.   Explain the differences between Mahayana Buddhism's and Hinduism's conceptions of women, especially with regard to liberation from samsara.

6.   How is Buddhism pluralistic?

Chapter 6

1.   Explain the main teachings of *The Lotus Sutra*, including skillful means, the bodhisattva way, and the long-lived/eternal Buddha.

2.   Must a Buddha be male-bodied? Cite specific examples in your answer.

Chapter 7

1.   Explain the importance of ahimsa in Jainist thought, including how it relates to the Jainist conception of reality and liberation from samsara.

2.   Discuss the similarities and differences among samadhi, prajna, and kevala.

3.   In what ways is Sikhism progressive?

Chapter 8

1.   What are some of the core concepts and teachings of ancient Chinese religion which predated and informed Confucianism and Taoism?

2.   Discuss the importance of the ruler, the Junzi, ren, and li in maintaining a harmonious and stable Confucian society.

3.   Discuss the differences between Confucianism and Taoism in their understanding of Tao, de, and the ideal course of human conduct.

4. Discuss Taoism's criticisms of Confucianism.

Chapter 9

1. Discuss the importance in Shinto of the kami.
2. Does Shinto have an ethic? What behaviors most concern the gods?

GLOSSARY

Adi Granth: The most sacred Sikh text; invested with supreme authority as Guru Granth Sahib after the death of Guru Gobind Sahib.

Advaita Vedanta: A prominent, monistic school of Hindu philosophy and religious practice. This tradition holds that the soul (Atman or Self) is identical to the one Divine Reality, Brahman.

Ahimsa: The avoidance of violence toward all life; the basic principle of Jainism, Hinduism, and Buddhism.

Ajiva: The nonliving component of the Jain universe which includes space, time, motion, rest, and all forms of matter.

Analects: A collection of sayings attributed to Confucius.

Anatman: Meaning "No-Self" or "no soul," the doctrine denying the reality of an independent, permanent, changeless, eternal soul underlying personal existence.

Arhat: In Buddhism, one who has attained enlightenment; an advanced disciple.

Asura: In Buddhism and Hinduism, the so-called angry gods, considered enemies of the devas, the benevolent gods.

Atman: In Hinduism, the eternal soul or Self that resides in the heart and transmigrates after death until released from samsara through moksha.

Avatar: An incarnation of a god (in Hinduism, this is usually Vishnu) that descends to Earth to defeat demons and overcome evil.

Bhagavad Gita: Hindu scripture inserted into the great epic, the *Mahabharata*, extolling the divinity of Krishna.

Bhagavata Purana: One of the major *Puranas* that focuses on Vishnu and his incarnations, in particular Krishna.

Bhakta: A devotee of a Hindu god.

Bhakti: Devotion to a Hindu god as a means to attain salvation and reside in the heaven of the chosen deity.

Bindi: A decorative Hindu forehead marking.

Bodhisattva: A Buddha-to-be; in the Mahayana tradition all individuals should aspire to be Buddhas.

Brahma: In Hinduism, the lesser creator god, born of Vishnu, who begins a new cycle of creation.

Brahman: In monistic Hinduism, the one Divine Reality that Hindus understand in either its impersonal form, Nirguna Brahman, or its personal form, Saguna Brahman.

Brahmin: A member of the priestly class of the Hindu varna or caste system.

Chandala: The lowest Hindu varna or caste, often called "outcastes," and traditionally considered to be "untouchable" since they engage in polluting jobs such as handling corpses.

Confucius: Also known as Master K'ung, founder of Confucianism.

Dalit: A word that means "oppressed" and refers to the lowest Hindu caste, the Chandala or "outcastes."

De (Confucianism): The charismatic power of the virtuous ruler or the man of virtue.

De (Daoism): The concrete manifestation or expression of the Tao in all things.

Dependent Origination: In Buddhism, twelve links which explain how individuals are bound to future rebirth in samsara until they eliminate desire and ignorance.

Deva: The benevolent gods in Buddhism and Hinduism.

Dharma (Hinduism): One's duty in society determined by one's caste or gender.

Dharma (Buddhism): Buddha's teaching.

Dukkha: Suffering, including physical suffering as well as mental suffering caused by desire and ignorance.

Dvija: Meaning "twice born," refers to members of the three upper castes or varnas in Hindu society: Brahmins, Kshatriyas, and Vaishyas.

Eightfold Path: In Buddhism, the practices required to reach nirvana, which include morality, meditation, and prajna (wisdom).

Five Classics: The five canonical works of Confucianism. They are *Book of Odes*, *Book of History*, *Book of Changes*, *Record of Rites, and Spring and Autumn Annals.*

Five Hierarchical Relationships: In Confucianism, the five relationships which, when properly served, lead society toward harmony and human flourishing.

Four Noble Truths: In Buddhism, the four truths about reality that diagnose the human condition as marked by suffering and caused by desire, and prescribe the Eightfold Path as the solution.

Gelugpa: A dominant school of Tibetan Buddhism whose head, the Dalai Lama, ruled Tibet until 1959.

Gui: Vengeful and malevolent ghosts and demons in ancient Chinese religion.

Guru Granth Sahib: The principal religious scripture of Sikhism, regarded as the final, eternal, living Guru.

Hun: In Chinese thought, the immaterial, spiritual aspect of the individual associated with the yang component.

Izanagi: In Shinto, one of the primordial pair credited with bringing the world out of its original chaos and creating the "grand eight islands" of the Japanese archipelago.

Izanami: The wife of Izanagi.

Jiva: In Jainism and Hinduism, the soul; also the category of living, as opposed to nonliving, entities of the universe.

Junzi: A Confucian gentleman; a person of noble character.

Kali Yuga: In Hinduism, the morally dark age the world has now entered.

Kalki: In Hinduism, the tenth avatar of Vishnu, foretold to appear at the end of Kali Yuga.

Kami: In Shinto, the gods or spirits of the whole of nature, the ancestors, and the emperor.

Karma: Action and the consequences of action, which determine the nature of one's reincarnation.

Karma yoga: In Hinduism, the yoga of action, of selfless service to others while pursuing the Self or Atman.

Kevala: In Jainism, perfect and complete knowledge or omniscience; enlightenment that marks the point at which one is liberated from samsara.

Khalsa: The Sikh organization for the defense of the faith, marked by: uncut hair covered with a turban, a small comb worn in the hair, a steel wristlet, a sword, and breeches.

Kojiki: *Record of Ancient Matters*; a collection of myths concerning the origin of Japan and the Kami.

Krishna: In Hinduism, the eighth avatar of Vishnu.

Kshatriya: A member of the warrior and ruling class of the Hindu varna or caste system.

Laozi: The reputed author of the *Tao Te Ching* and founder of Taoism.

Li: In Confucianism, rituals, etiquette, and proper manners.

Lotus Sutra: One of the earliest and most influential Mahayana Buddhist texts.

Mahabharata: One of the two major epics of ancient India, the other being *Ramayana*.

Mahavira: The twenty-fourth Tirthankara of Jainism.

Mahayana: Also known as the "Great Vehicle," the most prominent school of Buddhism in East Asia and Tibet.

Maitreya: The next Buddha.

Moksha: Liberation, the final release from samsara; freedom from future rebirth.

Mukti: In Sikhism, liberation from samsara; freedom from future rebirth.

Nam: In Sikhism, meditating on the divine nature of God.

Nanak: The founder of Sikhism and the first of ten Sikh gurus.

Nirvana: In Buddhism, a blissful state achieved by individuals who have extinguished desire, attachment and ignorance; after death they enter parinirvana, freed from future rebirth.

Om-kara: The "Divine One," one of the Sikh terms for God, understood as the impersonal ultimate reality.

Panth: The Sikh community; also known as Khalsa Panth.

Parinirvana: In Buddhism, the full entry into nirvana that occurs after death.

Po: In Chinese thought, the immaterial, spiritual aspect of the individual associated with the yin component.

Prajna: In Buddhism, the insight or wisdom necessary for enlightenment, comprising the ability to "see clearly" into the nature of existence (called the Three Marks of Existence).

Purānas: Ancient Hindu texts composed to glorify the gods, communicate their form of worship, and celebrate models of exemplary devotional faith (called bhaktas).

Qi: In Chinese philosophy, the vital life force or power within individuals and in nature.

Ramayana: One of the two major epics of ancient India, the other being *Mahabharata*.

Ren: The Confucian ideal of being "fully human" and which encompasses every aspect of human existence.

Rig Veda: The oldest of the *Vedas*, composed in the second millennium BCE.

Samadhi: In Hinduism, a trance state in which the yogi experiences a direct awareness of Atman; in the Advaita Vedanta school, the yogi experiences a direct awareness that Atman is identical to Brahman.

Samsara: The continuous cycle of birth, death, and rebirth according to karma; also this worldly realm in which the cycle recurs.

Sangha: In Buddhism and Jainism, the monastic community of monks and nuns.

Sat Guru: "True Teacher," one of the Sikh terms for God, understood as dwelling within all creation and bestowing grace and liberation upon those who approach him with devotion.

Shaivite: Devotees of the Hindu god Shiva.

Shakta: Devotees of the Hindu goddess Devi.

Shangdi: The Lord on High who presided over the early Chinese pantheon during the Shang period.

Shen: Benevolent gods and spirits in ancient Chinese religion.

Shiva: One of the main Hindu gods whose consort is the goddess Parvati.

Shramana: Wandering ascetic during the time of Buddha.

Shudra: A member of the servant class of the Hindu varna or caste system.

Siddhartha Gautama: Also Shakyamuni; the Buddha, on whose teachings Buddhism was founded.

Skandhas: In Buddhism, an aggregate identifying each of the five basic components that comprise a human being: the physical body, perceptions, feelings, innate tendencies (or dispositions shaped by karma), and consciousness.

Tao (Confucianism): Literally meaning the "Way," Tian's working in nature and the human world, and specifically referring to the ideal course of human conduct.

Tao (Taoism): The primordial entity that exists in an undifferentiated state and the ground of all being.

Tao Te Ching: The main Taoist text, attributed to Laozi, the traditional founder of Taoism.

Theravada: The traditionalists; the oldest surviving Buddhist school that is predominant in South and Southeast Asia.

Three Gems: The "Three Jewels" or "Refuges" that every Buddhist takes refuge in for all rituals: the Buddha, the Dharma, and the Sangha.

Three Marks of Existence: The Buddha's teachings on impermanence, suffering, and the nonexistence of an eternal, unchanging soul or Self (Anatman).

Three Poisons: Ignorance, hatred, and greed, considered to be the source of all evil and suffering and keeps a person in samsara.

Tian: In ancient Chinese religion, the transcendent, numinous entity that regulates the cosmos and intervenes in human affairs, often translated "Heaven."

Tianzi: "Son of Tian," the ancient Chinese ruler who was considered to be the chosen representative of Tian in the human world.

Tilaka: Hindu forehead mark.

Tirthankaras: The twenty-four sages of Jainism, mostly notably Mahavira, whose lives emulate the highest expression of the Jainist ideal.

Upanishads: Philosophical appendices to the *Vedas* which record early Hindu speculations on Brahman, Atman, and moksha.

Vahana: The "mount" of a Hindu god or goddess who uses it as a vehicle.

Vaishnavite: Devotees of the Hindu god Vishnu, his avatar Krishna, or his consort, Lakshmi.

Vaishya: A member of the farmer or merchant class of the Hindu varna or caste system.

Vajrayana: The "Thunderbolt School," often described as a form of Mahayana Buddhism, the most prominent form of Buddhism in Tibet and Nepal.

Varna: Caste or class; the four main castes that form the basis of the traditional hierarchical organization of Hindu society.

Vedas: The most ancient Hindu scriptures, composed of hymns, philosophy, and guidance on ritual. The four main texts are the *Rig Veda*, *Sama Veda*, *Yajur Veda*, and the *Atharva Veda*.

Vishnu: Considered one of the supreme Hindu gods, considered to have nine incarnations or avatars, including Rama, Krishna, and Buddha.

Xiao: In Confucianism, filial piety; respect and care for parents and ancestors.

Xin: The heart-mind in Confucian thought.

Yang: In Chinese philosophy, one of the twin forces, the active force or energy of the universe, characterized as male, and associated with light, dry, and heat.

Yin: In Chinese philosophy, one of the twin forces, the passive force or energy of the universe, characterized as female, and associated with dark, wet, and cold.

Yoga: Refers to the various moral, physical, and spiritual practices, including ascetic practices, to achieve union with the divine which leads to liberation.

Yuga: In Hinduism, one of the four stages of the four-stage cycle of the world; the fourth stage, the morally dark age, is called Kali Yuga.

Zhuangzi: The second great Taoist sage; the second great Taoist classic, named after the sage of the same name.

BIBLIOGRAPHY

Ames, Roger T. Ames and Henry Rosemont Jr., Henry. *The Analects of Confucius: A Philosophical Translation*. New York: Ballantine Books, 1999.

Brodd, Jeffrey, et al. *Invitation to Asian Religions*. New York: Oxford University Press, 2015.

Chen, Ellen M. *The Tao Te Ching: A New Translation with Commentary*. St. Paul, MN: Paragon House, 1998.

Dawson, Raymond. *The Analects (Oxford World Classics)*. Oxford: Oxford University Press, 2008.

Easwaran, Eknath. *The Bhagavad Gita*, 2nd ed. Tomales, CA: Nilgiri Press, 2007.

—————. *The Upanishads*, 2nd ed. Tomales, CA: Nilgiri Press, 2007.

Esposito, John, et al. *Religions of Asia Today*, 3rd ed. New York: Oxford University Press, 2014.

Harvey, Peter. *An Introduction to Buddhist Ethics: Foundations, Values, and Issues*. Cambridge: Cambridge University Press, 2000.

Johnson, Jay T. and Murton, Brian. "Re/placing Native Science: Indigenous Voices in Contemporary Constructions of Nature," *Geographical Research* 45(2) (June 2007).

Lifton, Robert. *Nazi Doctors*. New York: Basic Books, 1988.

Midgley, David and Lovelock, James. *The Essential Mary Midgley*. New York: Routledge, 2005.

Oxtoby, Willard, et al. *World Religions: Eastern Traditions*. Toronto: Oxford University Press, 2014.

Owen, Lisa Battaglia. "Toward A Buddhist Feminism: Mahayana Sutras, Feminist Theory, and the Transformation of Sex," *Asian Journal of Women Studies*, 3(4) (December 1997).

Parrinder, Geoffrey. *Avatar and Incarnation: The Divine in Human Form in the World's Religions*. London: One World Publications, 1997.

Reeves, Gene. *The Lotus Sutra: A Contemporary Translation of a Buddhist Classic*. Boston: Wisdom Publications, 2008.

Slingerland, Edward. *Confucius Analects: With Selections from Traditional Commentaries*. Indianapolis: Hackett Publishing, 2003.

Tedlock, Dennis. *Popol Vuh: The Definitive Edition of the Mayan Book of The Dawn of Life and The Glories of Gods and Kings*. New York: Touchstone Books, 1996.

Tomhave, Alan. "Cartesian Intuitions, Humean Puzzles, and the Buddhist Conception of the Self," *Philosophy East and West* (October 2010).

Ziporyn, Brook. *Zhuangzi: The Essential Writings with Selections from Traditional Commentaries*. Indianapolis: Hackett Publishing, 2009.

Made in the USA
San Bernardino, CA
28 April 2019